The Rohingya Crisis and the International Criminal Court

Hitomi Takemura

The Rohingya Crisis and the International Criminal Court

Springer

Hitomi Takemura
Graduate School of Law
Hitotsubashi University
Tokyo, Japan

ISBN 978-981-99-2736-4 ISBN 978-981-99-2734-0 (eBook)
https://doi.org/10.1007/978-981-99-2734-0

© The Editor(s) (if applicable) and The Author(s), under exclusive license to Springer Nature
Singapore Pte Ltd. 2023
This work is subject to copyright. All rights are solely and exclusively licensed by the Publisher, whether
the whole or part of the material is concerned, specifically the rights of translation, reprinting, reuse
of illustrations, recitation, broadcasting, reproduction on microfilms or in any other physical way, and
transmission or information storage and retrieval, electronic adaptation, computer software, or by similar
or dissimilar methodology now known or hereafter developed.
The use of general descriptive names, registered names, trademarks, service marks, etc. in this publication
does not imply, even in the absence of a specific statement, that such names are exempt from the relevant
protective laws and regulations and therefore free for general use.
The publisher, the authors, and the editors are safe to assume that the advice and information in this book
are believed to be true and accurate at the date of publication. Neither the publisher nor the authors or
the editors give a warranty, expressed or implied, with respect to the material contained herein or for any
errors or omissions that may have been made. The publisher remains neutral with regard to jurisdictional
claims in published maps and institutional affiliations.

This Springer imprint is published by the registered company Springer Nature Singapore Pte Ltd.
The registered company address is: 152 Beach Road, #21-01/04 Gateway East, Singapore 189721,
Singapore

Preface

As a result of the international community adopting a more institutional nature after World War II, progress has been made in the work of codifying customary international law, States have engaged in the formation of multilateral treaties, international law has expanded to cover a greater range of topics, and international law is being implemented ever more substantially on the international stage. Said implementation includes greater use of international courts and tribunals for inter-State dispute settlement and for improving human rights situations in States where the need for such may be evident. Such phenomena have become possible only with the proliferation of these selfsame courts and tribunals, as well as human rights treaty bodies being established in greater numbers.

Accordingly, today's international relations are becoming increasingly judicialized, although litigation as a means of remedying human rights violations, as well as for the pursuit of international public interest by third parties who are not directly concerned with a given country, may create a sense of disconnect between direct victims and legal judgment. Moreover, proceedings before the International Court of Justice (ICJ) and the International Criminal Court (ICC) typically take considerable time. In fact, identification of damage and satisfaction of victims through judicial remedies of international law may not happen as rapidly as one might think, any more than might political resolutions to such harms. However, understanding and clarifying deteriorating situations, and pursuing responsibility for same, through international law are important to rationally addressing current tragedies without letting emotions get in the way.

The impetus for writing this book came from a request from the Japanese Society of International Law (JSIL) for my expert commentary on the relationship between the plight of the Rohingya and the ICC. Ms. Juno Kawakami, who read that commentary, suggested that I write this book. I would like to express my appreciation to Ms. Kawakami, a senior editor of the publisher Springer, and my gratitude to the JSIL for providing me the opportunity to address this issue. It has taken me much time to finish, due to my own inability to get to the point. In the meantime, there has been a political upheaval in Myanmar, and an armed conflict in Ukraine on a scale not seen since the twentieth century. Yet, even in these difficult times of COVID-19 stagnation and world unrest associated with such conflict, international law reminds us all the more of the importance of rule of law. The Rohingya issue cannot be resolved overnight, but the fact that the international community is no longer tolerant of major human rights violations gives hope that there will be a resolution.

Given the scarcity of resources in the international community and the lack of a genuine unified world government, it is difficult to overcome bias in international criminal justice based on political dynamics. Such bias is incompatible with human dignity. If we are to enforce international law less arbitrarily with regard to gross human rights violations, we cannot be indifferent to human rights abuses anywhere.

The recent devastation of Rohingya and Ukrainians alike may have made the international community apathetic due to a lack of enforcement of international law. Yet, international law researchers have primary responsibility for examining the practice of their subject from a third-party perspective and to present both *lex lata* and *lex ferenda*. As Xi Jinping, President of China, reportedly spoke via video before the Davos Agenda of the World Economic Forum on January 25, 2021, "Without international law and international rules that are formed and recognized by the global community, the world may fall back to the law of the jungle, and the consequence would be devastating for humanity." Hence, international law is better than nothing; as mentioned above, it gives hope. The ultimate purpose of international law is to seek and maintain peace among nations, and sovereigns must interpret and apply that law in a manner that brings about peace. States must also respect the rights of their enemies in accordance with international human rights law, both within their States and in territory under their control.

Encouragement from family and friends was the most important driving force in completing this book. Without the support and encouragement of my family, I would not have embarked on this difficult English-language publishing project. And since 2008, when I began my academic career, I have been blessed with many fine coworkers, research associates, and students, to whom I am indebted. I take this opportunity to express my special gratitude to the faculty and staff of Hitotsubashi University, who provide me with a fine research environment. The excellent faculty, competent staff, and outstanding students of the Global Governance Program at Hitotsubashi University's Graduate School of International and Public Policy are always supportive and kind. In a class I taught at the school, which was conducted in English, I was struck by a Chinese graduate student remarking in late 2022, "I am not taking Russia's side, but I am getting tired of everyone blaming Russia so unilaterally." I was reminded once again that international conflicts will be more complicated unless we have rational discussions using international law, rather than assuming evil on the part of those who disagree with us. International law and studies thereof allow for a static and cogent view of ongoing conflicts, over which discussions tend to become heated. I am also grateful to Hitotsubashi University Library, for its unstinting efforts in purchasing books about the Rohingya. I am delighted by the fact that, thanks to this research project, the library is now well-stocked with English-written texts on the subject in both paper and electronic formats.

Preface

My interest in international criminal law was fostered by the opportunity I was afforded to study at Hitotsubashi University's Graduate School of Law in the early 2000s, when it was first being developed. I especially thank Profs. Emeriti Tetsuo Sato and Kyoji Kawasaki. It is no exaggeration to say that studying international law in Prof. Sato's seminar, surrounded by other good students ahead as well behind me, with whom I engaged in friendly debate, has made me the person I am today. I would also like to express my gratitude to Sonoko Nishitateno, Prof. Emerita of Tokyo University of Foreign Studies (TUFS), who was my supervisor during my undergraduate years there. I would not have been able to write this book if I had not encountered international law at TUFS. My colleagues at the Hitotsubashi University School of International and Public Policy's Global Governance Program are always very kind to me and understanding of my research. Professors Jiro Yashiki and Nobumasa Akiyama, deans of the Graduate School of Law and the School of International Public Policy, keep encouraging me to write in English. Professor Yumiko Nakanishi, specialist in EU law, and on the Hitotsubashi University faculty, supports my research and always has a friendly greeting for me whenever I see her in the halls. The natural surroundings of the university grounds also provide respite, and I feel joy each day I go to work there. At the same time, I am in a privileged position, and it hurts me to think of the harsh conditions that the people of Myanmar endure because of the conflict there, especially the persecuted Rohingya. Nevertheless, one must not see the matter as someone else's problem but must be sincere in addressing these and other human rights violations. As a law faculty member, I wish to continue my efforts to make international human rights more accessible and approachable to the Japanese, through such means as continuing to offer lectures on international human rights law at law schools in other Japanese universities. I hope that one day not far from now, when international criminal law is taught in more Japanese universities, many people will become increasingly familiar with the sorts of human rights violations that are disturbing the international community.

I would also like to express my heartfelt gratitude to Springer for publishing this short monograph. I especially thank the Ms. Kawakami for her patience and management. What with the COVID-19 crisis and the Myanmar *coup d'état* that occurred soon after I agreed to write this book, my writing schedule was significantly affected by the lack of progress in the international proceedings and investigations into the Rohingya crisis. This situation also implies a delay in justice for the Rohingya. In fact, it was only on December 21, 2022, that the first Security Council resolution (S/RES/2669) since the *coup* was adopted, allowing the international political community, rather than sitting on the sidelines, to show united concern by calling for a cessation of hostilities on the part of the junta.

In addition, I thank the Japan Society for the Promotion of Science (JSPS) for their generous financial support via JSPS KAKENHI Grant No. 21K01160.

In conclusion, I would like to express my deepest sympathy and solidarity with those who have been forced to flee their homes due to persecution, including the Rohingya.

Tokyo, Japan
December 2022

Hitomi Takemura

Contents

1	**Introduction**	1
	References	9
2	**Background to the Rohingya Crisis**	11
	2.1 Introduction	11
	2.2 Colonial Period	15
	2.3 Post-independence	19
	2.4 Conclusion	24
	References	25
3	**The Rohingya Crisis and the International Criminal Court**	27
	3.1 Procedural History	27
	3.1.1 The United Nations' and Myanmar's Initiatives for Dealing with the Rohingya Crisis	27
	3.2 The Good Offices of the United Nations Secretary-General	33
	3.3 Myanmar's Ratification of International Treaties	35
	3.4 Rising Awareness of the Pursuit of Individual Responsibility	37
	3.4.1 Prelude to the Pursuit of Individual Responsibility	37
	3.4.2 Proceedings Before the ICC	39
	3.5 Pros and Cons on the Jurisdiction of the ICC Over the Bangladesh/Myanmar Situation	45
	3.6 ASEAN and Chinese Efforts to Cope with the Rohingya Crisis	47
	3.7 Recent Developments	50
	3.8 Conclusion	54
	References	56
4	**The Relationship Between the Rohingya Case Before the International Court of Justice and the Bangladesh-Myanmar Situation Before the International Criminal Court**	63
	4.1 Proceedings Before the International Court of Justice	63

ix

		4.1.1	Institution of Proceedings by the Gambia	63

		4.1.1	Institution of Proceedings by the Gambia	63
		4.1.2	Desired Relief	65
		4.1.3	Myanmar's Counterargument	65
		4.1.4	Third-Party Intervention Before the ICJ	66
	4.2		Provisional Measures	68
	4.3		Preliminary Objections	72
		4.3.1	Myanmar's Preliminary Objections	72
		4.3.2	Rulings	73
	4.4		Related Developments	80
	4.5		Prospects for Establishing Genocide	83
	4.6		The Gambia V. Myanmar as Strategic Human Rights Litigation	86
	4.7		The Dynamic Relationship Between State and Individual Responsibility for Crimes Under International Law	87
		4.7.1	The ICJ and the ICC	87
		4.7.2	The ICC and Regional Human Rights Institutions	91
		4.7.3	Superior Responsibility	92
	4.8		Responsibility to Protect and the Gambia's Application	94
	4.9		Responsibility to Protect and the US Government	98
	4.10		Possible Effects Associated with the February 2021 *coup d'état*	100
	4.11		Implications of the Application of the Genocide Convention in Ukraine and Russia on the Application of the Genocide Convention in Myanmar	103
	4.12		Conclusion	104
	References			106
5	**The Legitimacy, Effectiveness, and Efficiency of the ICC**			**113**
	5.1		The Meaning and Indicators of the ICC's Legitimacy	113
		5.1.1	Legitimacy Discourse in International Law	113
		5.1.2	Legitimacy Discourse in International Criminal Law	115
		5.1.3	The Meaning of Legitimacy	118
		5.1.4	Legitimacy of the ICC	121
	5.2		ICC Effectiveness and Efficiency	126
	5.3		Evaluating Legitimacy and Effectiveness vis-à-vis Bangladesh/Myanmar	129
		5.3.1	Evaluating Legitimacy	129
		5.3.2	Effectiveness: Likelihood of Trials in Domestic Courts	131
	5.4		Conclusion	134
	References			135

Contents

6 Conclusion 141
   6.1   Rule of Law in a World in Chaos 141
   6.2   Proposed Solutions 143
   6.3   Dual-Track Pursuit of State and Individual Responsibility
        in the International Legal System 146
   References 147

Index 149

About the Author

Hitomi Takemura is a professor of law at Hitotsubashi University in Japan. She has amassed a solid research record in the fields of international criminal and international human rights law both in Japanese and English and has consistently held tenured academic positions since April 2008. Dr. Takemura obtained a bachelor's degree at Tokyo University of Foreign Studies, LL.M. degrees from Hitotsubashi University and Leiden University (Netherlands), and a Ph.D. from the Irish Centre for Human Rights, National University of Ireland, Galway (Ireland).

Chapter 1
Introduction

Abstract This book looks at the current situation in Myanmar and how the International Criminal Court is dealing with the Rohingya crisis, as well as possibilities for its future. The Rohingya are considered the most vulnerable stateless persons in the world today. The first part of this chapter is an overview of what the Rohingya issue is and how it has become a concern for the international community today. From there, it examines how the treaty system addresses the human rights situation in the Republic of the Union of Myanmar (Myanmar), which is not a party to the International Criminal Court (ICC). As the Rohingya issue is pending before the International Court of Justice (ICJ), this study will provide a concise history of the pursuit of state responsibility on the part of Myanmar at the ICJ. In summary, individual and state responsibility for Myanmar's alleged human rights violations are being pursued simultaneously at present, and the significance and timeliness of these efforts need to be reconsidered.

The purpose of this book is to critically examine the activities of the International Criminal Court (ICC) on the eve of the twentieth year since its founding, with a focus on its relationship to the Rohingya crisis in the Republic of the Union of Myanmar. Even though Myanmar is not a State Party to the ICC, a case involving Myanmar is taking shape at the ICC. Myanmar is one of a number of developing countries that has undergone significant democratization in recent years. Some 90 percent of its population are Buddhists, and it is in the international spotlight because of its northwestern Muslim inhabitants, the Rohingya, who are inhumanely treated as a stateless minority.[1] They are considered the most persecuted minority in the world.[2] The Rohingya may be characterized as both an ethnic and a religious group, as they are both an ethnic and a religious minority in Myanmar.[3] The 1982 Citizenship Law that was promulgated under the regime of Ne Win's Burma Socialist Programme Party created various categories of Myanmarese citizenship and narrowed the grounds on

---

[1] The Office of the United Nations High Commissioner for Refugees, "Rohingya Emergency," available at <https://www.unhcr.org/rohingya-emergency.html> (last accessed, 1 March 2022).

[2] UN Human Rights Office of the High Commissioner (2017).

[3] Pérez-León-Acevedo, Pinto (2022), p. 459.

© The Author(s), under exclusive license to Springer Nature Singapore Pte Ltd. 2023
H. Takemura, *The Rohingya Crisis and the International Criminal Court*,
https://doi.org/10.1007/978-981-99-2734-0_1

which citizenship could be acquired.[4] This law has been assessed as discriminating against the Rohingya, as it effectively bars from receiving citizenship,[5] because section 3 of the law does not recognize the Rohingya as an indigenous ethnic identity.[6] The law prescribes three categories of citizenship: full citizens, associate citizens, and naturalized citizens. In 1989, the government distributed Citizens Scrutiny Cards (CSC) to its residents: pink for full citizens, blue for associate citizens, and green for naturalized citizens. With the result that no cards were issued to the Rohingya.[7] At the urging of the UNHCR, the Rohingya were issued with Temporary Registration Cards (TRC), but this card type does not indicate nationality and thus cannot be used as proof of citizenship.[8]

Even though the 1954 Convention relating to the Status of Stateless Persons provides stateless persons certain rights, Myanmar has not acceded to the 1954 Convention, nor to the 1961 Convention on the Reduction of Statelessness. Nor has it ratified either the 1951 Refugee Convention or the 1967 Protocol. In the Asia–Pacific region, however, this is not unusual: the majority of states there remain outside the Refugee Convention's regime.[9] Only the Philippines and Cambodia have ratified the Refugee Convention, and that under pressure from the United States of America.[10] While the jurisprudence and refugee policies of countries such as Bangladesh, Indonesia, and Thailand have been influenced by the Refugee Convention regime,[11] Bangladesh has only occasionally officially recognized Rohingya arrivals as 'refugees,' instead labeling the majority 'Undocumented Myanmar Nationals.'[12] Thus, the Rohingya's stateless status makes it even more difficult for many countries to accept them as refugees. For example, Japanese courts have been cautious in considering whether a finding of discrimination against Rohingya as stateless persons constitutes persecution that should be afforded protection under the Refugee Convention.[13]

Myanmar has a complex history of inter-ethnic conflicts, with the main Rohingya domains having been inhabited by the Bengali population for a prolonged period. The country also has a history of foreign interventions. The contemporary Rohingya crisis has become problematic because the manner in which the current regime treats the Rohingya has created a large number of Rohingya refugees. While Myanmar ratified

---

[4] Brett, Hlaing (2020), p. 1.

[5] ibid.

[6] Haque (2017), p. 457. 135 groups were recognized under the 1982 Citizenship Law as ethnic identities. See Chowdhory, Mohanty (2020), p. 23.

[7] Kaveri (2020), p. 77.

[8] ibid.

[9] Moretti (2021), p. 215.

[10] Ibid.

[11] Ibid, p. 229; Hossain (2021), pp. 59–61.

[12] Janmyr (2021), p. 206; UNHCR Submission on Bangladesh: 30th UPR session, (May 2018) p. 2.

[13] Arakaki (2015), p. 85. Japanese court precedents interpret 'persecution' under the Refugee Convention as "aggression or oppression which causes intolerable pain, in general, and it is appropriate to recognize persecution as representing a violation or oppression of freedom to life or physical integrity," ibid., p. 79.

1 Introduction

the Convention on the Prevention and Punishment of the Crime of Genocide as far back as March 14, 1956, it is not currently a party to the ICC Statute. The question thus arises as to how to hold states and individuals accountable for inhumane acts in such a situation.

The United Nations Human Rights Council made an urgent decision to dispatch an independent international fact-finding mission on recently alleged human rights violations and abuses by military and security forces in Myanmar, particularly in Rakhine State, under the terms of resolution 34/22 of March 24, 2017. The mission found that there was a non-international armed conflict between the Arakan Rohingya Salvation Army (ARSA) and the Myanmar security forces in Rakhine State,[14] and that mopping-up operations led by Myanmarese authorities were targeting the entire Rohingya population. As a result, 725,000 Rohingya had fled to Bangladesh.[15] Based on these findings, the mission has repeatedly recommended, in the interest of justice for victims and accountability of perpetrators, that the Security Council either refer the situation of Myanmar to the ICC or establish an ad hoc tribunal. Nonetheless, the People's Republic of China (PRC) and Russia have refused to allow the Security Council to intervene in the domestic human rights situation in Myanmar because of their position against foreign interference in the internal affairs of states. Therefore, there is little hope of either of these actions being taken. This situation is deplored as one in which geopolitics prevails over humanitarian values and ethics.[16]

In the face of this stalemate in the international community with regard to holding Myanmar accountable over the Rohingya crisis, there were some notable developments in 2019. Specifically, on November 11, the Republic of The Gambia instituted proceedings against Myanmar before the International Court of Justice (ICJ) on behalf of the Organization of Islamic Cooperation (OIC). On November 13, the Burmese Rohingya Organization UK (BROUK) filed a complaint in Argentina over alleged human rights abuses on behalf of the corresponding ethnic group in Myanmar on the basis of universal jurisdiction. On the following day, the Pre-Trial Division of the ICC granted an application which had been filed by the Prosecutor of the ICC to open an investigation into the Bangladesh-Myanmar situation. On December 27, two weeks after the International Court of Justice (ICJ) heard a request by The Gambia for a provisional measures order against Myanmar, the UN General Assembly adopted a resolution (UN Doc. A/RES/74/246) condemning human rights violations and abuses in Myanmar, especially against the Rohingya, by a vote of 134 for and 9 against.[17] This action signifies the dramatic turn that the Rohingya crisis had taken at the time. Then, on January 23, 2020, the ICJ unanimously issued the requested order of provisional measures against Myanmar, holding that the Rohingya people appear to constitute a protected group within the terms of Article II of the Genocide Convention. In September 2020, two Myanmar soldiers reportedly held by the Arakan Army of the Rohingya were sent to the Hague, the Netherlands, where the ICC is located.

---

[14] UN Doc. A/HRC/39/64, para. 11.

[15] Ibid., para. 33.

[16] Karim (2020), p. 94.

[17] UN Doc. A/RES/74/246 (15 January 2020). Granville (2021), p. 178.

It was also reported that the Myanmar armed forces were investigating allegations of wider patterns of human rights violations before and during a 2017 operation in Rakhine State. Considering the principle of complementarity, by which the ICC complements state jurisdiction, there remains a theoretical possibility that domestic criminal proceedings may take precedence over investigation and prosecution of the case at the ICC. The situation depends on the status of future domestic investigations in Myanmar. If Myanmar does not conduct a genuine investigation and prosecution into the Rohingya human rights situation, the ICC could intervene.

It is noteworthy that the ICJ and the ICC were established to deal with different crimes, even though they deal with the same situation of the treatment of the Rohingya in Myanmar. The ICC Office of the Prosecutor is expected to limit the scope of its investigation and prosecution of the treatment of the Rohingya to crimes against humanity and war crimes of a transboundary nature, such as "deportation," for the time being. It is thus unlikely that the ICC will take up charges of genocide in the matter. By contrast, the case before the ICJ is one in which The Gambia is suing Myanmar under the Dispute Settlement Clause of the Genocide Convention, and the issue before the ICJ is solely one of alleged genocide by Myanmar against the Rohingya. While both the ICC and the ICJ can take sometimes as long as five years, to conclude a case, victims have little hope of a resolution of the Rohingya crisis by the Security Council, a political body, whereas they may have at least some hope for proceedings before these courts.[18]

As 2022 marks the 20th anniversary of the Rome Statute entering into force, we are presented with an opportune moment to reflect on the work of the ICC. As with any organization, the effectiveness and efficiency of the court are critical to its undertakings. However, the ICC is a criminal court, and one must examine its effectiveness and efficiency with respect to the rights of accused persons on the principle of presumption of innocence. Therefore, a difficult and careful balance is needed in examining the effectiveness and efficiency of the ICC between pursuing the truth about mass violations of human rights and ensuring due process of law. On the one hand, the democratic legitimacy of the ICC is guaranteed to a certain extent by the agreement of the parties to the Rome Statute, which established the ICC, and by domestic democratic control over the right of each state's government to conclude the treaty based on their constitutional laws. On the other hand, the ICC deals either with cases referred to it by the Security Council in relation to Non-State Party situations, or with cases concerning Non-State Party nationals, when a national of a Non-State Party is considered to have committed at least one aspect of a crime in a State Party, as in the case of Bangladesh/Myanmar. Hence, the issue of democratic legitimacy remains complicated as long as the ICC deals with a Non-State Party, as with the present Bangladesh/Myanmar situation.

The COVID-19 pandemic and the February 2021 Myanmar coup have further jeopardized the human rights of the Rohingya. As is well known, on February 1, 2021, the Tatmadaw (Myanmar armed forces), overthrew the National League for Democracy (NLD) government in a *coup d'état*. They acted out of dissatisfaction

---

[18] Lee (2021), p. 116.

1 Introduction

with the November 8, 2020 general election in Myanmar, in which the NLD, led by Aung San Suu Kyi, won majorities in both houses of the parliament. The coup was carried out under the direction of Min Aung Hlaing, Senior General of the Tatmadaw, who became the first Chairman of the State Administration Council established by the Tatmadaw on February 2, making him the new head of State. Aung San Suu Kyi was ousted as State Counsellor and has been under arrest since that time.[19] A popular uprising has also been violently suppressed by the Tatmadaw. As a result of these actions, the situation on the ground in Myanmar remains in chaos. In July 2021, Aung San Suu Kii was sent to prison in Naypyidaw.[20] On December 6, 2021, Aung San Suu Kii was sentenced by a special court established by the Tatmadaw to four years' imprisonment after being found guilty of incitement and violating COVID-19 restrictions.[21] On January 10 2022, Aung San Suu Kii was found guilty of multiple charges including possession of unlicensed walkie-talkies and further violations of COVID-19 restrictions, and sentenced to a further four years' imprisonment.[22] On August 15 2022, the special court convicted her again, this time on four counts of corruption, adding another six years to her sentence.[23] She had already been sentenced to 11 years in prison on sedition, corruption, and other charges in earlier trials.[24] The special court sentenced her on September 2, 2022 to another three years in prison at hard labor for election fraud in relation to her political party's 2020 electoral victory.[25] On October 12, 2022, Aung San Suu Kyi was sentenced to another three years in prison by the special court for corruption.[26] These trials and sentencing hearings were conducted behind closed doors,[27] and very little information about them has been made public. On December 30 2022, the special court sentenced Aung San Suu Kyi to a further seven years in prison over five additional corruption cases, completing the series of trials and bringing Suu Kyi's total sentence to 38 years' imprisonment.[28] It is reported that the total prison time the Myanmar junta has imposed on Aung San Suu Kyi is tantamount to a life sentence, and is believed to be aimed at reducing her influence in new elections, which the junta has scheduled for August 2023.

On July 25 2022, the military-owned newspaper Global New Light of Myanmar reported that four pro-democracy activists, Ko Jimmy (aka Kyaw Min Yu), Phyo Zayar Thaw, Hla Myo Aung, and Aung Thura Zaw were executed on March 14, 2021 after closed-door trials, in accordance with death sentences handed down by

---

[19] Beech (2021).

[20] Paddock (2022).

[21] Ratcliffe (2021).

[22] Ibid.

[23] Ibid.

[24] Grant Peck, 'Myanmar court convicts Suu Kyi on more corruption charges', AP News (15 August 2022).

[25] Wee (2022).

[26] Ratcliffe (2022).

[27] Beech, Gladstone, Paddock (2021).

[28] Ives, Stevens (2022); Mao (2022).

military tribunal for involvement with brutal and inhuman terror acts.[29] These were the first such executions in Myanmar in 30 years, and were condemned by the United Nations High Commissioner for Human Rights.[30] Nicholas Koumjian, head of the Independent Investigative Mechanism for Myanmar, also issued a statement that "[o]ne of the most fundamental attributes of a fair trial is that it be held in public to the greatest extent possible. [...] The secrecy of proceedings is itself a violation of one of the most basic principles of a fair trial, and casts doubt on whether any of the other fair trial guarantees have been respected, such as the requirement that the tribunal was impartial and independent."[31] The above criticisms of the procedural legitimacy aspect of the closed hearing process apparently applies to the of trials of Aung San Suu Kyi. According to Koumjian, "Imposing a prison or death sentence in such circumstances could constitute crimes against humanity or war crimes,"[32] such as persecution or murder in particularly egregious situations. This inability to conduct open and fair trials would reflect poorly on the junta's legitimacy, and suggests that it is not meeting the minimum requirements of international human rights and criminal law as established under customary international law.

Given the current internal turmoil, in Myanmar under the junta, sometimes seemingly tantamount to armed conflict, together with the COVID-19 pandemic, the Rohingya refugees in Bangladesh are neither willing nor able to return to Myanmar.[33] Even more unfortunately, on March 22, 2021, a fire raced through four Rohingya refugee camps. It is reported that 11 people were killed, including three children, while 50 children were separated from their parents, and 300 people are unaccounted for.[34] Although no decision has been made by an international judicial body on whether the situation in post-coup Myanmar constitutes a non-international armed conflict, it is worth listening to the opinion of the key figures of concerned human rights organizations that they have so designated the situation as of October 2021.[35] As will be addressed in detail in Chap. 4, the U.S., the EU, and the U.K. have shown their condemnation of the human rights violations in Myanmar after the coup by repeatedly introducing targeted sanctions.

Some Rohingya living in exile hope that the growing criticism of the coup by the international community will add to momentum to turn Myanmar into a multi-ethnic federal state.[36] At the same time, the Ukrainian crisis that began in February 2022, in which neighboring countries have rapidly accepted refugees, has once again evoked the importance of hosting all people fleeing persecution without giving the appearance of playing favorites.

---

[29] The Global New Light of Myanmar (2022).

[30] The UN Human Rights Office of the High Commissioner (2022a).

[31] The Independent Investigative Mechanism for Myanmar (2022).

[32] Ibid.

[33] International Crisis Group (2021), p. 15.

[34] UNICEF (2021).

[35] Christine Schraner Burgener referred to the situation after the *coup* as internal armed conflict prior to stepping down as UN Special Envoy to Myanmar. *See* Nichols (2021).

[36] Hussein (2021).

1 Introduction

In this book, I attempt to make novel observations by identifying potential and contemporary challenges that the ICC faces while focusing on the relationship between the Rohingya issue and the ICC. This relationship is worth engaging with because it is fraught with these selfsame contemporary challenges, examples of which include relations between the ICC and Non-States Parties and between the ICC and high government officials. The novelty here lies in addressing the relationship between the Rohingya crisis and the ICC by staying current with information. With the case pending at the ICJ, State as well as individual responsibility may be sought for the most serious human rights violations. This is the first time the ICC and the ICJ have simultaneously had to deal with the same situation, that being the inhumane treatment of the Rohingya in Myanmar, though arguably from different perspectives. The Rohingya crisis is of great international concern, and one can expect that related issues will be discussed within the purview of international human rights, humanitarian, and criminal law. Accordingly, the structure of this book is as follows. First, it explains the history of the Rohingya crisis. Second, it addresses the relationship between the Rohingya crisis and the ICC. Third, it discusses the relationship between the ongoing case of *The Gambia v. Myanmar* at the ICJ and the proceedings of the ICC. Finally, the book concludes with an assessment of the legitimacy, effectiveness, and efficiency of the ICC in recent years.

In 2022, another case was also brought before both the ICC and the ICJ besides the Myanmar genocide case following Russia's military action against Ukraine. Whereas Ukraine filed an application before the ICJ to establish that Russia has no lawful basis to take action in and against Ukraine for the purpose of preventing and punishing any purported genocide as early as 26 February 2022,[37] The Gambia purports to establish a manifest violation of the Genocide Convention by the Myanmar government in the former case.[38] In other words, Ukraine is seeking to confirm in its ICJ case that it has not committed genocide and is not in violation of the Genocide Convention, while The Gambia is seeking to confirm in its ICJ case that Myanmar has committed genocide in violation of the Genocide Convention. And both parties are using the same aspect of the Genocide Convention to make their cases: the compromissory clause. On February 8 2022, the Office of the Prosecutor of the ICC decided to seek authorization from the Pre-Trial Chamber of the Court to open an investigation into the international armed conflict in Ukraine on the basis of a declaration made by the Ukraine government in 2015 to accept the jurisdiction of the ICC under Article 12(3) of the Rome Statute, despite Ukraine being a Non-State Party to the Rome Statute, like Myanmar.[39] This event points to a situation in international law in which State and individual responsibility are being pursued simultaneously, and also suggests that the ICC will become increasingly involved in situations concerning Non-States Parties. It is important to see how situations pending simultaneously at the ICJ and the ICC may impair understanding of relations between them and the impact this may have on the fragmentation of international law. While a thorough treatment of

---

[37] Government of Ukraine (2022), para. 3.

[38] Ibid., para. 2.

[39] International Criminal Court News (2022).

8   1 Introduction

the latter topic is beyond the scope of this book, the author takes this opportunity to provide an overview of how international rule of law deals with ongoing issues.

Now that the world's attention is focused on Ukraine, it is high time to examine the Rohingya issue critically in the context of international law. Human rights abuses by the junta against Myanmar citizens and non-Rohingya minorities as well as the Rohingya have become an issue in post-coup Myanmar. On October 23, 2022, the Kachin Independence Organization (KIO) was holding a concert to celebrate its 62nd anniversary at a military base in Hpakant, Kachin State, Myanmar, when the Tatmadaw carried out its largest air strike since the coup, reportedly killing some 60 people.[40] The United Nations released a statement the following day in which held that it "is deeply concerned and saddened by reports of airstrikes. […] What would appear to be excessive and disproportionate use of force by security forces against unarmed civilians is unacceptable and those responsible must be held to account."[41] Prior to this, at the 51st session of the Human Rights Council in September 2022, the UN Acting High Commissioner for Human Rights was concerned that military operations by the Myanmar military were becoming increasingly indiscriminate and violent.[42] The Commissioner claimed that "[u]rgent action is needed to reverse this catastrophic situation and to restore peace, democracy, and sustainable development" in Myanmar.[43]

"Whataboutism" and "bothsidesing," in which the West is criticized for showing excessive interest in human rights violations against Europeans while passing over what is happening in Palestine or Myanmar, have proliferated particularly since the outbreak of the international armed conflict in Ukraine.[44] Proponents of whataboutism also express doubts that international law is being applied and enforced equitably. However, as there are others in Myanmar, such as the Kachin, who also suffer human rights abuses at the hands of the junta, whataboutism backfires by instead becoming a justification, rather than a refutation, of such abuses. Since there is no single world government, it becomes impossible to avoid being tarred with the brush of whataboutism regarding the application of international law unless international law is imposed impartially. Even so, it is wrong to tolerate any serious violation of international law because of whataboutism. If we are to defeat whataboutism, we must all stop being indifferent to human rights violations and other injustices, and be constantly on the alert wherever in the world they may occur. With this in mind, this book examines the issue of persecution of the Rohingya from an international law perspective.

---

[40] Holmes (2022).

[41] UN Myanmar (2022).

[42] The UN Human Rights Office of the High Commissioner (2022b).

[43] Ibid.

[44] *See* Labuda (2022) for an introduction to arguments about such biases in applying law.

References

Arakaki O, Akiyama H (trans.) (2016) Statelessness conventions and Japanese laws. UNHCR Representation in Japan, Tokyo

Beech H (2021 January 31) Myanmar's leader, Daw Aung San Suu Kyi, is detained amid coup. International New York Times. https://www.nytimes.com/2021/01/31/world/asia/myanmar-coup-aung-san-suu-kyi.html

Beech H, Gladstone R, Paddock RC (2021 November 29) Judge delays Aung San Suu Kyi Trial in Myanmar. The New York Times. https://www.nytimes.com/live/2021/11/29/world/myanmar-coup-verdict-aung-san-suu-kyi

Brett P, Hlaing KY (2020) Myanmar's 1982 citizenship law in context. TOAEP Policy Brief Ser 122:1–4

Chowdhory N, Mohanty B (2020) Contextualizing citizenship, nationalism and Refugeehood of Rohingya: an introduction. In: Chowdhory N, Mohanty B (eds) Citizenship, nationalism and refugeehood of Rohingyas in Southern Asia. Springer, Singapore, pp 1–30

Glanville L (2021) Sharing responsibility: the history and future of protection from atrocities. Princeton University Press, Princeton

Government of Ukraine (2022) Application instituting proceedings. Dispute relating to allegations of genocide (Ukraine v. Russian Federation), the international court of justice

Haque MM (2017) Rohingya ethnic Muslim minority and the 1982 citizenship law in Burma. J Muslim Minor Aff 37(4):454–469

Holmes O (2022) Myanmar airstrike kills 60 people at concert, says Kachin separatist group. The Guardian. https://www.theguardian.com/world/2022/oct/24/myanmar-military-air-strike-kills-dozens-at-concert-says-kachin-separatist-group

Hossain MS (2021) Bangladesh's judicial encounter with the 1951 refugee convention. Forced Migr Rev 67:59–61

Hussein R (2021 March 18) Some exiled Rohingya see "Rare Opportunity" in Myanmar coup. Voice of America News. https://www.voanews.com/a/extremism-watch_some-exiled-rohingya-see-rare-opportunity-myanmar-coup/6203482.html

International Criminal Court News (2022) Statement of ICC Prosecutor, Karim A. A. Khan QC, on the Situation in Ukraine: "I Have Decided to Proceed with Opening an Investigation." https://www.icc-cpi.int/Pages/item.aspx?name=20220228-prosecutor-statement-ukraine

International Crisis Group (2021) The cost of the coup: Myanmar edges toward state collapse. Crisis Group Asia Briefing 167. https://www.crisisgroup.org/asia/south-east-asia/myanmar/b167-cost-coup-myanmar-edges-toward-state-collapse

Ives M, Stevens M (2022) Myanmar's ousted leader gets 33 years in prison, a likely life sentence. The New York Times. https://www.nytimes.com/2022/12/29/world/asia/myanmar-aung-san-suu-kyi-trial.html

Karim MA (2020) Genocide and geopolitics of the Rohingya crisis. NOVA Science Publishers, New York

Janmyr M (2021) The 1951 refugee convention and non-signatory states: charting a research agenda. Int J Refug Law 33(2):188–213

Kaveri (2020) The politics of marginalization and statelessness of the Rohingyas in India. In: Chowdhory N, Mohanty B (eds) Citizenship, nationalism and refugeehood of Rohingyas in Southern Asia. Springer, Singapore, pp 71–95

Labuda PI (2022) On Eastern Europe, "Whataboutism" and "West(s)plaining": some thoughts on international lawyers' responses to Ukraine. EJIL: Talk! https://www.ejiltalk.org/on-eastern-europe-whataboutism-and-westsplaining-some-thoughts-on-international-lawyers-responses-to-ukraine

Lee R (2021) Myanmar's Rohingya genocide: identity, history and hate speech. I.B. Tauris, London

Mao F (2022) Aung San Suu Kyi jailed for a further seven years. BBC News. https://www.bbc.com/news/world-asia-64123149

Moretti S (2021) Southeast Asia and the 1951 convention relating to the status of refugees: substance without form? Int J Refug Law 33(2):214–237

Nichols M (2021) Outgoing U.N. envoy says Myanmar has spiraled into civil war. Reuters. https://www.reuters.com/world/asia-pacific/outgoing-un-envoy-says-myanmar-has-spiraled-into-civil-war-2021-10-21/

Paddock RC (2022) Myanmar widens arrests and slaps Aung San Suu Kyi with more prison time. The New York Times. https://www.nytimes.com/2022/08/15/world/asia/myanmar-trial-coup-arrests.html

Pérez-León-Acevedo J, Pinto TA (2022) Disentangling law and religion in the Rohingya case at the international criminal court. Nord J Hum Rights 39(4):458–480

Ratcliffe R (2021) Myanmar's junta condemned over guilty verdicts in Aung San Suu Kyi trial. The Guardian. https://www.theguardian.com/world/2021/dec/06/aung-san-suu-kyi-sentenced-to-four-years-in-prison-for-incitement

Ratcliffe R (2022) Aung San Suu Kyi faces total of 26 years in prison after latest corruption sentencing. The Guardian. https://www.theguardian.com/world/2022/oct/12/aung-san-suu-kyi-faces-total-of-26-years-in-prison-after-latest-corruption-sentencing

The Global New Light of Myanmar (2022 July 25) Punishment conducted for four death-sentenced prisoners under the law. https://cdn.myanmarseo.com/file/client-cdn/gnlm/wp-content/uploads/2022/07/25_July_22_gnlm.pdf

The Independent Investigative Mechanism for Myanmar (2022 June 20) Death sentences announced by Myanmar military may constitute a serious international crime—Statement by Nicholas Koumjian, Head of Independent Investigative Mechanism for Myanmar. https://iimm.un.org/death-sentences-announced-by-myanmar-military-may-con stitute-a-serious-international-crime/

UN Human Rights Office of the High Commissioner (2017) Press release: human rights council: human rights council opens special session on the situation of human rights of the Rohingya and other minorities in Rakhine state in Myanmar: HRC opens special session on situation of human rights in Myanmar. https://www.ohchr.org/en/press-releases/2017/12/human-rights-cou ncil-opens-special-session-situation-human-rights-rohingya?LangID=E&NewsID=22491

UN Human Rights Office of the High Commissioner (2022a) Press release: Myanmar: Bachelet condemns executions, calls for release of all political prisoners. https://www.ohchr.org/en/press-releases/2022a/07/myanmar-bachelet-condemns-executions-calls-release-all-political-prisoners

UN Human Rights Office of the High Commissioner (2022b) Oral update on the human rights situation in Myanmar to the human rights council: opening statement by Nada Al-Nashif UN acting high commissioner for human rights. https://www.ohchr.org/en/statements-and-speeches/2022b/09/oral-update-human-rights-situation-myanmar-human-rights-council

UNICEF (2021 March 26) Statement by UNICEF executive director Henrietta fore on the fire at Rohingya refugee camps in Cox's Bazar, Bangladesh. https://www.unicef.org/press-releases/sta tement-unicef-executive-director-henrietta-fore-fire-rohingya-refugee-camps-coxs

UN Doc. A/HRC/39/64 (2018)

UN Doc. A/RES/74/246 (2020)

UN Myanmar (2022) Statement by the united nations in Myanmar on reported airstrikes in Hpakant, Kachin State (24 October 2022). Available at https://myanmar.un.org/en/204444-statement-uni ted-nations-myanmar-reported-airstrikes-hpakant-kachin-state. Last accessed 25 Oct 2022

Wee SL (2022) Myanmar gives more prison time to its best-known convict. The New York Times. https://www.nytimes.com/2022/09/02/world/asia/myanmar-coup-trial-guilty.html

Chapter 2
Background to the Rohingya Crisis

Abstract This chapter sets out the facts and history leading up to the Rohingya crisis, based on UN reports and recommendations. We begin with the history of coexistence between the Buddhist and Muslim populations; that is to say, the Buddhist dynasty of the Arakan Kingdom (present-day Rakhine State), where the people known as the Rohingya have lived, has a long history of integration and prosperity with the Bengal region. Nonetheless, the dispute between the Rohingya and the central Burmese authority dates back as far as the 1784 Burmese conquest of the Arakan Kingdom by the Konbaung dynasty. Myanmar also has a history of British and Japanese colonial rule respectively, and such rule has been pointed out as a root cause of the Rohingya problem today. The United Nations Security Council, to say nothing of Europe, has been slow to respond to the Rohingya crisis, and the absence of states with which the Rohingya can form alliances has led to a long confrontation with no solution in sight and the continued displacement of the Rohingya population from Myanmar to Bangladesh. The immediate impetus for Myanmar's most recent alleged persecution of the Rohingya was the killing of a Buddhist woman in May 2012. This incident led to intensified conflict among Buddhists and Muslims in Myanmar, and to conflict between state armed forces and the Rohingya.

2.1 Introduction

As of this writing, the very name Rohingya has become a political issue in Myanmar, raising, for instance, the question of whether that name can legally refer to a specific group protected under the Genocide Convention.[1] From the perspective of restorative justice, suggestions may be made that the world move beyond historical narratives.[2] Nonetheless, it may still be wise to look into the historical background of those peoples who call themselves Rohingya. International institutions, including the ICJ and the ICC, use the term "Rohingya" in their rulings and orders. Yet, neither the

---

[1] Ware and Laoutides (2018), p. xv.

[2] Advisory Commission on Rakhine State (2017), p. 18.

© The Author(s), under exclusive license to Springer Nature Singapore Pte Ltd. 2023
H. Takemura, *The Rohingya Crisis and the International Criminal Court*,
https://doi.org/10.1007/978-981-99-2734-0_2

11

ICJ nor the ICC has inquired into the historical origins of the Rohingya. The former mentioned cursorily that "[the ICJ's] references in this Order to the 'Rohingya' should be understood as references to the group that self-identifies as the Rohingya group and that claims a longstanding connection to Rakhine State, which forms part of the Union of Myanmar,"[3] whereas the latter held that "the Chamber will employ the term 'Rohingya' in the present decision to refer to the alleged victims individually and collectively,"[4] taking consideration into the fact that the United Nations General Assembly has used the same term for these people.[5]

On the other hand, neither the former government of Myanmar nor Aung San Suu Kyi, the former State Counsellor, used the term "Rohingya" to refer to the people in question. Instead, they used either "Muslims in Rakhine State" or "Bengalis" to refer to them in order to indicate that the Rohingya were not ethnic Rakhines,[6] but rather, were immigrants from Bangladesh.[7] That is to say, both the Rakhine Burmese and the Myanmarese state authorities consider the Rohingya to be immigrants imported into their country by British colonial rule in the nineteenth and twentieth centuries.[8] For its part, the government of Bangladesh claims that the Rohingya did not in fact originate there.[9]

Inevitably, the historical origins of the Rohingya and the history of the Rakhine region are also contested in Myanmar between the Rohingya origin narrative and Rakhine Burmese narratives.[10] The contradictory narratives are partially due to "the poor state of archaeology" in the area.[11]

To begin with, the name "Rohingya" is said to have originated from the old name of the Arakan Kingdom, Rohang/Roshang, and Rohingya refers to the inhabitants of Rohang.[12] The term Rohingya is said to have come into use only recently.[13] According to one theory, it dates back to 1799.[14] Modern usage, by contrast, is said to have started in 1950.[15] This post- World War II period was also when the people in question began seeking recognition as Muslims in what was then Burma.[16]

A typical rendering of the Rohingya origin narrative claims that there have been four waves of Muslim migration into, and presence in, the region.[17] The aim of all

---

[3] International Court of Justice (2020), para. 15.

[4] Pre-Trial Chamber III of the International Criminal Court (2019). p. 9, para. 17.

[5] UN Doc. A/RES/73/264 (22 January 2019).

[6] Myanmar State Counsellor Daw Aung San Suu Kyi (2017).

[7] Ware and Laoutides (2018), p. xv.

[8] Bari (2018), p. 2.

[9] Farzana (2017), p. 2.

[10] Ware and Laoutides (2018), pp. 75–136.

[11] Ware and Laoutides (2018), p. 108.

[12] Velath and Chopra (2018), p. 75.

[13] Chaudhury and Samaddar (2018), p. 6.

[14] De Lang (2019), p. 159.

[15] Leider (2018). Chan (2005), p. 397.

[16] Leider (2020), p. 1.

[17] Ware and Laoutides (2018), p. 79. Bari (2018), p. 2.

2.1 Introduction

such efforts is to show that there is a historical basis to the Rohingya claim to being indigenous to Arakan.[18] It is thought that the first king of Arakan ruled in 2666 B.C,[19] while the first Arakan Kingdom was founded in the fifth century.[20] A king of the Chandra Dynasty established the capital of the Arakan Kingdom at Dinnyawadi.[21] Today, Muslims in Arakan are divided into Thambaikkya, Zerbadi, Kamanchi and Rohingya.[22]

The first wave of Muslim presence in the region is marked by Arab traders traveling from the Red Sea region to trade over an extensive area including the Chinese coast and Arakan, supposedly as early as the ninth century.[23] It is said that Arab merchant ships reached and settled in Arakan due to bad weather, and that these Arabs married the indigenous Burmese people, leading to the growth of the Muslim population in Burma.[24] There is, however, a lack of critical examination of that period of the early history of Arakan when this first wave would have occurred, and it is difficult to believe that Muslims were genuinely present in the region at that time.[25]

The second wave of Muslim migration took place mainly in the fifteenth century and largely came from India,[26] when European merchants began to trade along the coast, making it difficult for the Arabs to maintain their historical occupation of Southeast Asian waters.[27] King Narameikhia (also called Min Saw Mun) assumed the in Arakan circa 1404, but was overthrown after two years due to Burmese resistance to his kingship.[28] He regained his throne in 1430 with the help of the Sultan of Bengal, establishing the Mrauk-U dynasty.[29] The dynasty was so named because Narameikhia moved his capital and his court from Launggyet to the town of Mrauk-U near the eastern coast of the Bay of Bengal, as part of an effort to establish strong tie with the Sultan.[30] Thereafter, many Bengali traders and craftsmen visited the court at Mrauk-U,[31] and Islam became a significant religion in this area beginning at this time, one which would remain popular among later generations of the Mrauk-U dynasty.[32] If nothing else, Muslims lived in the court at Mrauk-U, which was indifferent to the religious origin of the peoples in its domain.[33]

---

[18] Ware and Laoutides (2018), p. 78.

[19] Yimprasert (2004), p. 66.

[20] Yimprasert (2004), p. 66.

[21] Yimprasert (2004), p. 66.

[22] Karim (2016), p. 95.

[23] Ware and Laoutides (2018), pp. 79–81; Bari (2018), p. 2; Ahmed and Mohiuddin, (2020), pp. 4–5.

[24] Bari (2018), pp. 2–3; Ahmed and Mohiuddin, (2020), pp. 4–5.

[25] Ware and Laoutides (2018), pp. 80–81.

[26] Chowdhory and Mohanty (2020), p. 6.

[27] Ahmed and Mohiuddin, (2020), p. 5.

[28] Ware and Laoutides (2018), p. 82.

[29] Chaudhury and Samaddar (2018), p. 8.

[30] Bari (2018), p. 25.

[31] Chaudhury and Samaddar (2018), p. 9.

[32] Chowdhory and Mohanty (2020), p. 6; Ibrahim (2016), p. 39.

[33] Ware and Laoutides (2018), p. 86.

The third wave is believed to have been caused by the Portuguese slave trade, mainly during the seventeenth century,[34] and it appears to the largest such wave.[35] It is believed that the Portuguese first arrived in the Arakan Kingdom in 1501–1523.[36] Initially, it was Bengal that depended on Portuguese power, but when Bengal was defeated by the Mughal Kingdom, Portugal approached Arakan, which became friendly to the Portuguese.[37] In the 1560 and 70 s, Portuguese merchants even began to serve in the Arakanese navy.[38] Portuguese merchants, serving Arakan but not controlled by Arakan, soon engaged in piracy in the neighboring waters. The Bengalis captured during this period were sold in Arakan, which is said to have contributed to the migration of Muslims to the region.[39] These Bengali slaves were sometimes sold to Dutch merchants who first arrived in Arakan in 1608.[40] The Rohingya narrative stresses "the impact of slave capture, transport, and resettlement on a massive scale" on the Arakan Kingdom throughout the seventeenth century.[41] By contrast, non-Rohingya narratives have contested the size of this purported forced migration.[42]

According to the Rohingya narrative, this fourth wave of Muslim migration prior to the colonial era was "during the time the Mughal Emperor's son Shah Shuja sought refuge in Arakan," that is, when the Mughals ruled Bengal.[43] Although Shuja became governor of Bengal in 1639 with the support of his father, the Mughal Emperor, his brother ousted him upon the Emperor's death,[44] whereupon Shuja fled with his family, property and army to Mrauk-U[45] in May 1660.[46] The king of Arakan welcomed Shuja, giving him shelter.[47] Although the particulars remain a subject of debate, Shuja's plot to rebel against King Arakan, who had begun to mistreat him, failed, and he and his family were massacred.[48] Whatever the case, Shuja was killed on February 7, 1661.[49] It is said that the arrival of Shuja's forces came to Arakan marks an influx of Muslims into the region.[50] These soldiers of Shuja's later became the Kaman, who, following Burmese independence, were designated a "taing yin

---

[34] Ware and Laoutides (2018), p. 86.

[35] Ware and Laoutides (2018), p. 86.

[36] Yimprasert (2004), p. 67.

[37] Ware and Laoutides (2018), p. 86.

[38] Yimprasert (2004), p. 68.

[39] Ware and Laoutides (2018), pp. 86–87.

[40] Yimprasert (2004), p. 79.

[41] Ware and Laoutides (2018), p. 87.

[42] Ware and Laoutides (2018), p. 87.

[43] Ware and Laoutides (2018), p. 88.

[44] Ware and Laoutides (2018), p. 88.

[45] Ware and Laoutides (2018), p. 88.

[46] Nurul (1953), p. 392.

[47] Ware and Laoutides (2018), p. 88; Das and Das (1966), p. 164.

[48] Ware and Laoutides (2018), p. 88; Das and Das (1966), pp. 166–167.

[49] Das and Das (1966), p. 167.

[50] Ware and Laoutides (2018), p. 88.

tha" (indigenous) ethnic Muslim group in Rakhine State.[51] By these events, Shuja's family is said to have played a role in the settlement of Muslims in Arakan.[52] While the Kaman and the Rohingya comprise the two main Muslim groups in Rakhine State,[53] only the former, currently living on Ramree Island,[54] is a recognized ethnic group in Myanmar. Shuja's feud with the King of Arakan and its aftermath was later used by both Rohingya and non-Rohingya in Myanmar as an excuse to explain their acrimonious relations.[55]

In 1784–85, the Burmese King Bodawpaya conquered and incorporated the Arakan Kingdom into the Kingdom of Ava in Upper Burma.[56] The Arakanese people turned to rebellion against Burma because Bodawpaya enslaved and oppressed them.[57] Consequently, the Arakanese are said to have fled to Bengal in their thousands.[58] Arakan was ceded to Great Britain in 1826 by virtue of the latter's victory in the First Anglo-Burmese War (1824–26).[59] Freed from Burmese oppression, the Arakanese gave their allegiance to the British.[60]

2.2 Colonial Period

The colonial period, especially British rule, may be treated as the fifth wave of immigrants into Burma. It is believed that British colonial rule only intensified the historical hatred between Burmese and Arakanese.[61] Following the aforementioned First Anglo-Burmese War, the British would fight two more wars for the acquisition and colonization of Burma, in 1852–53 and 1885,[62] expanding their colonial holdings each time. In addition to Arakan, Britain also annexed Tenasserim in the First Anglo-Burmese War.[63] The British established a new seat of government at Akyab, also called Sittwe, and which is the capital of present-day Rakhine State.[64] The British then requested that farmers move from neighboring Chittagong to cultivate Arakanese

---

[51] Ware and Laoutides (2018), p. 88.

[52] Bari (2018), p. 5.

[53] Mohajan (2018), p. 30.

[54] Mohajan (2018), p. 29.

[55] Ahmed and Mohiuddin, (2020), p. 9.

[56] Ware and Laoutides (2018), p. 109; Farzana (2017), p. 43; Chowdhory, Mohanty (2020), p. 41.

[57] Farzana (2017), p. 43.

[58] Farzana (2017), p. 43.

[59] Bari (2018), p. 27.

[60] Farzana (2017), p. 44.

[61] Chowdhory, Mohanty (2020), p. 41.

[62] Bergsmo (2019), p. 7; Chowdhory and Mohanty (2020), p. 207.

[63] Farzana (2017), p. 44; Bergsmo (2019), p. 7, fn. 20.

[64] Bari (2018), p. 9.

land.[65] In this way, the farmers from Chittagong and migrants from the British Raj contributed to increases in the number of Muslims in Arakan.[66]

The Second Anglo-Burmese War of 1852–53 resulted in the British annexation of Pegu,[67] with Burma falling entirely to the British in the third Anglo-Burmese War of 1885.[68] The British had used Arakan as a buffer zone until they established control over Burma,[69] and it is reported that the British took advantage of the fact that the Arakanese were rebelling against Burma by using the Arakanese as a guerilla force.[70] The new colonial administration redrew the map of the region, creating a separation between Ministerial Burma and the Frontier Areas.[71]

The region known today as Burma is an ethnic archipelago, with a central lowland area inhabited by the Burmese, Mon, and some Karen, and many ethnic minorities with their own languages and cultures living in the surrounding mountains.[72] Whereas Ministerial Burma consisted of the lowlands and valleys, the mountains constituted the Frontier Areas.[73] Although the former was controlled by the colonial central authority, the latter was indirectly ruled by the British Empire itself. This is known as the 'direct-indirect rule' model of colonial rule.[74] In this mode of governance, local leaders in the Frontier Areas remained in power, under the Empire's watchful eyes.[75] The difference in degree of colonial rule is said to stem from the British interest in the production and export of rice, and to be related to the fact that only Central Burma was suitable for rice cultivation.[76] This differentiation also caused an ethnic tension between communities.[77] For these reasons, this policy is also known as 'divide and rule'.[78]

The British moved many people from the Raj to Burma.[79] It is said that the British brought more immigrants to this area than the total number of Israeli settlers in the West Bank.[80] This policy led to increased friction between the immigrants and the indigenous Burmese. It is said that this influx of economic migrants came at a time of unemployment for those already living there, causing the Burmese to feel antagonistic

---

[65] Bari (2018), p. 9.

[66] Bari (2018), p. 9; Ahmed and Mohiuddin, (2020), p. 9.

[67] Bergsmo (2019), p. 7, fn. 20; Farzana (2017), p. 44.

[68] Clarke, et al. (2019), p. 16; Bergsmo (2019), p. 7, fn. 20.

[69] Farzana (2017), p. 44.

[70] Farzana (2017), p. 44.

[71] Clarke et al. (2019), p. 16.

[72] Selth (1986), pp. 484–485.

[73] Clarke et al. (2019), p. 16.

[74] Ahmed and Mohiuddin (2020), p. 112.

[75] Clarke et al. (2019), p. 16.

[76] Clarke et al. (2019), p. 16.

[77] Farzana (2017), p. 44; Clarke et al. (2019), p. 16.

[78] Bari (2018), p. 29.

[79] Bergsmo (2019), p. 7.

[80] Bergsmo (2019), p. 8. *See also* Federman (2019).

2.2 Colonial Period

toward the Indian migrants.[81] The nationalist Buddhists deliberately began calling the Indians *Kala*, meaning foreigners.[82]

On April 1, 1937, Burma formally split from India.[83] Muslims living in Burma took this opportunity to try to gain autonomy therein.[84] By 1938, both the anti-colonial movement that began in 1937 and anti-Muslim sentiment reached a peak,[85] with the former targeting the Rohingya as well as colonial rule.[86] Prior to separation, "there were no Burmans in the regular Burma Army and, until shortly before separation, none in the military police."[87] To counter British occupation, Marxist groups in Burma gathered together to form the Communist Party of Burma (CPB) on August 15, 1939.[88] After the Japanese invaded Burma, the CPB took part in anti-Japanese resistance.[89] Following a mutiny in March–April 1989, the CPB ultimately ceased to exist.[90]

World War II and the Japanese invasion of Burma further complicated the Burmese ethnic consciousness. At the time, the Japanese military contributed to the further escalation of ethnic conflict in the region.[91] The Japanese incursion divided the people into two hostile camps, with the Rakhines backing the Japanese and the Muslims supporting the British.[92] Thus, while many Muslims remained loyal to the British during World War II, some of the Arakanese forged ties with the Burmese nationalists and the Japanese.[93] The British established a unit called 'V Force,' which was a guerrilla army composed of Arakanese Muslims.[94] The resulting ethnic conflict of colonial origin led to massive killing on both sides.[95] It is reported that Japan instigated the Burma Independence Army (BIA), headed by General Aung San, to attack minorities which rebelled against the Japanese army.[96] The Japanese army itself is said to have attacked those Rohingya who showed allegiance to the British army.[97] The full extent to which these Muslims and Rakhines were killed in the war

---

[81] Bari (2018), p. 11.

[82] Bari (2018), p. 11.

[83] Guyot-Réchard (2021), p. 296.

[84] Chowdhory and Mohanty (2020), p. 8.

[85] Chowdhory and Mohanty (2020), p. 8.

[86] Bari (2018), p. 12.

[87] Selth (1986), p. 488.

[88] Communist Party of Burma (1964).

[89] Lintner (1994, 2019), p. xv.

[90] Lintner (1994, 2019), p. 297.

[91] Selth (1986), p. 494.

[92] Chowdhory and Mohanty (2020), p. 8.

[93] Ware and Laoutides (2018), p. 14.

[94] Bari (2018), p. 12.

[95] Ware and Laoutides (2018), p. 15.

[96] Chowdhory and Mohanty (2020), pp. 8–9. Clarke et al. (2019), p. 19.

[97] Bari (2018), p. 12.

remains unclear to this day.[98] In any event, it is probable that some of the hostilities between Buddhists and Rohingya were formed in the colonial period.[99]

Near the end of World War II, the BIA approached the Allies with the aim of overthrowing the Japanese military occupation. The Anti-Facist People's Freedom League (AFPFL) was also founded to resist the Japanese occupation in league with the BIA.[100] After negotiating with the British, Aung San revolted against the Japanese on March 27, 1945.[101] When Japan was defeated, Britain offered Aung San a generalship in the newly established Burmese Army, but he declined the offer in order to maintain his position as a revolutionary outsider and head of the AFPFL.[102] When Japan surrendered, the BIA turned around and made a token resistance to British rule. Following independence, the BIA became the core of the Burmese national army.[103]

After concluding an agreement with British Prime Minister Clement Atlee in London which promised Burmese independence on January 27, 1947, Aung San, keenly aware of the need to unite different ethnic groups, held a conference. He envisioned post-independence Burma as an inclusive state that would treat all of its people as equal citizens.[104] Nonetheless, there were other within the military, such as Ne Win, with a strong preference for continued military control of the state.[105] Many Burmese nationalists also resented the fact that ethnic minorities in the country had aligned themselves with British colonial rule.[106] It is also said that the British granted independence to the Burmese nationalists on the condition that they consult with the non-Burmese on the frontier, rather than spontaneously on the part of Aung San.[107] This led to the Panglong Conference, which was held on February 12, 1947,[108] the outcome of which was the Panglong Agreement (Panglong Accord). In its preamble, the Accord stipulated that "freedom will be more speedily achieved by the Shans, the Kachins and the Chins by their immediate co-operation with the Interim Burmese Government." However, other ethnic groups, such as the Karen, Mon, and Arakanese were not represented at the conference and did not sign the Accord.[109]

A Constituent Assembly was elected in Burma in April 1947.[110] At the May 1947 Convention of the AFPFL, Aung San revealed that the draft Constitution submitted to the conference had been modeled on the Yugoslav Constitution and the USSR.[111]

---

[98] Ware and Laoutides (2018), p. 15.

[99] Williams et al. (2020), p. 545.

[100] Clarke et al. (2019), p. 20.

[101] Ibrahim (2016), p. 28.

[102] Ackerman (2019), p. 284.

[103] Ibrahim (2016), p. 28.

[104] Ibrahim (2016), p. 36.

[105] Ibrahim (2016), p. 36.

[106] Bari (2018), p. 13.

[107] Clarke et al. (2019), p. 20.

[108] Ahmed and Mohiuddin (2020), p. 112.

[109] Clarke et al. (2019), p. 20.

[110] The Burma Constitution (1948), p. 99.

[111] The Burma Constitution (1948), p. 98.

2.3 Post-independence

On July 19 1947, Aung San was assassinated together with five of his colleagues.[112] Despite these killings, the Constituent Assembly managed to adopt the Constitution, advancing the core principles envisioned by Aung San.[113] This constitution took into account the autonomy of ethnic minorities,[114] but lacked reference to the Rohingya.

World War II brought many immigrants from India and elsewhere to Burma,[115] as well as the migration of the Rakhine people northern Rakhine.[116] As a result, it has been said that "Britain, with its historic links with Myanmar as the main colonial power and as a permanent member of the UN Security Council, has a huge moral and global responsibility to initiate some practical steps to resolve the Rohingya crisis."[117]

2.3 Post-independence

Japan withdrew from Burma in 1945. The British colonial occupation ended with Burma gaining independence on January 4, 1948, in accordance with the Panglong Agreement. In 1949, conflict broke out between the Karen armed forces and the Burmese government, and the security situation in Burma deteriorated from there.[118] Thus, the pre-existing situation of skirmishes between the central and peripheral forces in Burma remained the same even after independence.[119] At the time, Buddhist nationalists, communists, and a Rohingya insurgency emerged in Arakan.[120] Not surprisingly, the new government was hostile to the Rohingya and did not grant them citizenship until 1948.[121]

In the 1950s, the U Nu administration recognized the Rohingya as an indigenous ethnic group.[122] It is reported that there is evidence that under Burmese law, the Rohingya were treated no differently than any other minority group therafter until 1962.[123] In fact, the Rohingya are said to hold seats in the parliament, and that a Rohingya-dialect radio station was established.[124] However, the *coup* of March 2, 1962 made the situation worse for the Rohingya.[125] Even though the change of

---

[112] Clarke et al. (2019), p. 20.

[113] Ackerman (2019), p. 285.

[114] The Burma Constitution (1948), p. 100.

[115] Chaudhury and Samaddar (2018), p. 10.

[116] Ware and Laoutides (2018), p. 15.

[117] Bari (2018), p. 18.

[118] Clarke et al. (2019), p. 22.

[119] Chaudhury and Samaddar (2018), p. 6.

[120] Bari (2018), p. 14.

[121] Ibrahim (2016), p. 8.

[122] Bari (2018), p. 14.

[123] Ibrahim (2016), p. 8.

[124] Bari (2018), p. 14.

[125] Bari (2018), p. 14.

the situation is described as having happened gradually,[126] the political and civil rights of the most of the Rohingya were violated under the Ne Win regime.[127] The resistance movement that took place between 1950 and 1954 to demand citizenship for the Rohingya and an end to the discriminatory treatment against them was ultimately contained by the government.[128] The junta established the Burma Socialist Programme Party (BSPP), a one-party state. The 1974 Constitution emphasized the nation-state and denied the Rohingya the status they had been given since independence.[129] In accordance with the constitution, the government began to try to undermine the political base of the Rohingya.[130] Although there are many theories about when it started,[131] the citizen registration operation known as Dragon King or Nagamin, which pushed 200,000–250,000 Rohingya refugees into Bangladesh within three months,[132] was carried out in 1978 by Ne Win for the sake of national unity. At the same time, the military launched operation "Ye The Ha" north Arakan, driving Muslims to take refuge elsewhere.[133] Burma allowed refugees to return in 1979 under pressure from Muslim countries in the UN and mediation by the UN High Commissioner for Refugees. However, the Burmese government maintained its hardline stance against the Rohingya.[134]

In 1982, the Burmese government amended and promulgated the Citizenship Law to designate the Rohingya as Foreigners.[135] The law recognizes 135 ethnicities, excluding the Rohingya. This law remains in effect and this is the reason why Rohingya do not have citizenship in Myanmar. The Rohingya have since been frequently called Bengalis and considered illegal immigrants consequently.

A 1988 student protest against the Ne Win dictatorship led to the 8888 Uprising.[136] In the face of the resulting domestic turmoil, Ne Win stepped down in July.[137] On August 8, there was a demonstration against the government which the military suppressed, imposing martial law, which resulted in many casualties.[138] On

---

[126] Ibrahim (2016), p. 8.

[127] Bari (2018), p. 14.

[128] Barany (2018), p. 142.

[129] Ibrahim (2016), p. 8.

[130] Farzana (2017), p.49; Bari (2018), p. 14.

[131] *E.g.*, Holt describes that the Dragon Strategy under Ne Win began in the early 1970s after the establishment of Bangladesh in order to expel the Bengalis of Maungdaw and Buthidaung. Holt (2019), p. 195. Bari described Dragon King or Nagamin as having started on February 6, 1978. *See* Bari (2018), p. 15. Several authors also endorse 1978 as the start of the operaion. Thawnghmung (2016), p. 531; Martin et al. (2018), p. 341. Others claim that the operation was carried out in 1977. Farzana (2017), p.49.

[132] Thawnghmung (2016), pp. 531–532; Bari (2018), p. 15; Martin et al. (2018), p. 341; Chaudhury and Samaddar (2018), pp. 10–11; Clarke et al. (2019), p. 25.

[133] Chaudhury and Samaddar (2018), p. 11.

[134] Bari (2018), p. 15; Thawnghmung (2016), p. 532.

[135] See 2(e) of the Burmese Citizenship Law 1982.

[136] Bari (2018), p. 16.

[137] Clarke et al. (2019), p. 26.

[138] Clarke et al. (2019), p. 26.

2.3 Post-independence

September 18, 1988, General Saw Maung led a *coup* that replaced the BSPP with a new junta: the State Law and Order Restoration Council (SLORC),[139] which also suspended the 1974 Constitution.[140] In 1989, SLORC replaced many Burmese place names, including the country itself, with those derived from the national language, with Burma and Burmese becoming Myanmar and Myanmarese, respectively.[141] At the same time, the Rohingya were allowed to form political parties in 1989, whereupon they established the Students and Youth League for Mayu Development (SYLMD) and the National Democratic Party for Human Rights (NDPH).[142] On May 27, 1990, SLORC held a general election.[143] Despite the repressive atmosphere, a movement calling itself the National League for Democracy (NLD), led by Aung San Suu Kyi, won a landslide victory.[144] However, SLORC refused to recognize the results of the election until a new constitution was enacted.[145] The resulting popular backlash was suppressed by the military. This failure of democratization led to the activation of Rohingya militias,[146] which was met with a massive Rohingya clearance operation by the Tatmadaw in 1991–92, which resulted in another 250,000 refugees in Bangladesh.[147]

The military campaign was dispersed in April 1992 when the generals were replaced.[148] General Than Shwe replaced Saw Maung that month[149] and began work on a new constitution, which was drafted between 1993–2007, with a suspension from 1996–2004.[150] He also renamed SLORC the State Peace and Development Council (SPDC). In May 2003, Aung San Suu Kyi's convoy was attacked by thugs, the NLD was suppressed, and she was placed under house arrest.[151]

In August 2003, General Khin Nyunt developed a seven-step roadmap to "disciplined democracy." These steps were: (1) reconvening the National Convention; (2) step by step implementation of the process necessary for the emergence of a genuine and disciplined democracy; (3) drafting of a new constitution in accordance with the basic principles laid down by the National Convention; (4) adoption of the Constitution through national referendum; (5) holding of free and fair elections for Pyithu Hluttaws (legislative bodies) according to the new Constitution; (6) convening of Hluttaws attended by Hluttaw members in accordance with the new Constitution; and (7) the building of a modern, developed, and democratic nation by state leaders

---

[139] Clarke et al. (2019), p. 26.

[140] Clarke et al. (2019), p. 26.

[141] Clarke et al. (2019), p. 26.

[142] Haque (2020), p. 65.

[143] Bari (2018), p. 16.

[144] Bari (2018), p. 16; Clarke et al. (2019), p. 26.

[145] Clarke et al. (2019), p. 26.

[146] Ware and Laoutides (2018), p. 78.

[147] Ware and Laoutides (2018), p. 78; Bari (2018), p. 16; Farzana (2017), p. 120.

[148] Ware and Laoutides (2018), p. 17.

[149] Clarke et al. (2019), p. 27.

[150] Clarke et al. (2019), p. 27.

[151] Ewing-Chow (2007), p. 154.

elected by the Hluttaws together with the government and other central organs formed by the Hluttaws.[152]

In October 2004, Khin Nyunt was disgraced by corruption charges and replaced by the more conservative Lieutenant General (later General) Soe Win.[153] The new government, finding itself increasingly isolated, moved the capital from Yangon to the remote city of Naypyidaw, Pyinmana, in a previously planned transition.[154] Anti-government momentum grew, especially among the poor, in the wake of gas and oil price hikes, resulting in demonstrations by Buddhists against the junta, in what has been called the Saffron Revolution.[155] In response to the demonstrations, a final draft of the constitution was presented in February 2008.[156] Although the SPDC had scheduled a referendum on the new constitution for early May 2008, Cyclone Nargis struck Myanmar on May 2–3, reportedly killing some 140,000 Burmese.[157] At the time, the Rohingya were allowed to vote in the referendum.[158] Then the SPDC postponed voting in areas hit by the cyclone until May 24, and set May 10 as the date for the vote in the rest of the country.[159] The new constitution was adopted with the support of more than 90 percent of the population, according to the government.[160] In April 2009, after the adoption of the 2008 Constitution, the SPDC declared that all groups and militias that agreed to lay down arms would be reorganized as Border Guard Forces in accordance with Section 338 of the new constitution.[161] The junta was come to an end after the next general election was held, in 2010.

In 2010, the generals formed the Union Solidarity and Development Party (USDP).[162] Aung San Suu Kyi met directly with the USDP and initiated a peace process with them.[163] Shwe Maung (a/k/a Abdul Razak) was elected in 2010 on a USDP ticket, and he spoke in parliament on behalf of the Rohingya.[164] Midterm elections held in 2012 were said to be more transparent and democratic than these general elections.[165]

---

[152] Thawnghmung and Myoe (2008), p. 15, fn. 5.

[153] Ewing-Chow (2007), p. 155.

[154] Ewing-Chow (2007), p. 155.

[155] Steinberg (2008), p. 53.

[156] Nardi (2014), p. 650.

[157] Nardi (2014), p. 650.

[158] Haque (2020), p. 65.

[159] Nardi (2014), p. 650.

[160] Nardi (2014), p. 650.

[161] Clarke et al. (2019), p. 44.

[162] Kipgen (2021), p. 3.

[163] Clarke et al. (2019), p. 44.

[164] Haque (2020), p. 66.

[165] Marston (2013), pp. 282–283.

2.3 Post-independence

During this period, the armed struggle between the Myanmar army and the Karen National Union (KNU), the Karenni National Progressive Party (KNPP), and the Shan State Army-South (SSA-S) continued in eastern Myanmar.[166] The plight of the Rohingya remained as serious as ever.[167] In 2012, violent clashes between Buddhists and Rohingya in Rakhine State led to the declaration of a state of emergency there,[168] as well as the latest wave of Rohingya refugees.

It was not until 2013 that the Rohingya themselves founded the Arakan Rohingya Salvation Army (ARSA) in an attempt to address their own plight. There had been previous attempts by the Rohingya to unite politically, but they were quickly stifled by the government due to lack of financial resources and the overall vulnerability of the Rohingya.[169] The leaders of the ARSA are said to be from Pakistan or Bangladesh, and counts less than six hundred active members.[170]

The NLD won the 2015 elections, forming a government in March 2016.[171] After Aung San Suu Kyi became State Counsellor, her Office, that of the State Counsellor, and the Kofi Annan Foundation established an Advisory Commission on Rakhine State to examine the challenges facing the region.[172] The Commission presented its final report and recommendations to the Government of Myanmar in August 2017. No progress was made, however, in the repatriation of Rohingya refugees.[173] The Myanmar government stepped up its offensive against the ARSA during 2016–17,[174] after labeling the group a terrorist organization.[175]

In the next general election, held on November 8, 2020, amid the COVID-19 crisis,[176] the NLD won another five-year term.[177] The USDP made allegations of electoral fraud.[178] According to USDP spokesman Thein Tun Oo, the NLD ministers claimed that they were in an advantageous position because they had been campaigning since July 2020, while other political parties in Myanmar were subject to various COVID-19-related restrictions.[179]

---

[166] Haacke (2009), p. 177.

[167] Bari (2018), p. 17.

[168] Clarke et al. (2019), p. 45.

[169] Barany (2018), p. 142.

[170] Barany (2018), pp. 142–143.

[171] Bari (2018), p. 21.

[172] Bari (2018), p. 21.

[173] Bari (2018), p. 28.

[174] Parveen and Sahana (2022), p. 362.

[175] Lee (2021), p. 61.

[176] Kipgen (2021), p. 1.

[177] Kipgen (2021), p. 1.

[178] Kipgen (2021), p. 1.

[179] Kipgen (2021), p. 3.

On 1 February 2021, a few hours before the National Assembly was to convene, the military staged a *coup d'état*, taking the NLD leaders into custody.[180] The military justified this act with further claims of election fraud. This *coup* was seen as backsliding on the road to democracy in Myanmar and an obstacle to peace negotiations between the government and ethnic minorities.[181]

2.4 Conclusion

It has been pointed out that inter-communal conflict in Rakhine State is a clash of narratives.[182] This may also be true of the history of Rakhine State itself, given that both the Burmese Buddhists and the Muslims keep trying to legitimize their political claims[183] and residency status to the area. Myanmar is a multi-ethnic polity that has been struggling to govern itself for many years, with the military growing in power over that time. It should also be remembered that British colonial rule and the World War II Japanese occupation of Myanmar have resulted in indifference on the part of the Myanmarese majority to the Rohingya crisis in their midst.[184] The true history of the Rohingya is not easily identified, and conclusions are not ready to hand. This situation is a microcosm of Myanmar as whole: being a multi-ethnic country, its likewise does not have a unified history. This does not provide justification for ongoing subjugation and persecution of minorities, however. It is precisely because of Myanmar's complicated history that a path of peaceful coexistence must be found.

Myanmar has seen frequent armed clashes between ethnic minorities and the junta since the 1960s, particularly in Kachin and Shan States.[185] Despite the overall difficult situation facing Myanmar's minorities, the fact that the persecution of the Rohingya has attracted the attention of the international community is a sign of that their plight is even more serious. As suggested by the former United Nations High Commissioner for Refugees, there may be no humanitarian solutions of Rohingya crisis, only political solutions.[186] The 2021 *coup* took the humanitarian crisis a long way away from any such political resolution. In these circumstances, the international community's efforts to address the Rohingya crisis are being closely watched. In the next chapter, we will examine these very efforts, particularly in the arena of international criminal justice.

---

[180] Kipgen (2021), p. 12.

[181] Kipgen (2021), p. 14.

[182] Advisory Commission on Rakhine State (2017), p. 19.

[183] Advisory Commission on Rakhine State (2017), p. 19.

[184] Parveen and Sahana (2022), pp. 360–361.

[185] Ochi and Matsuyama (2019), p. 340.

[186] Ogata (2005), p. 25.

References

Ackerman B (2019) Revolutionary Constitutions: charismatic leadership and the rule of law. Belknap Press of Harvard University Press, Cambridge, Mass

Advisory Commission on Rakhine State (2017) Towards a peaceful, fair and prosperous future for the people of Rakhine: final report of the advisory commission on Rakhine State. https://www.rakhinecommission.org/app/uploads/2017/08/FinalReport_Eng.pdf

Ahmed K, Mohiuddin H (2020) The Rohingya crisis. Lexington Books, Maryland

Barany Z (2018) Where Myanmar went wrong: from democratic awakening to ethnic cleansing. Foreign Aff 97(3):141–154

Bari MA (2018) The Rohingya crisis: a people facing extinction. Kube Publishing, Markfield

Bergsmo M (2019) Myanmar, colonial aftermath, and access to international law. Toaep's Occas Paper Ser 9:1–24

Chan A (2005) The development of a Muslim enclave in Arakan (Rakhine) State of Burma (Myanmar). SOAS Bull Burma Res 3(2):396–420

Chaudhury SBR, Samaddar R (2018) Introduction. In: Chaudhury SBR, Samaddar R (eds) The Rohingya in South Asia: people without a state. Routledge, London, pp 1–19

Chowdhory N, Mohanty B (2020) Contextualizing citizenship, nationalism and refugeehood of Rohingya: an introduction. Springer, Singapore

Clarke SL, Myint SAS, Siwa ZY (2019) Re-examining ethnic identity in Myanmar. Centre for Peace and Conflict Studies, Siem Reap

Communist Party of Burma (1964) A short outline of the history of the Communist Party of Burma. https://digital.lib.washington.edu/researchworks/bitstream/handle/1773/24715/A_short_outline.pdf;jsessionid=4EAC11135A5AC5FDE0FBEBF00C8CE68F?sequence=1

Das RK, Das RK (1966) The end of prince Shuja and his family. Proc Indian Hist Cong 28:164–168

De Lang NE (2019) The Rohingya and other Muslim minorities in Myanmar: human rights and the marginalisation of the most vulnerable. In: De Varennes F, Gardiner CM (eds) Routledge handbook of human rights in Asia. Routledge, London, pp 158–183

Ewing-Chow M (2007) First do no harm: Myanmar trade sanctions and human rights. Northwestern Univer J Int Human Rights 5(2):153–180

Farzana KF (2017) Memories of Burmese Rohingya refugees: contested identity and belonging. Palgrave Macmillan, New York

Federman J (2019) West Bank settlers report surge in population growth. The Times of Israel

Guyot-Réchard B (2021) Tangled lands: Burma and India's unfinished separation, 1937–1948. J Asian Stud 80(2):293–315

Haacke J (2009) Myanmar, the responsibility to protect, and the need for practical assistance. Glob Responsib Protect 1(2):156–184

Haque MM (2020) A future for the Rohingya in Myanmar. In: Swazo NK, Tawfique S, Haque M, Haque MM, Nower T (eds) The Rohingya crisis: a moral, ethnographic, and policy assessment. Routledge, Abingdon, pp 52–78

Holt JC (2019) Myanmar's Buddhist-Muslim crisis: Rohingya. In: Arakanese, and Burmese narratives of siege and fear. Honolulu. University of Hawai'i Press

Ibrahim A (2016) The Rohingyas: inside Myanmar's hidden Genocide. Hurst and Company, London

International Court of Justice (2020) Order. Application of the Convention on the Prevention and Punishment of the Crime of Genocide (the Gambia v. Myanmar)

Karim A (2016) The Rohingyas: a short account of their history and culture. Jatiya Sahitya Prakash, Dhaka

Kipgen N (2021) The 2020 Myanmar election and the 2021 coup: deepning democracy or widening division. Asian Aff 52(1):1–17

Lee R (2021) Myanmar's Arakan Rohingya Salvation Army (ARSA): an analysis of a New Muslim Militant Group and its strategic communications. Perspect Terrorism 16(6):61–75

Leider J (2018) Rohingya: the history of a Muslim identity in Myanmar. In: Ludden D (ed) Oxford Research Encyclopedia of Asian History. Oxford University Press, Oxford. https://doi.org/10.1093/acrefore/9780190277727.013.115

Leider JP (2020) Rohingya: the foundational years. Toaep's Policy Brief Series 123:1–4

Lintner B (1994, 2019) Burma in revolt: opium and insurgency since 1948. Routledge, New York

Marston H (2013) Myanmar's electoral system: reviewing the 2010 and 2012 elections and looking ahead to the 2015 general elections. Asian J Polit Sci 21(3):268–284

Martin MF, Margesson R, Vaughn B (2018) The Rohingya Crises in Bangladesh and Burma. Curr Polit Econ South, Southeastern Central Asia 27(3–4):333–375

Mohajan HK (2018) History of Rakhine State and the origin of the Rohingya Muslims. Indonesian J Southeast Asian Stud 2(1):19–46

Myanmar State Counsellor Daw Aung San Suu Kyi (2017) In an exclusive interview with Ani, Spoke About The ongoing Rohingya refugee crisis, counter-terrorism, The Dalai Lama's "Buddha To Help Rohingyas" assertion and the way forward. https://www.statecounsellor.gov.mm/en/node/1032, https://www.aninews.in/news/world/asia/myanmar-state-councillor-aung-san-suu-kyis-interview-with-ani-full-transcript201709201439310001/

Nardi DJ (2014) Finding Justice Scalia in Burma: constitutional interpretation and the impeachment of Myanmar's constitutional tribunal. Pac Rim Law Policy J 23(3):633–682

Nurul KM (1953) Fate of Shah Shuja- his flight to Arakan and death. J Pakistan Hist Soc 1(4):392–397

Ochi M, Matsuyama S (2019) Ethnic Conflicts in Myanmar: The Application of the Law of Non-International Armed Conflict. In: Linton S, McCormack T, Sivakumaran S (eds) Asia-Pacific perspectives on international humanitarian law. Cambridge University Press, Cambridge, pp 338–355

Ogata S (2005) The Turbulent Decade: Confronting The Refugee Crises of The 1990s. Norton, New York

Parveen S, Sahana M (2022) Identity and humanitarian-based approach: resolution and resolving the Rohingya Refugee Crisis. In: Bülbül K, Islam MN, Khan MS (eds) Rohingya Refugee Crisis in Myanmar: ethnic conflict and resolution. Palgrave Macmillan, Singapore, pp 357–378

Pre-Trial Chamber III of the International Criminal Court (2019) Decision Pursuant to Article 15 of the Rome Statute on the Authorisation of an Investigation into the Situation in the People's Republic of Bangladesh/Republic of the Union of Myanmar

Selth A (1986) Race and resistance in Burma, 1942–1945. Mod Asian Stud 20(3):483–507

Steinberg D (2008) Globalization, dissent, and orthodoxy: Burma/Myanmar and the Saffron Revolution. Geo J Int Aff 9(2):51–58

Thawnghmung AM (2016) The politics of indigeneity in Myanmar: competing narratives in Rakhine State. Asian Ethnicity 17(4):527–547

Thawnghmung AM, Myoe MA (2008) Myanmar in 2007: a turning point in the "roadmap"? Asian Surv 48(1):13–19

The Burma Constitution (1948) Australian J Int Aff 2:98–101

UN Doc. A/RES/73/264 (2019)

Velath PM, Chopra K (2018) The stateless people: Rohingya in Hyderabad. In: Chaudhury SBR, Samaddar R (eds) The Rohingya in South Asia: people without a state. Routledge, London, pp 74–90

Ware A, Laoutides C (2018) Myanmar's 'Rohingya' conflict. Oxford University Press, New York

Williams P, Buchwald TF, Domino J, Hamilton R, Scharf MP (2020) The Rohingya Genocide. Case Western Res J Int Law 52(1–2):543–571

Yimprasert S (2004) The Portuguese in Arakan in the sixteenth and seventeenth centuries. MANUSYA: J Humanit 7(4):66–82

Chapter 3
The Rohingya Crisis and the International Criminal Court

Abstract This chapter discusses how the International Criminal Court (ICC) has dealt with the Rohingya crisis and the challenges that lie ahead, even though that is essentially a domestic matter for Myanmar, which is not a party to the Rome Statute. Bangladesh, the main refuge for Rohingya, has been a party to the International Criminal Court Code since 2010, however. On September 6, 2018, the Pre-Trial Chamber I of the ICC found that it has jurisdiction over the crime against humanity of deportation and other crimes with transboundary elements. On November 14, 2019, the Pre-Trial Chamber III of the ICC authorized the Prosecutor to proceed with an investigation for the alleged crimes within the ICC's jurisdiction in the situation in Bangladesh/Myanmar. In 2020, video footage was made public of two former members of Tatmadaw confessing their complicity in a sweeping operation against the Rohingya, whereupon they were transferred to the ICC. In January 2021, the military staged a *coup d'état*, and the possibility of holding Myanmar accountable for gross human rights violations against the Rohingya in Myanmar has since been at an impasse. In an effort to avoid giving the appearance of legitimacy to the junta, the National Unity Government (NUG) was created in exile, based on the ousted civilian government. As mentioned above, Myanmar is not a party to the Statute of the ICC, and thus, there is no legal basis obligating Myanmar to cooperate with the ICC. Hence, the extent to which the Office of the Prosecutor (OTP) of the ICC will be able to obtain Myanmar's cooperation is of interest. Meanwhile, the exiled regime has declared its acceptance of ICC jurisdiction and has shown a cooperative attitude toward the ICC in general.

3.1 Procedural History

3.1.1 The United Nations' and Myanmar's Initiatives for Dealing with the Rohingya Crisis

Myanmar is not a State Party to the Rome Statute which established the International Criminal Court (ICC), though it did ratify the Genocide Convention on March 14, 1956, albeit with reservations to Articles 6 and 8 of the Convention. Article

© The Author(s), under exclusive license to Springer Nature Singapore Pte Ltd. 2023
H. Takemura, *The Rohingya Crisis and the International Criminal Court*,
https://doi.org/10.1007/978-981-99-2734-0_3

6 mandates prosecution before an international criminal tribunal that has jurisdiction and that exercises the territorial jurisdiction of the state in which the crime occurred. Thus, while Article 6 is irrelevant to the proceedings of the International Court of Justice (ICJ), it has the potential to impede ICC proceedings, although how or to what extent is uncertain. Under one interpretation, Myanmar's reservation is seen as not disclaiming the obligation to prosecute perpetrators of genocide but indicating that Myanmar considers its own courts to have exclusive jurisdiction over such cases.[1] Another interpretation, however, asserts that "Myanmar and Venezuela stand out as the only two countries refusing any jurisdiction of the IPT [international penal tribunal]."[2] Some of the ICC's own views on this issue will not be known until the Office of the Prosecutor (OTP) of the ICC commences specific prosecutions. Of particular importance will be whether OTP will include genocide in subsequent charges, as well as whether the Chambers of the ICC agree with the Pre-Trial Chamber's findings that the ICC may exercise its jurisdiction so long as at least one element of a crime under ICC jurisdiction takes place on the territory of a State Party.[3] Article 8 of the Genocide Convention suggests that a competent UN body may take up the issue of genocide, and the Myanmar government interprets its reservation to this article to be an impediment to litigation before the ICJ. The ICJ is the principal judicial organ of the UN under Article 92 of the UN Charter. It should be noted that Bangladesh, a major refuge for the Rohingya, signed the Rome Statute on September 16, 1999, and deposited its instrument of ratification of the Rome Statute on March 23, 2010. Bangladesh had also previously acceded to the Genocide Convention, on October 5, 1998.

Repeated gross violations of human rights by the Myanmar junta led the United Nations Commission on Human Rights (UNHCR), and the United Nations Human Rights Council (UNHRC), which replaced the UNHCR in March 2006, to appoint six special rapporteurs on the situation of human rights in Myanmar[4] between 1992 and March 2021.[5] The UN Secretary General has also appointed a special envoy since 2018 to facilitate good offices with Myanmar and all other interested groups, as will be discussed hereinafter.

In this way, we see how the Rohingya crisis initially attracted the attention of the UNHRC.[6] Then on May 28, 2012, a 27 year-old woman was killed in the south of Rakhine State.[7] On June 5, the New Light of Myanmar reported the case as one

---

[1] Becker M F (2019), p. 2. *See also* Islam Md R (2019).

[2] Khan (2019), p. 13.

[3] Pre-Trial Chamber III of the International Criminal Court (2019), hereinafter, 'Authorisation Decision', pp. 20, 26, paras. 43, 56.

[4] UN Doc. E/CN.4/1992/58 (3 March 1992), para. 3.

[5] The special rapporteurs in order of appointment are Yozo Yokota of Japan (1992–1996), Rajsoomer Lallah of Mauritius (1996–2000), Paulo Sergio Pinheiro of Brazil (December 2000–April 2008), Tomás Ojea Quintana of Argentina (2008–2014), Yanghee Lee of the Republic of Korea (2014–2020), and Thomas Andrews of the United States (2020–).

[6] UN Doc. A/HRC/RES/13/25 (15 April 2010), para. 12.

[7] UN Doc. A/HRC/39/64 (12 September 2018), para. 625.

3.1 Procedural History

of rape and murder,[8] and that suspects in the case were "Bengali/Muslim."[9] This alleged attack is said to have triggered the latest atrocities against the Rohingya.[10] In June 2013, the UNHRC expressed its deep concern at the gross violations of human rights against Muslims in Myanmar, including against Rohingya Muslims in Rakhine State, and urged the Government of Myanmar to take immediate measures to put an end to all acts of violence and all violations of human rights against Muslims.[11] However, in interactive dialogue during a UNHRC Universal Periodic Review (UPR), the attitude of the Government of Myanmar was that "[i]n Myanmar, there was no minority community under the name of 'Rohingya'."[12]

Under pressure from the international community, Aung San Suu Kyi, then the Chief State Counselor in Myanmar, decided to establish an Advisory Commission on Rakhine State September 2016, with participation by the Office of the State Counsellor and the Kofi Annan Foundation. The Commission was accordingly hybrid in nature: six of its members were native Myanmarese, and the other three from outside Myanmar, as follows:

- Kofi Annan (Chair), Chair of the Kofi Annan Foundation, Secretary-General of the United Nations (1997–2006), Nobel Peace Laureate (2001)
- U Win Mra, Chair of the Myanmar National Human Rights Commission
- Dr. Thar Hla Shwe, former President of the Myanmar Red Cross Society
- Ghassan Salamé, Special Representative and Head of the United Nations Mission in Libya, Lebanese Minister of Culture (2000–2003), UN Special Advisor to the Secretary-General (2003–2006)
- Laetitia van den Assum, Special Advisor to UNAIDS (2005–2006), Ambassador of the Netherlands to the United Kingdom (2012–2015)
- U Aye Lwin, Core Member and Founder of Religions for Peace, Myanmar
- Dr. Mya Thida, President of the Obstetrical and Gynaecological Society of Myanmar Medical Association, Member of the Myanmar Academy of Medical Science
- U Khin Maung Lay, Member of the Myanmar National Human Rights Commission
- Daw Saw Khin Tint, Chairperson (Rakhine Literature and Culture Association, Yangon) and Vice-Chairperson (Rakhine Women Association).

Although the commission had the aforementioned hybrid domestic-international membership, it was still described as being a domestic national agency,[13] and as such, was mandated to examine the complex challenges facing Rakhine State and propose

---

[8] UN Doc. A/HRC/39/64 (12 September 2018), para. 625.

[9] Ibid.

[10] Ibid.

[11] "President's Statement, Situation of human rights of Muslims in Myanmar (2013)," UN Doc. A/HRC/23/L.26.

[12] "Report of the Working Group on the Universal Periodic Review," UN Doc. A/HRC/31/13 (2015), p. 11, para. 133.

[13] Advisory Commission on Rakhine State (2017), p. 12.

responses.[14] Therefore, the commission's mandate did not include the criminal investigation of specific cases, but rather focused on examining structural challenges to bringing peace to Rakhine State.[15]

The Commission submitted its final report to the Government of Myanmar on August 23, 2017. It was carefully drafted in accordance with the wishes of Aung San Suu Kyi, in her role as Chief State Counselor. For instance, the commission uses neither the term "Bengali" nor "Rohingya," substituting "Muslims" or "the Muslim community in Rakhine" instead.[16] The report was praised to a certain extent by the international community,[17] as the commission presented the Myanmar government with moderate recommendations on a wide range of issues. For instance, the commission urged the government to increase the participation of Rakhine's local communities in decision-making affecting the development of the state, and find ways to ensure that these same local communities benefit from investment, including natural resource extraction. Although the report was assessed as offering "the best proposals to date towards resolution of the underlying issues and long-term drivers of the conflict,"[18] it failed to address the key incident, precisely, the 'clearance operations' against the Rohingya in northern Rakhine that commenced on August 25, 2017, just two days after the report was submitted to the government.[19]

In March 2017, the UNHRC urgently dispatched an independent international fact-finding mission to establish the facts and circumstances of alleged recent human rights violations and abuses by military and security forces in Myanmar, particularly in Rakhine State.[20] While the Security Council failed to adopt a resolution due to opposition from China and Russia,[21] it issued its own presidential statement in November.[22]

In September 2018, the Independent International Fact-Finding Mission on Myanmar (IIFFMM) released a full account of the findings of its examination of the crisis in Rakhine State and the hostilities in Kachin and Shan States.[23] The nature of the Rohingya group, particularly whether it is an ethnic or religious group, is at issue in what constitutes persecution of a crime against humanity and what constitutes the crime of genocide, and the report suggests that the Rohingya are indeed an ethnic and religious group when it asserts that "[t]he lack of legal status and identity of the Rohingya] is State-sanctioned and in violation of Myanmar's obligations under international law because it discriminates on the basis of race, ethnicity and

---

[14] Ibid., p. 6.

[15] Ibid., p. 13.

[16] Ibid., p. 12.

[17] UN News (2017). Delegation of the European Union for the Pacific (2017).

[18] Ware, Laoutides (2018), p. 198.

[19] UN Doc. A/HRC/42/CRP.3 (12 September 2019), 37, para. 105.

[20] UN Doc. A/HRC/RES/34/22 (3 April 2017), para. 11.

[21] Barkholdt, Winkelmann (2019), para. 30.

[22] UN Doc. S/PRST/2017/22 (6 November 2017).

[23] UN Doc. A/HRC/39/64 (12 September 2018). A more detailed report is contained in UN. Doc. A/HRC/39/CRP.2 (17 September 2018).

3.1 Procedural History

religion."[24] After having found gross human rights violations in these states, the mission recommended that the Security Council ensure accountability for crimes under international law committed in Myanmar, preferably by referring the situation to the ICC or failing that, by creating an ad hoc international criminal tribunal.[25] Yet, the Security Council could not have agreed to either recommendation,[26] owing to the aforementioned Chinese and Russian vetoes, which may have been motivated by Myanmar's geographic importance to both China and Russia in terms of security, transit rights, natural resources, and energy policy.[27] On the other hand, Myanmar lacks such geopolitical considerations for either the US or the UK, making it difficult for them to give much priority to the protection of the Rohingya.[28] The situation does appear to be changing as of late 2022, however, with the US at least beginning to show a positive attitude toward such referrals as were recommended in the report.[29]

For its part, Myanmar took two steps prior to the release of the report. The first was to set up its own domestic commission of inquiry. On July 30, 2018, the Government of Myanmar wrote to the President of the UN Security Council and announced the establishment of the Independent Commission of Inquiry (ICOE) as part of a national initiative to address reconciliation, peace, stability and development in Rakhine State.[30] As listed hereinafter, the commission comprised four members, two each Myanmarese and non-Myanmarese, with the latter being a Filipino diplomat and a Japanese ambassador. The main purpose of the commission was to investigate allegations of human rights violations and related issues following terrorist attacks by the ARSA.[31] The ICOE final report was submitted to the President and the State Counselor of Myanmar on January 20, 2020, three days before the ICJ issued its order of provisional measures to Myanmar. Although the ICOE website is defunct as of October 2021, the executive summary of its report, including its 22 recommendations, remains available online.[32] These recommendations include accountability for responsible military personnel throughout the chain of command. It is also noteworthy that the report referred to "Muslims in northern Rakhine State" instead of "Rohingya" wherever possible.

- Rosario Manalo (Chair)
  Former Undersecretary of Foreign Affairs of the Philippines
  Former Chair and current Representative of the Philippines to the Committee on the Elimination of Discrimination against Women
- U Mya Thein

---

[24] UN Doc. A/HRC/39/CRP.2 (17 September 2018), p. 118, para. 491.

[25] UN Doc. A/HRC/39/64 (12 September 2018), para. 105.

[26] UN Doc. S/PV.8381 (24 October 2018).

[27] Gepp (2021), p. 92.

[28] Ibid.

[29] U.S. Mission to the United Nations (2022); U.S. Department of State (2022).

[30] "Letter dated 30 July 2018 from the Permanent Representative of Myanmar to the United Nations addressed to the President of the Security Council" UN Doc. S/2018/748 (30 July 2018).

[31] Ibid.

[32] ReliefWeb (2020).

Former Chair of the constitutional tribunal of the Republic of the Union of Myanmar
- Kenzo Oshima
  Former Under-Secretary-General for Humanitarian Affairs and Emergency Relief Coordinator
  Former Permanent Representative of Japan to the United Nations
- Aung Tun Thet
  Former Senior Official, United Nations International Children's Emergency Fund
  Former Principal Officer, United Nations System Staff College

The second step taken by the Myanmar government was to argue, in statements addressed to the President of the Security Council dated April 13[33] and August 9, 2018,[34] respectively, that the ICC has no significant jurisdiction in Myanmar. Anticipating this gesture, the ICC Prosecutor filed "Prosecution's Request for a Ruling on Jurisdiction under Article 19(3) of the Statute" on April 9, 2018.[35]

In September 2018, the UNHRC opted to establish the Independent Investigative Mechanism for Myanmar (IIMM, or "Myanmar Mechanism").[36] This mechanism became operational on August 30, 2019, with a mandate "to collect, consolidate, preserve and analyse evidence of the most serious international crimes and violations of international law committed in Myanmar since 2011, and to prepare files in order to facilitate [...] criminal proceedings, in accordance with international law standards, in national, regional or international courts or tribunals that have or may in the future have jurisdiction over these crimes."

As the attention of UN human rights bodies has thus focused on Myanmar, the country has begun to emphasize the principle of exhaustion of domestic remedies. In August 2019, the Myanmar government wrote to the President of the Security Council that "we strongly reject any attempt to take the matter to any international judicial or legal body unless it is patently clear that national remedies have been exhausted."[37] At the same time, the government revealed that the Tatmadaw had also established its own Court of Inquiry to address the allegations of human rights violations in northern Rakhine.[38]

---

[33] Government of the Republic of the Union of Myanmar (2018).

[34] "Letter dated 9 August 2018 from the Permanent Representative of Myanmar to the United Nations addressed to the President of the Security Council," UN Doc. S/2018/507 (13 August 2018).

[35] Office of the Prosecutor of the International Criminal Court (2018).

[36] UN Doc. A/HRC/RES/39/2 (3 October 2018), para. 22.

[37] "Letter dated 22 August 2019 from the Permanent Representative of Myanmar to the United Nations addressed to the President of the Security Council," UN Doc. S/2019/676 (22 August 2019).

[38] Ibid.

3.2 The Good Offices of the United Nations Secretary-General

In September 2019, the IIFFMM issued another report on its detailed findings of the situation in Myanmar.[39] The report appears to emphasize the ethnic group aspect of the Rohingya,[40] while also recognizing the Rohingya's religious attribution.[41] The report alleges that the "government's accountability efforts are woefully inadequate."[42] It also criticizes the ICOE for not constituting an effective independent investigations mechanism,[43] asserting that "[t]he ICOE lacks a clear mandate. Its chairperson has said that it is not an accountability mechanism. Its methodology is opaque. Its operating procedures are questionable. It is dependent on the Myanmar Government. There is no possibility that its investigations will identify perpetrators, promote accountability and justice, and provide redress to victims." It denounces Myanmars unwillingness to address impunity and declares that Myanmar is in breach of its obligation to conduct effective investigations as a State Party to the Genocide Convention.[44]

3.2 The Good Offices of the United Nations Secretary-General

Along with these UNHRC initiatives, the Secretary-General appointed former Guatemalan Foreign Minister and UN Ambassador Gert Rosenthal to carry out a "comprehensive, independent inquiry into the involvement of the United Nations in Myanmar from 2010 to 2018, as well as to how different parts of the UN system responded to events that took place during that time.[45] This appointment was in accordance with the recommendations of the IIFFMM report, which was published in September 2018.[46] On May 17, 2019, the so-called Rosenthal report was delivered to the Secretary-General.[47] The report dealt with the challenges the UN is facing in its efforts to protect the Rohingya.[48]

Over the past three decades, each successive Secretary-General has contributed to facilitating diplomatic relationships between the Myanmar junta and the outside

---

[39] "Detailed Findings of the Independent International Fact-Finding Mission on Myanmar," UN Doc. A/HRC/42/CRP.5 (16 September 2019).

[40] Ibid., p. 175, para. 663. This report concludes that "[t]he victims are predominantly people from ethnic minorities: the Rohingya, Kachin, Shan, Ta'ang, ethnic Rakhine, Chin, Karen or Kokang and many more not mentioned in this report."

[41] Ibid., p. 68, para. 210. The report notes that "[h]ateful and divisive language targeted the Rohingya on the basis of their ethnicity, religion and status."

[42] Ibid., p. 81, para. 230.

[43] Ibid., p. 81, para. 231.

[44] Ibid., pp. 81–82, paras. 232–233.

[45] UN News (27 October 2021).

[46] UN Doc. A/HRC/39/64 (12 September 2018) para. 111.

[47] UN News (27 October 2021).

[48] Rosenthal (29 May 2019).

world. Indeed, the General Assembly adopted resolution 48/150 by consensus at its 85th plenary meeting on December 20, 1993,[49] in which the UN urges the Government of Myanmar to ensure full respect for human rights and fundamental freedoms, and calls upon Myanmar to respect fully the obligations of the Geneva Conventions of August 12, 1949.[50] With respect to these obligations on the part of Myanmar under human rights and humanitarian law, the General Assembly further requests, by this resolution, that the Secretary-General assist in the implementation thereof.[51] The Secretary-General's good offices on Myanmar is described elsewhere as "one of the longest such diplomatic efforts in the history of the world organization."[52]

Despite the many years of these selfsame good offices, however, the Rohingya human rights situation has not improved, and in 2017 the UN General Assembly decided to establish a special envoy of the Secretary-General to Myanmar. On December 24, 2017, the General Assembly expressed its great concern "at the outbreak of violence in Rakhine State in August 2017 that has caused hundreds of thousands of Rohingya civilians to flee towards Bangladesh" in resolution 72/248, which was adopted by recorded vote of 122 in favor to 10 against, with 24 abstentions.[53] By this resolution, the General Assembly requested "the Secretary-General to continue to provide his good offices and to pursue his discussions relating to Myanmar, involving all relevant stakeholders and including the concerns addressed herein, and in this regard to appoint a special envoy on Myanmar and to offer assistance to the Government of Myanmar."[54] On April 26, 2018, Secretary-General António Guterres announced the appointment of Christine Schraner Burgener, a Swiss diplomat, as United Nations Special Envoy on Myanmar.[55] In this capacity, she engaged in shuttle diplomacy between Bangladesh and Myanmar at the request of both governments, and encouraged Myanmar's greater international cooperation towards the effective and holistic implementation of all of the recommendations of the Annan Advisory Commission on Rakhine State.[56] She also urged the Security Council in closed session to act against the calamity in Myanmar, especially after the 2021 *coup*.[57] However, the Security Council was prevented from condemning

---

[49] UN Doc. A/RES/48/150 (31 January 1994).

[50] Ibid., paras. 6 and 13.

[51] Ibid., para. 15.

[52] Magnusson, Pedersen (2012), p. 1.

[53] UN Doc. A/RES/72/248 (23 January 2018). Against were Belarus, Cambodia, China, Lao People's Democratic Republic, Myanmar, Philippines, Russian Federation, Syrian Arab Republic, Viet Nam, and Zimbabwe. Abstentions were Bhutan, Cameroon, Côte d'Ivoire, Dominican Republic, Ecuador, Equatorial Guinea, Ethiopia, India, Japan, Kenya, Lesotho, Mongolia, Mozambique, Namibia, Nauru, Nepal, Papua New Guinea, Singapore, South Africa, and Sri Lanka. Thailand, Timor-Leste, Togo, Venezuela. *See* UN Doc. A/72/PV. 76 (2017), p.7.

[54] Ibid., para. 10.

[55] *See* SG/A/1802-BIO/5081, UN Secretary General Press Release (2018).

[56] UN Doc. S/PV.8477 (28 Fenruary 2019), p. 2.

[57] UN News (18 June 2021).

3.3 Myanmar's Ratification of International Treaties

the *coup* or taking stronger action due to the Chinese veto.[58] On October 25, 2021, Noeleen Heyzer of Singapore was appointed to succeed Burgener in this role.[59]

The efforts of these human rights organizations would have undoubtedly facilitated the investigations of the OTP and encouraged Myanmars own domestic efforts to investigate and prosecute, even though there was no guarantee that Myanmars efforts in this regard would be sincere. Ultimately, however, it seems fair to say that the February 2021 *coup* turned the relationship between Myanmars junta and the UNHRC hostile, and the human rights situation in Myanmar has become even more difficult as a consequence. For instance, on July 7, 2022, the UNHRC adopted a resolution on the human rights situation of Rohingya Muslims and other minorities in Myanmar, in which it calls upon "Myanmar to end immediately all violence and violations of international law in Myanmar, to ensure full protection of the human rights and fundamental freedoms of all persons in Myanmar, including Rohingya Muslims."[60] In response, the Myanmar junta's Ministry of Foreign Affairs objected strongly, describing the resolution as amounting to "hate speech with politically and religiously motivated languages along with fictitious allegations."[61]

3.3 Myanmar's Ratification of International Treaties

While Myanmar has not ratified the Rome Statute, it has ratified other binding treaties. First of all, as mentioned previously, Myanmar ratified the Genocide Convention[62] on March 14, 1956, albeit with the following reservations:

(1) With reference to Article VI, the Union of Burma makes the reservation that nothing contained in the said Article shall be construed as depriving the Courts and Tribunals of the Union of jurisdiction or as giving foreign Courts and tribunals jurisdiction over any cases of genocide or any of the other acts enumerated in Article III committed within the Union territory.

(2) With reference to Article VIII, the Union of Burma makes the reservation that the said Article shall not apply to the Union.

On the basis of the foregoing, Myanmar challenged the jurisdiction of the ICJ when The Gambia filed suit in 2019, claiming that The Gambia could not validly call upon the Court because of Myanmar's reservation to Article VIII of the Genocide Convention, which specifically deals with the right of any of the contracting parties to

---

[58] Mahaseth, Tulsyan (2022), p. 6.

[59] *See* UN Secretary General Statements, SG/A/2070, "Ms. Noeleen Heyzer of Singapore—Special Envoy on Myanmar (25 October 2021)," available at <https://www.un.org/sg/en/content/sg/per sonnel-appointments/2021-10-25/ms-noeleen-heyzer-of-singapore-special-envoy-myanmar> (last accessed, 9 September 2022).

[60] UN Doc. A/HRC/50/L.21 (4 July 2022).

[61] Myanmar, Information Sheet, vol. II, issue 3 (11 July 2022), pp. 20–21.

[62] 78 UNTS 277.

the convention to call upon any competent organ of the United Nations.[63] Regardless, the ICJ interpreted Article VIII as not referring to the submission of disputes between contracting parties to the Genocide Convention to the ICJ for adjudication.[64]

Second, Myanmar has been a State Party to the Geneva Conventions of 1949 since August 25,1992. Nonetheless, it has not ratified the Additional Protocols I and II of the Conventions.[65] All of the Geneva Conventions call on the High Contracting Parties to the conventions to ensure that they are able to prosecute perpetrators of war crimes, including grave breaches of the Geneva Conventions under Article 49 of the First Convention, Article 50 of the Second Convention, Article 129 of the Third Convention, and Article 146 of the Fourth Convention.[66] Even though such duty to prosecute is not an absolute obligation, because it is for the competent national authorities to conclude whether there exist sufficient grounds to proceed to criminal proceedings following investigation,[67] Article 129, paragraph 2 of the Third Convention "puts the onus to investigate the facts, and, when so warranted, to prosecute or extradite alleged perpetrators"[68] on said High Contracting Parties.

Third, Myanmar acceded the Convention on the Rights of the Child on July 15, 1991, and the Convention on the Elimination of All Forms of Discrimination Against Women on July 22, 1997. On September 27 2019, Myanmar further ratified the Optional Protocol to the Convention on the Rights of the Child on the Involvement of Children in Armed Conflict, albeit with the following declarations. First is Myanmar's declaration under Article 3(2) of the protocol, as follows: "With reference to Article 3(2) of the Optional Protocol, the Government of the Republic of the Union of Myanmar declares that citizens may freely present themselves for voluntary military service provided they have attained a minimum age of 18 years, whereas citizens above 16 and under 18 years of age may voluntarily join military academies and military vocational training courses, if furnished with the proof of their age and the prior written consent of their parents or guardians." Second is Myanmar's interpretative declaration with respect to Article 4 of the protocol, as follows: "With reference to Article 4 of the Optional Protocol, the Government of the Republic of the Union of Myanmar considers that any responsibility deriving from recruitment of children under 18 years of age or their use in hostilities by non-state armed groups lies solely with such groups. In the prevention of underage military recruitment, the Government would collaborate with the ethnic armed groups which have signed the NCA (Nationwide Ceasefire Agreement). The latter shall also have a duty to apply at all times the principles governing international humanitarian law." The governments of the Netherlands, Romania, and Portugal objected.[69]

---

[63] International Court of Justice (2020), para. 32.

[64] Ibid., para. 35.

[65] Ochi, Matsuyama (2019), p. 339.

[66] International Committee of the Red Cross (2021), p. 1848, para. 5124.

[67] Ibid., p. 1849, para. 5127.

[68] Ibid., p. 1852, para. 5135.

[69] Netherlands (2020); Romania (2020).

Fourth, Myanmar ratified the Biological Weapons Convention on December 1, 2014,[70] and the Chemical Weapons Convention on July 8, 2015.[71] According to Nuclear Threat Initiative (NTI), a non-profit organization, "Myanmar is not believed to have either nuclear or biological weapons programs, and, despite accusations, there is no conclusive evidence of a chemical weapons program."[72] Indeed, the United States suspects that Myanmar does possess a chemical weapons arsenal by reason of its failure to declare its past chemical weapons program and destroy its chemical weapons plants.[73] Myanmar also acceded to the Treaty on the Non-Proliferation of Nuclear Weapons (NPT) on February 12, 1992.

Fifth, Mynamar ratified both the Hague Convention for the Protection of Cultural Property and the Hague Protocol for the Protection of Cultural Property on February 10, 1956. Myanmar did not have a World Heritage Site until 2014, when the Pyu Ancient Cities were registered as a World Heritage Site. In 2019, Bagan was also added to the World Heritage List.

In sum, it is evident from Myanmars treaty ratifications that applicable international law regulating the non-international armed conflict in Myanmar is limited to common Article 3 of the Geneva Conventions of 1949[74] and related customary international law.

3.4 Rising Awareness of the Pursuit of Individual Responsibility

3.4.1 Prelude to the Pursuit of Individual Responsibility

As part of an international wave of calls for accountability for Myanmar, The Gambia filed a complaint against Myanmar with the ICJ on November 11, 2020. The, Abubacarr Marie Tambadou, Minister of Justice of The Gambia and as of this writing a Registrar of the International Residual Mechanism for Criminal Tribunals (MICT), played a leading role in bringing the case to the ICJ, motivated by his personal experience as a member of the Organization of Islamic Cooperation (OIC) delegation that visited the overcrowded Rohingya refugee camps in Cox's Bazar, Bangladesh.[75] As is well known, The Gambia claims that the jurisdiction is based on Article IX of the Genocide Convention, to which both The Gambia and Myanmar are parties.[76] The Gambia appears to justify its standing to institute these proceedings

---

[70] UN Office for Disarmament Affairs (2022).

[71] Organisation for the Prohibition of Chemical Weapons (2015).

[72] Nuclear Threat Initiative (2015).

[73] U.S. Department of State (2019), p. 2.

[74] Ochi, Matsuyama (2019), p. 341.

[75] Ross (2019).

[76] International Court of Justice (2019), paras. 24, 120.

on the grounds: (1) the *jus cogens* character of the prohibition of genocide and the *erga omnes* and *erga omnes partes* character of the obligations under the Genocide Convention[77], and (2) solidarity with Rohingya as fellow Muslims with the support of the OIC.[78] As previously mentioned, the ICJ issued issued its provisional measures order on January 23, 2020, with some changes to the content of the order that were requested by The Gambian government.[79] On September 2, 2020, the Ministers of Foreign Affairs of Canada and the Netherlands issued a joint statement regarding their intention to intervene in the case of The Gambia v. Myanmar before the ICJ.[80]

Starting with The Gambias lawsuit against Myanmar in the International Court of Justice, the movement to pursue state responsibility on Myanmar's part has also become a movement to pursue individual criminal responsibility. On November 13, 2019, two days after The Gambia filed suit with the ICJ, a UK-based Rohingya organization filed criminal charges in Argentina over Myanmars persecution of the Rohingya on behalf of six Rohingya women,[81] claiming a basis of universal jurisdiction.[82] Although the Court of First Instance in Buenos Aires rejected the case in December 2019, owing to a risk of duplicating the relevant investigation launched by the ICC, the federal Appeal Court overturned this decision on May 29, 2020, and requested more information from the ICC in order not to duplicate other justice efforts.[83] On July 12, 2021, another Argentinian lower court ruled against investigating crimes committed against the Rohingya in Myanmar.[84] The court held that Argentinian courts were not the appropriate forum to adjudicate the alleged crimes, as the OTP of the ICC was already investigating the matter.[85] The complainants appealed the decision, and a hearing was held on the appeal in August. On November 26, 2021, the Second Chamber of the Federal Criminal Court in Buenos Aires affirmed that it would launch a case against senior Myanmar officials under the principle of universal jurisdiction.[86] After the Federal Criminal Court heard from the six women in refugee camps in Bangladesh via remote video, it reversed the lower court's denial, as an investigation by Argentinian authorities would encompass a broader range of crimes than that of the ICC.[87]

---

[77] Ibid., para. 15.

[78] Van den Berg (2019).

[79] International Court of Justice (2020).

[80] Joint Statement (2020).

[81] UN Independent Investigative Mechanism for Myanmar (2022), p. 4.

[82] *See* Burma Campaign UK (2019). *See also*, Khin (2020).

[83] BROUK UK (2020).

[84] TRIAL International (2021).

[85] Fortify Rights (2021).

[86] BROUK UK (2021).

[87] UN Independent Investigative Mechanism for Myanmar (2022), p. 4.

3.4 Rising Awareness of the Pursuit of Individual Responsibility

3.4.2 Proceedings Before the ICC

3.4.2.1 Jurisdiction Rulings

On November 14, 2019, the day before the Rohingya NGO launched its action in the Argentinian courts, the Pre-Trial Chamber III of the ICC authorized the Prosecutor to open an investigation into the situation in Bangladesh/Myanmar.[88] In its ruling, the chamber declared that "the Prosecutor may extend the investigation into crimes allegedly committed at least in part on the territory of other States Parties after the date of entry into force of the Statute for those States Parties, insofar as the alleged crimes are sufficiently linked to the situation as described in this decision."[89]

Prior to this decision, on April 9, 2018, the Prosecutor sought a ruling on a question of jurisdiction: whether the Court may exercise jurisdiction over the alleged deportation of the Rohingya people from Myanmar to Bangladesh.[90] The authorization decision by the Pre-Trial Chamber III of 2019 essentially follows the ruling by the Pre-Trial Chamber I of September 2018, which held that the ICC may assert jurisdiction under Article 12(2)(a) of the Rome Statute if at least one element of a crime within the jurisdiction of the Court were committed on the territory of a State Party.[91] Responding to the Prosecutor's request on the question of the jurisdiction at the time, the Pre-Trial Chamber I ruled 2 to 1 that the Pre-Trial Chamber I was able to entertain the Prosecutor's request.[92] Judge Perrin de Brichambaut appended a partially dissenting opinion.

This ruling accordingly raises the procedural issue of whether a Pre-Trial Chamber can make such determinations at such stages of proceedings, as well as the substantive issue of whether it can exercise international criminal jurisdiction over crimes that cross borders between States Parties and Non-States Parties. Taking the procedural issue on which the judges were divided first, although the Prosecutor relied on Article 19(3) of the Statute to lodge the request for the ruling, the majority found that its authority to rule on the motion rested instead on Article 119(1) of the Statute as well as an established principle of international law, that of the ICC's inherent power to determine its own competence, pursuant to Article 21(1)(b) of the Statute.[93] Article 119(1) provides that "[a]ny dispute concerning the judicial functions of the Court shall be settled by the decision of the Court." While the Myanmar government did not formally participate in the proceedings, it did issue a statement claiming that it is not a party to the Rome Statute, and thus, the ICC lacks jurisdiction.[94] Accordingly,

---

[88] *See* "Authorisation Decision" (2019).

[89] "Authorisation Decision" (2019), p. 56, para. 131.

[90] Office of the Prosecutor of the International Criminal Court (2018).

[91] Pre-Trial Chamber I of the International Criminal Court (2018), hereinafter, "Jurisdiction Decision," pp. 36, 44–45, paras. 64, 79. *See* Spadaro (2020), p. 616.

[92] "Jurisdiction Decision."

[93] "Jurisdiction Decision" (2018), pp. 11–12, paras. 28–29.

[94] Ibid., p. 11, fn 36.

the majority concluded that the jurisdiction of the Court is clearly subject to dispute with Myanmar.[95]

However, the partial dissent asserted that neither Article 19(3) nor Article 119(1) is applicable to the present instance.[96] It held that at this juncture, the Court could not rule on the question of jurisdiction over the alleged deportation of the Rohingya people from Myanmar to Bangladesh.[97]

Myanmar's argument has been consistent on this point: under the Statute, Myanmar is a Non-State Party, and therefore, pursuant to Article 34 of the Statute, the OTP cannot conduct a *proprio motu* investigation of a situation in a Non-State Party.[98] Thus, the crux of the matter is how the effect of a treaty on a Non-State Party can be justified under Article 34 of the Vienna Convention on the Law of Treaties.

Concerns about the impact of Article 12 of the Rome Statute on Non-State Party nationals have been consistently expressed by the United States in relation to the provisions of the Article 34. At the signing of the Rome Statute, President William J. Clinton emphasized that the jurisdiction of the ICC over US personnel should only be exercised if the United States ratified the Statute,[99] stressing that "[t]he treaty requires that the ICC not supersede or interfere with functioning national judicial systems; that is, the ICC prosecutor is authorized to take action against a suspect only if the country of nationality is unwilling or unable to investigate allegations of egregious crimes by their national. The U.S. delegation to the Rome Conference worked hard to achieve these limitations, which we believe are essential to the international credibility and success of the ICC."[100] This delegation identified "the flaw" of the Rome Statute that military and civilian personnel of a Non-State Party to the treaty could be ensnared by the Court's jurisdiction without the non-party's consent.[101] As is well known, against the backdrop of such US concerns, the relationship between the US and the ICC has become more adversarial over time. On May 6, 2002, the Bush Administration sought to unsign the Statute by sending a letter to the then UN Secretary-General Kofi Annan, stating that "the United States does not intend to become a party to the treaty. Accordingly, the United States has no legal obligations arising from its signature on December 31, 2000."[102] After a judgment by the Appeals Chamber of the ICC on March 5, 2020 to authorize the Prosecutor to commence an investigation into alleged crimes in relation to the situation in Afghanistan,[103] for which the Prosecutor had determined that there was a reasonable basis to believe that war crimes were committed by members of the U.S. armed forces and by members of the US Central Intelligence Agency (CIA) in Afghanistan, President Donald J. Trump

---

[95] Ibid., p. 11, para. 28.

[96] "Partially Disenting Opinion" (2018), pp. 4–12.

[97] "Partially Disenting Opinion" (2018), p. 21.

[98] "Jurisdiction Decision" (2018), pp. 16–17, para. 35.

[99] U.S. President William J. Clinton, Statement by the President (2000).

[100] Ibid.

[101] Ambassador David J. Scheffer (2001), p. 4.

[102] U.S. Department of State (2002).

[103] Appeals Chamber of the International Criminal Court (2020).

3.4 Rising Awareness of the Pursuit of Individual Responsibility

issued Executive Order 13,928, "Blocking Property of Certain Persons Associated with the International Criminal Court" on June 11, 2020, imposing targeted sanctions on ICC Prosecutor Fatou Bensouda and Phakiso Mochochoko, Head of the Jurisdiction, Complementarity and Cooperation Division of the OTP.[104] On April 1, 2021, President Joseph R. Biden Jr. terminated this Executive Order and lifted the sanctions thereby with Executive Order 14,022, "Termination of Emergency with Respect to the International Criminal Court."[105] Nonetheless, President Biden reasserted the position that the US "continues to object to the International Criminal Court's (ICC) assertions of jurisdiction over personnel of such Non-States Parties as the United States and its allies absent their consent or referral by the United Nations Security Council and will vigorously protect current and former United States personnel from any attempts to exercise such jurisdiction."[106]

The Pre-Trial Chamber I answered the question of whether the Convention is binding on Non-States Parties by relying on the concept of objective legal personality, noting that Article 34 of the Convention on the Law of Treaties has an exception, which is written into Article 38.[107] When confirming the objective legal personality of the ICC, the Pre-Trial Chamber I referred to a leading case on the discussion of objective legal personality, the International Court of Justice Case for Reparations for Injuries Suffered in the Service of the United Nations.[108] The majority found that when at least an element of another crime within the jurisdiction of the Court or part of the crime of deportation is committed on the territory of a State Party, the Court may assert jurisdiction pursuant to Article 12(2)(a) of the Statute.[109] This decision has been criticized as constituting a de facto advisory opinion.[110] It also does not bind the Prosecutor and cannot force the Prosecutor to open an investigation in such a situation.[111]

This jurisdiction decision by the Pre-Trial Chamber I justifies the view that jurisdiction pursuant to Article 12(2)(a) of the Statute is satisfied if at least one legal element of a crime within the jurisdiction of the Court or part of such a crime is committed on the territory of a State Party for the following reasons: First, a contextual interpretation of Article 12(2)(a) of the Statute justifies this interpretation in accordance with Article 31(3)(c) of the Vienna Convention on the Law of Treaties.[112] For this interpretation, the Court relied on the judgment of the Permanent Court of International Justice in the 1927 Lotus case, which found that "[t]he territoriality of criminal law [...] is not an absolute principle of international law

---

[104] U.S. President Donald J. Trump (2020), pp. 36,139 36,142.

[105] U.S. President Joseph R. Biden Jr (2021), pp. 17,895–17,896.

[106] Ibid., p. 17, 895.

[107] "Jurisdiction Decision" (2018), p. 18, para. 36. McIntyre (2021), p. 528.

[108] Ibid., p. 18, para. 37.

[109] "Jurisdiction Decision" (2018), p. 42, para. 74.

[110] "Partially Dissenting Opinion" (2018), pp. 17–20, paras. 33–39.

[111] Vagias (2019), p. 373.

[112] "Jurisdiction Decision" (2018), p. 36, para. 65.

and by no means coincides with territorial sovereignty."[113] The Pre-Trial Chamber I also cited as a basis for its interpretation the fact that a number of states allow, by legislation, the exercise of criminal jurisdiction over crimes where at least some of the constituent elements of the offense are committed within the state. To wit, the Pre-Trial Chamber I cited the fact that a number of national jurisdictions, including Bangladesh and Myanmar, have adopted legislation to the effect that the exercise of criminal jurisdiction requires the commission of at least one legal element of the crime on the territory of the state.[114] Second, the Pre-Trial Chamber I determined that the object and purpose of the Statute supports this interpretation[115] in that "the drafters of the Statute intended to allow the Court to exercise its jurisdiction pursuant to Article 12(2)(a) of the Statute in the same circumstances in which States Parties would be allowed to assert jurisdiction over such crimes under their legal systems."[116]

Originally, the Prosecutor proposed "a creative extension of jurisdiction with respect to the crime against humanity of deportation,"[117] and the impact of the Pre-Trial Chamber's ruling appears to have extended the jurisdiction of the ICC beyond this crime, affecting all crimes within its jurisdiction.[118] Accordingly, the ICC's territorial jurisdiction under Article 12(2)(a) applies if at least one legal element is committed on the territory of a State Party to the Statute.[119] Still, the Pre-Trial Chamber hints that such an expansive interpretation of Article 12(2)(a) is justified because of "the inherently transboundary nature of the crime of deportation."[120]

A cautionary note is raised with respect to the understanding of one legal element of a crime within the Court's jurisdiction as a criterion for the exercise of the ICC's territorial jurisdiction. It is claimed that one must distinguish between facts that are necessary to constitute a crime under certain conditions, and facts that are remotely connected to what has become a crime.[121] In other words, under the extended territoriality principle, a single criminal act may allow many states to exercise jurisdiction, making it difficult for an individual to foresee which state's criminal law may apply to them.[122]

In response, the Government of Myanmar resolutely rejected the ICCs ruling of 6 September 2018 in connection with Rakhine State at the 73rd session of the UN General Assembly,[123] declaring that "The ICC decision was made on dubious

---

[113] Ibid., p. 37, para. 66.

[114] Ibid., pp. 37–40, paras. 66–68.

[115] Ibid., p, 40, para. 69.

[116] Ibid., p, 41, para. 70.

[117] Schabas (2020), p. 74.

[118] *See e.g.*, Mascarenhas, Jacobi, O'Connell and San Martin (2019).

[119] *See* Gallant (2022), p. 195.

[120] "Jurisdiction Decision" (2018), p, 41, para. 71.

[121] Gallant (2022), pp. 195–195.

[122] *See* ibid., p. 196.

[123] Government of the Republic of the Union of Myanmar (2018), p. 4.

3.4 Rising Awareness of the Pursuit of Individual Responsibility

legal grounds and applied to a situation where domestic remedies have not yet been exhausted."[124]

3.4.2.2 Authorization to Investigate the Bangladesh/Myanmar Situation

On July 4 2019, the ICC Prosecutor officially requested authorization to investigate the Bangladesh/Myanmar situation.[125] In this instance, the OTP asked for permission to open an investigation into crimes against humanity, not genocide,[126] which likely resulted from the OTP's determination that crimes against humanity are the most transboundary crimes by nature. The situation in Myanmar, even though it is not a Security Council referral, goes directly to crimes committed by a Non-State Party, and the OTP is thus forced to take up crimes of a transboundary nature as a basis for exercising jurisdiction. The Prosecutor submitted that there is a reasonable basis to believe that crimes against humanity under the jurisdiction of the Court—in particular, deportation, other inhumane acts, and persecution contrary to Article 7 of the Statute—have been committed by the Myanmar armed forces ("Tatmadaw") jointly with the Border Guard Police ("BGP") and/or Myanmar Police Force ("MPF") ("other Security Forces") with some participation of non-Rohingya civilians, and by other Myanmar authorities, since at least August 25, 2017.[127] According to the Prosecutor, there is a reasonable basis to believe that the following crimes against humanity were committed in the context of the 2017 wave of violence: (1) deportation under Article 7(1)(d); (2) other inhumane acts under Article 7(1)(k), namely, the infliction of great suffering or serious injury by means of intentional and severe violations of the customary international law right of displaced persons to return safely and humanely to the state of origin with which they have a sufficiently close connection; and (3) persecution on ethnic and/or religious grounds under Article 7(1)(h) by means of deportation and violation of the right to return.[128] It is noteworthy that the Prosecutor shows a broad understanding of the group attributes of the Rohingya, stating that the Rohingya group was persecuted on "ethnic and/or religious grounds." This is consistent with the position of the United Nations. It should be noted that the term ethno-religious has been proposed to describe a fusion of the ethnic and religious nature of a group on this issue, but that it is an ambiguous term and poses legal problems as a consequence.[129] Therefore, if the ICC were to recognize persecution on ethnic and religious grounds, however, the background of human rights violations

---

[124] Ibid.

[125] Office of the Prosecutor of the International Criminal Court (2019).

[126] Ibid., p. 6, para. 4.

[127] Ibid., p. 6, para. 4.

[128] Ibid., p. 40, para. 75.

[129] Pérez-León-Acevedo, Pinto (2021), p. 465.

based on each of these grounds would need to be brought to light separately in the Court's decision.[130]

In addition, the OTP also sought permission to open investigations into other crimes sufficiently related to crimes against humanity, at least one element whereof could be said to have occurred in Bangladesh.[131] In other words, the OTP suggested that the scope of crimes to be investigated could be expanded by as the investigation progressed. The question once again became whether the ICC would be allowed to exercise jurisdiction over human rights violations against Rohingya in Myanmar, given that Myanmar is a Non-State Party to the Rome Statute.

The Pre-Trial Chamber III accepted that there exists a reasonable basis to believe widespread and/or systematic acts of violence may have been committed that could qualify as the crimes against humanity of deportation across the Myanmar-Bangladesh border and persecution against the Rohingya population. The Chamber essentially concurred with the earlier mentioned Pre-Trial Chamber I decision of September 6, 2018,[132] holding that as long as part of the conduct of the crime, the *actus reus*, takes place within the territory of a State Party, the Court may exercise territorial jurisdiction within the limits prescribed by customary international law.[133]

The Pre-Trial Chamber III authorized "the commencement of the investigation in relation to any crime within the jurisdiction of the Court committed at least in part on the territory of Bangladesh, or on the territory of any other State Party or state making a declaration under Article 12(3) of the Statute, if the alleged crime is sufficiently linked to the situation as described in this decision,"[134] thereby avoiding having to make initiating the investigation conditional on the transboundary nature of the crimes to be investigated. The Chamber also emphasized that "the Prosecutor is not restricted to the incidents identified in the Request and the crimes set out in the present decision but may, on the basis of the evidence gathered during her investigation, extend her investigation to other crimes against humanity or other Article 5 crimes, as long as they remain within the parameters of the authorized investigation."[135] This implies that the OTP may investigate acts of violence allegedly committed in Myanmar by the ARSA.[136]

Even if the ICC's jurisdiction theoretically extends to Non-State Party nationals, however, some have questioned whether suspects would voluntarily appear before the ICC in the face of this decision and the associated possibility of conviction.[137] In 2013, the Assembly of States Parties of the ICC ("the Assembly") adopted Rules 134*bis*, 134*ter* and134*quaeter*, bearing in mind that President Uhuru Kenyatta and Vice President William Ruto of Kenya had official duties that would make it difficult

---

[130] Ibid., p. 479.

[131] Office of the Prosecutor of the International Criminal Court (2019), p. 11, para. 20.

[132] "Jurisdiction Decision."

[133] "Authorisation Decision" (2019), pp. 27–28, paras. 61–62.

[134] "Authorisation Decision" (2019), p. 54, para. 126.

[135] "Authorisation Decision" (2019), p. 54, para. 126.

[136] Kittichaisaree (2022) p. 156.

[137] Ibid., p. 212.

for them to appear in court. These amendments are said to be difficult to reconcile with the wording of Article 63, which clearly requires the presence of the accused at trial.[138] Rule 134*quarter* seems especially problematic in this sense, as it allows an accused who is "mandated to fulfil extraordinary public duties at the highest international level" to be excused from being present at their trial.[139] It is said that there is no guarantee that the ICC's Trial Chamber will apply this rule to Myanmar key figures.[140] It is also noted that the only people who would voluntarily appear before the ICC would be those who are convinced that the OTP has no chance of winning its case against them.[141] The difficulty of investigating and prosecuting key government officials from Non-States Parties is illustrated by the case of Sudanese President Omar Al-Bashir, who was not handed over to the ICC for more than a decade after the court's warrant was issued, and despite being ousted in April 2019.

3.5 Pros and Cons on the Jurisdiction of the ICC Over the Bangladesh/Myanmar Situation

The ICC faces criticism for inserting itself into a situation where there is no chance of gaining the cooperation of Non-States Parties.[142] In the first place, there is the question of whether Myanmars obligation to cooperate with the ICC arises under the Statute. Under Article 87(5) (a), "The Court may invite any State not party to this Statute to provide assistance under this Part on the basis of an ad hoc arrangement, an agreement with such State or any other appropriate basis." In this regard, the ICC's Questions and Answers on the situation of Bangladesh/Myanmar also points out that "States Parties to the Rome Statute have a legal obligation to cooperate fully with the ICC. Other non-party States, such as Myanmar, may be invited to cooperate with the ICC and may decide to do so on a voluntary basis."[143] The de facto expansion of the territorial jurisdiction of the ICC would invite rejections from states Parties too, because the ICC has its hands full with its current caseload.[144] Even if the ICC does extend its jurisdiction to Non-States Parties, continued noncooperation by these would call into question the ICC's effectiveness, which in turn would affect its performance-based social legitimacy.[145]

Another issue is the concern the crime of deportation may be used as a rationale to extend the ICC's territorial jurisdiction over Non-States Parties inexhaustibly,[146]

---

[138] Stahn (2015), p. 417.

[139] Ibid.

[140] Kittichaisaree (2022), p. 212.

[141] *Ibid.*

[142] Guilfoyle (2019), pp. 2–8.

[143] "Questions and Answers" (2019).

[144] Freuden (2019), p. 122.

[145] *See* Foysal (2022).

[146] Gomez (2019), p. 193.

though this aspect could also be seen as a green light for similar expanded jurisdiction over Non-States Parties by those who wish to see the ICC become a truly universal court. It is pointed out that "it was this mass deportation and not the other crimes that provoked the need for a humanitarian response."[147] Eventually, the Chamber determines that the "persecution" and "other inhumane acts" fall within the Court's jurisdiction in the Rohingya case.[148] Conversely, it is also pointed out that the crime of persecution or other inhuman acts "for preventing Rohingya people from returning to their country will not have the jurisdictional issues that there are for the crime of deportation, since these crimes are committed in Bangladesh as the ICC's Member State."[149] That the ICC's Bangladesh/Myanmar jurisdiction decision suggests the possibility of exerting its jurisdiction over crimes committed in Non-States Parties has also been assessed in a positive light.[150] Indeed, Syrian refugees who fled to Jordan, which is a State Party of the Rome Statute, communicated thorough lawyers with the OTP under Article 15 of the Rome Statute to request that the Prosecutor exercise jurisdiction over the crime of deportation and other crimes against humanity committed against them as well, based on the ICC's Bangladesh/Myanmar jurisdiction decision.[151] One negative aspect of the current decision is the possibility that Non-States Parties to the ICC may prevent border crossings of refugees to State parties and persecute them within their own borders for fear of falling foul of ICC jurisdiction.[152]

Other opinions have been issued in support of the ICC's jurisdictional decision, including that the ruling was necessary for the ICC to act as a truly universal court and to ensure the fulfillment of the prosecutor's obligation to prosecute.[153] From the perspectives of victims of human rights abuses and human rights activists alike, the authorization to investigate is a welcome development, as it could lead to redress for the former.[154] This expansive interpretation of the Rome Statute is hailed as "amenable to the purpose of the ICC," putting an end to legal impunity, and to contributing to forestalling such crimes in future.[155] For proponents of a strong and truly universal ICC, the potential for sovereignty infringement by the ICC against Non-States Parties that might arise from this expansive interpretation of the Statute is not to be feared, so long as all States understand the purpose of the ICC and exercise their criminal jurisdiction to properly address gross human rights violations.[156]

The European Union (EU) is particularly supportive of the OTP of the ICC in its investigation of the Bangladesh/Myanmar situation, as evidenced by the European

---

[147] Ibid., p. 194.

[148] Bazzar (2022), p. 52.

[149] Ibid., pp. 52–53.

[150] Fisher (2020), p. 398.

[151] Ibid. *See also* Saleh (2019); Cadman, Bucklay (2019).

[152] Fisher (2020), pp. 407–408.

[153] Hale, Rankin (2019), pp. 22–28.

[154] Freuden (2019), p. 121.

[155] Nagakoshi (2021), p. 289.

[156] Ibid.

Parliament resolution on Myanmar, notably the situation of the Rohingya,[157] of September 19, 2019, which was adopted by a vote of 546 in favor to 12 against, with 94 abstentions. Its paragraph 10 provides that the Parliament:

> [w]elcomes the decision of the International Criminal Court (ICC) regarding its jurisdiction over the deportation of Rohingya people from Myanmar and the decision of the ICC Chief Prosecutor to open a preliminary investigation into crimes committed against the Rohingya population under the court's jurisdiction since October 2016; calls on the authorities of Myanmar to cooperate with the ICC; calls on Myanmar to becoming a signatory of the Rome Statute of the ICC; calls on the UN Security Council to refer the situation in Myanmar to the ICC, including all crimes under its jurisdiction committed against the Rohingya, or to create an hoc international criminal tribunal; reiterates its call for the EU and its Member States to take the lead on the UN Security Council on the request to refer the situation in Myanmar to the ICC; further calls for the EU and its Member States to join and support efforts to open a case on Myanmar's possible violation of the UN Genocide Convention before the International Court of Justice[.]

On February 11 2021, the European Parliament adopted another resolution on the situation in Myanmar by a vote of 667 in favor to 1 against, with 27 abstentions,[158] in which the parliament "[s]trongly condemns the military takeover of 1 February 2021 orchestrated by the Tatmadaw, under the leadership of General Min Aung Hlaing, as a *coup d'état* and calls on the Tatmadaw to fully respect the outcome of the democratic elections of November 2020,"[159] and "[r]eiterates its support for the decision of the ICC Chief Prosecutor to open a preliminary investigation into crimes committed against the Rohingya population and for any suitable initiative contributing to holding those responsible for atrocities, including General Min Aung Hlaing and General Soe Wen, to account."[160]

3.6 ASEAN and Chinese Efforts to Cope with the Rohingya Crisis

While the EU is supportive of the fight against impunity for crimes against Rohingya, member states of the Association of Southeast Asian Nations (ASEAN) are less monolithic in their positions. At the, While Myanmar joined ASEAN on July 3, 1997, at the urging of European countries,[161] ASEAN has never had a unanimous policy on either the Rohingya issue or the refugee issue.[162] Reasons include the fact out of all the ASEAN member states, only the Philippines and Cambodia are States parties to the 1951 Refugee Convention,[163] and that ASEAN has adhered to a principle of

---

[157] European Parliament (2019).

[158] European Parliament (2021).

[159] Ibid., para. 2.

[160] Ibid., para. 32.

[161] Haque, Nower (2021), p. 44.

[162] Ibid., p. 45.

[163] Ibid.

non-interference in domestic affairs since it was founded in 1967. However, concerns about the Rohingya issue have been expressed by individual ASEAN member states and influential parties therein,[164] including Malaysia and Bangladesh. In January 2021, ASEAN Parliamentarians for Human Rights (APHR) urged the foreign ministers of the ASEAN States to grant the ASEAN Intergovernmental Commission on Human Rights (AICHR) a mandate to address human rights concerns in Rakhine State and recommend that any further plans by ASEAN especially the Comprehensive Needs Assessment on the repatriation of refugees, are developed with the meaningful consultation and participation of the Rohingya community and its representatives.[165] At its April 24, 2021 summit, ASEAN adopted a Five-Point Consensus on Myanmar aimed at countering the rising violence in Myanmar following the February 2021 *coup*, as follows[166]:

- First, there shall be immediate cessation of violence in Myanmar and all parties shall exercise utmost restraint.
- Second, constructive dialogue among all parties concerned shall commence to seek a peaceful solution in the interests of the people.
- Third, a special envoy of the ASEAN Chair shall facilitate mediation of the dialogue process, with the assistance of the Secretary-General of ASEAN.
- Fourth, ASEAN shall provide humanitarian assistance through the AHA Centre.
- Fifth, the special envoy and delegation shall visit Myanmar to meet with all parties concerned.

Although the Five-Point Consensus does not directly refer to the Rohingya issue, it can be interpreted that in order to properly address the Rohingya issue, ASEAN first of all seeks to restore security in Myanmar as a whole, and to ensure reasoned dialogue between the parties to the conflict within Myanmar. In following up the implementation of the Five-Point Consensus, ASEAN leaders conducted reviews and made decisions regarding the Five-Point Consensus at their November 2022 summit,[167] in which they "reaffirmed that Myanmar remains an integral part of ASEAN,"[168] and "that the situation in Myanmar remains critical and fragile, with growing violence as a major concern which affects not only Myanmar but also ASEAN's Community-building efforts."[169] At the same time, they found "little progress" toward the implementation of the Five-Point Consensus and that "it is therefore incumbent on the Myanmar Armed Forces to comply with its commitments to the ASEAN Leaders."[170] The Myanmar junta immediately refuted the ASEAN summit's decision, issuing a press release through its Ministry of Foreign Affairs that Myanmar objected to

---

[164] Ibid.

[165] ASEAN Parliamentarians for Human Rights (2021).

[166] Chairman's Statement on the ASEAN Leaders' Meeting (2021).

[167] ASEAN Leaders' Review and Decision on the Implementation of the Five-Point Consensus (2022).

[168] Ibid., para. 2.

[169] Ibid., para. 4.

[170] Ibid., para. 5.

3.6 ASEAN and Chinese Efforts to Cope with the Rohingya Crisis

any discussions or decisions without the involvement of the Myanmar junta. From the outset, the junta was furious that a non-political representative from Myanmar was invited to the summit in response to demands from some member states.[171] In the junta's view, "the ASEAN Leaders' review and decision on the implementation of the five-point consensus did not factually reflect the on-ground situation and did not include any constructive efforts made by the Myanmar government in the implementation of the five-point consensus."[172]

Although China has been reluctant to engage with the Rohingya issue in the Security Council because of its own domestic minority relations issues and its position that human rights issues are domestic issues, it is worth noting that China, as well as ASEAN, has been lobbying Myanmar and neighboring States to help alleviate the Rohingya crisis. To begin with, in 2016 China inaugurated the Panglong Peace Conference with the aim of arriving at a ceasefire in the civil war between Myanmarese ethnic minorities and the country's military.[173] The name "Panglong" derives from the 1947 Panglong Agreement, which was signed by Aung San.[174] Although two more such conferences were held in 2017 and 2018, collectively they produced no significant progress, and Tatmadaw staged the 2021 *coup* as a result. Next, it is reported that "China had been engaged in mediation diplomacy over the Rohingya issue even before this Rohingya crisis erupted, and offered to mediate when Sun Guoxiang [Beijing's special envoy for Asian affairs] visited Bangladesh from April 24 to 27, 2017."[175] In November 2017, the Chinese Government launched a three-phased approach for the return of Rohingya refugees: ceasefire, return, and development.[176] Although this approach did not yield concrete results either, China remained committed to a peace process in the region, as evidenced by a tripartite meeting conducted online between Bangladesh, China, and Myanmar in January 2021, which was instigated by the Chinese Vice Minister of Foreign Affairs.[177] It was reportedly decided among the participants to hold future meetings periodically, and to avoid internationalizing or politicizing the Rohingya issue.[178]

---

[171] Ministry of Foreign Affairs of Myanmar Nay Pyi Taw (2022).

[172] Ibid.

[173] Aoyama (2022), p. 2.

[174] Nitta, Hlahtway (2018).

[175] Aoyama (2022), p. 3.

[176] Ibid.

[177] Ibid.

[178] Ibid.

3.7 Recent Developments

In September 2019, the two Myanmar soldiers who had reportedly deserted the Tatmadaw and crossed over into Bangladesh to be captured by the ARSA confessed before the ICC to a campaign against Rohingya by Tatmadaw.[179] They were sent to the Hague on September 7.[180] In January 2020, the Pre-Trial Chamber III ordered the Registry to institute a system of public information and outreach activities with affected communities and particularly with the victims of the Bangladesh/Myanmar situation, following the issuance of the decision authorizing the OTP investigation, and in consultation and collaboration with the OTP.[181] The Chamber also ordered the Registry to inform the Chamber periodically about the progress of and challenges to these outreach and information activities.[182] In accordance with this order, the Registry filed four reports between July 6, 2020 and December 17, 2022.[183] Additionally, the Public Information and Outreach Section (PIOS) held a series of online Open Dialogues to provide general information about the ICC.[184] Although these attempts at dialogue between the ICC and the communities affected by the core crimes deserve praise, they have also been harshly criticized. Reasons given for this criticism are that the outreach materials prepared by the ICC are unfamiliar to, and hard to understand by, those without legal training,[185] and that even experts have a hard time finding the materials in question on the ICC website.[186]

The relationship between the ICC and Myanmar changed following the 2021 *coup*, with the ousted regime demonstrating more willingness to cooperate than it had before its overthrow. One possible aim of this change in attitude may be to demonstrate the continued democratic legitimacy of the ousted government against the post-*coup* junta. Another may be to achieve some degree of catharsis, domestically as well as internationally, by having the ICC hold the Myanmar junta accountable. On 17 July 2021, Acting President Duwa Lashi La of the National Unity Government (NUG) of Myanmar of the Republic of the Union of Myanmar lodged a declaration with the Registrar of the ICC in accordance with Article 12(3) of the Statute, in which he accepted the jurisdiction of the ICC with respect to international crimes committed in Myanmar territory since July 1, 2002.[187] However, neither the ICC nor the OTP has taken any significant action in response. Some authorities in international law and international criminal law have pointed out that the ICC should have acknowledged the NUG's declaration of acceptance of the ICC's jurisdiction and, as in Ukraine, immediately dispatched investigators to Myanmar with the intent of opening an

---

[179] Ellis-Petersen (2020).

[180] Beech, Nang, Simons (2020).

[181] Pre-Trial Chamber III (2020), p. 7.

[182] Ibid.

[183] Registry of the International Criminal Court (2022), p. 4, para. 3.

[184] Ibid, p. 5, para. 7.

[185] Hilllebrecht (2021), p. 165.

[186] Ibid.

[187] Min (2021). Legal Action World Wide (2021).

3.7 Recent Developments

investigation there.[188] At present, the prevailing view is that the ICC is avoiding making a ruling to assess the NUG's unilateral move because the junta has seized real power in Myanmar. As of February 2022, the UN is also reserving its position on the issue of succession of the Myanmar government, though the ICJ allowed the junta to appear at oral arguments on the provisional measures order in February 2022, as will be discussed in Chap. 4.

By contrast, the ICC has been proactive, or at least transparent, on the issue of government recognition for the situation in Afghanistan, which is a State Party to the ICC. On March 5, 2020, the Appeals Chamber authorized an investigation into the matter.[189] In a letter dated March 26, 2020, the Afghanistan government responded by attempting to defer said investigation pursuant to Article 18(2) of the Statute, which stipulates that "[...] a State may inform the Court that it is investigating or has investigated its nationals or others within its jurisdiction with respect to criminal acts which may constitute crimes referred to in Article 5 and which relate to the information provided in the notification to States. At the request of the State, the Prosecutor shall defer to the State's investigation of those persons unless the Pre-Trial Chamber, on the application of the Prosecutor, decides to authorize the investigation."[190] In August 2021, the Taliban announced the establishment of a new Afghan government. On September 27, the Prosecutor requested that the Chamber authorize resumption of its Afghan investigation pursuant to the aforementioned Article 18(2).[191] The Pre-Trial Chamber II noted that "It is of the essence, for this dialogue to take place and the principle of complementarity to be orderly, meaningfully and effectively implemented, that there be no uncertainty as to the representation and competent authorities of the concerned State." Contrary to the Prosecutor's argument, its request could not be legally adjudicated without addressing the "question of which entity actually constitutes the State authorities of Afghanistan since 15 August 2021; rather, this question is central to the triggering of the procedure under Article 18(2) of the Statute."[192] The Chamber went on to add that "the Chamber considers that, for it to be in a position to make an informed decision and hence properly establish the procedure under Article 18(2) of the Statute, it needs to receive reliable and updated information as to the identification of the authorities currently representing Afghanistan,"[193] and concluded by identifying both the UN Secretary-General and the Bureau of the ICC's Assembly of States Parties as "the entities suitable to provide this type of information at this stage."[194] To date, however, neither of these bodies has provided the requested information. The UN Secretary-General replied that neither they, nor the United Nations Secretariat more broadly, engage in acts of recognition

---

[188] Dugard, Gunness, Thomas, Wahyuningrum, Wilde (2022).

[189] Appeals Chamber of the International Criminal Court (2020).

[190] Pre-Trial Chamber II (2021), p. 3, para. 3.

[191] Office of the Prosecutor of the International Criminal Court (2021).

[192] Pre-Trial Chamber II (2021), p. 6, para. 16.

[193] Ibid., p. 7, para. 19.

[194] Ibid.

of governments, which is a matter for individual member states.[195] For its part, the Bureau of the Assembly of States Parties wrote that "the Bureau regrets to inform that due to its nature and functions, it does not hold the type of information that is requested."[196] Ultimately, the ICC Pre-Trial Chamber II did not get what it wanted from these requests. The abovementioned situation in Afghanistan suggests that in the absence of a world government, there is no unified authority for government recognition, and that in a situation such as that of Bangladesh/Myanmar, there may be fragmentation between the ICC and the ICJ regarding what constitutes the legitimate government.

On July 22, 2022, the Pre-Trial Chamber II ordered the Prosecution to communicate to the Chamber any materials received from Afghanistan in support of the Deferral Request and to submit an assessment of the merits of the Deferral Request, or any other relevant observations and information pertaining thereto.[197] The Prosecutor replied that "conduct of the authorities currently representing Afghanistan abundantly demonstrates that they are not continuing any such activity, nor will they do so."[198] Accordingly, the Prosecutor requested that the Pre-Trial Chamber II "authorise the resumption of the Court's investigation in the Situation in the Islamic Republic of Afghanistan."[199] The delay in the ICC's decision on Afghanistan's right to representation has been condemned by international human rights groups as resulting in delays in justice for crimes under international law.[200] On October 31, 2022, the Chamber authorized the Prosecution to resume investigation into the Afghanistan situation, having determined that in accordance with the above cited view expressed by the Prosecutor, the material transmitted by the Afghanistan government indeed did not show that Afghanistan has investigated, or was investigating, in a manner that covered the full scope of the Prosecutor's intended investigation.[201]

On September 13, 2021, Legal Action Worldwide (LAW) and the law firm of Debevoise and Pimpton filed a communication with the ICC Prosecutor on behalf of Rohingya clients who were victims of the 2017 military operation against the Rohingya.[202] It will be interesting to see how the ICC deals with the declaration by the NUG's declaration in this regard, but as of this writing, neither the Court nor the OTP have shown any significant response.

In late 2021, the UN Credentials Committee decided to defer its decision on the representation of Myanmar and Afghanistan, which had each nominated two individuals to represent their governments at the UN General Assembly.[203] In response, the General Assembly also adopted a resolution without a vote to accept the committee's

---

[195] Registry of the International Criminal Court (2021).

[196] Ibid.

[197] Pre-Trial Chamber II (2022a).

[198] Office of the Prosecutor of (26 August 2022) p. 42, para. 116.

[199] Ibid., p. 42, para. 117.

[200] Evenson (2022).

[201] The Pre-Trial Chamber II (2022b).

[202] Mulvey (2021).

[203] UN Doc. A76/550 (1 December 2021), p. 2, para. 9.

3.7 Recent Developments

decision to defer.[204] In the meantime, as mentioned above, the Myanmar participated in oral arguments before the ICJ.[205] Therefore, when the Security Council called an emergency special session of the General Assembly for February 28–March 3, 2022 over the Ukraine situation, Myanmar's representative to the UN was Kyaw Moe Tun, who had been appointed by the previous civilian government,[206] a situation that persists as of September 2022.

As indicated above, however, it was the post-*coup* junta that represented Myanmar before the ICJ when the ICJ handed down its judgment on the country's preliminary objections, a situation that fueled further criticism as follows[207]: the ICJ's preliminary objection procedure in this instance "marked the first time that a different government represented the same member state before the General Assembly and the ICJ during the same Assembly session."[208] Nor is there a united front vis-à-vis the junta among other States. For example, the UK did not invite Myanmar's head of state to the state funeral of Queen Elizabeth II. By contrast, Japan invited a diplomat appointed by the Myanmar junta to attend the state funeral of former Prime Minister Shinzo Abe, drawing criticism from civil society at home and abroad.[209]

Given that General Assembly Resolution 396(V) stipulates that whenever the question of state representation arises, UN organs should take into account the "attitude adopted by the General Assembly",[210] it was to be hoped that the Credentials Committee would reach a final decision one way or another on Myanmar's representation at the General Assembly's 2022 session. The outcome of the committee's deliberations remains unknown as of this writing, however.

Thus, with the Myanmar government's representation in the international arena still uncertain, the OTP concluded its first five-day visit to Bangladesh on February 27, 2022.[211] It was reported that the Chief Prosecutor spoke directly to survivors and affected communities during his visit to the Kutupalong refugee camp in Cox's Bazar, emphasizing the need to accelerate the collection and analysis of evidence.[212]

---

[204] UN Doc. A/RES/76/15 (7 December 2021).

[205] Verbatim Record (2022), pp. 6–7.

[206] Tiezzi (2022).

[207] Special Advocacy Council for Myanmar (2022).

[208] Amirfar, Zamour, Pickard (2022).

[209] Hirano (2022).

[210] UN Doc. A/RES/396(V) (1951), para. 3. *See* Barber (2022).

[211] International Criminal Court (2022).

[212] Ibid.

3.8 Conclusion

The Pre-Trial Chamber's affirmation of its jurisdiction over the Bangladesh/Myanmar situation and its authorization to open an investigation are generally seen not as persuasive, but rather as self-aggrandizement on the part of the ICC.[213] Given these circumstances, it would not be easy for the ICC to conduct a site visit even if it recognizes the previous Myanmar government in place of the ruling junta. That is, it is obvious that it would be extremely difficult to conduct an investigation of a situation involving a Non-State Party without the consent of the Non-State Party in question. Even though the State Party, in this case Bangladesh, would be a willing participant in this situation, the lack of cooperation from the Non-State Party to the matter will instead necessitate, in addition to interviewing witnesses in Bangladesh, reliance on evidence from social media, such as videos posted online, if progress is to be made in the said investigation. As the Report of the Independent International Fact-finding Mission on Myanmar (IIFFMM) suggests, "The role of social media is significant. Facebook has been a useful instrument for those seeking to spread hate."[214]

It is important to reiterate that the ICC is not able to fully investigate all crimes against the Rohingya in Myanmar, and in fact is only authorized by the Pre-Trial Chamber to open investigations into those crimes whereof at least some element can be said to have been committed in Bangladesh.[215] Thus, even if Bangladesh cooperates, only partial evidence of the crimes in question is available in Bangladesh, meaning that much of the information needed to prosecute the Myanmar ruling junta would be in the hands of that selfsame junta, including evidence of Myanmar's deportation of the Rohingya.[216] When evidence is scarce, as indicated herein, the OTP may instead rely on UN reports, NGO reports, and the testimony and evidence-gathering activities of activists and UN personnel working in the field in furtherance of its investigation. Reliance on intermediaries of this sort has been criticized, however, by the ICC judges in the Lubanga case as a dereliction of duty by the OTP, meaning that the OTP must strive to conduct its investigations as independently as possible.[217]

It has also been suggested that effective accountability for the situation in Myanmar could be achieved by going one step further than a *proprio motu* investigation by the ICC Prosecutor and referring the situation to the UN Security Council. In fact, even after the ICC Pre-Trial Chamber III authorized the Prosecutor on November

---

[213] McIntyre (2021), p. 541; Kieldgaard-Pedersen (2021), p. 943.

[214] UN Doc. A/HRC/39/64 (2018), para. 74.

[215] "Authorisation Decision" (2019), para. 124, p. 53.

[216] Williams, Buchwald, Domino, Hamilton, Scharf (2020), p. 566.

[217] Trial Chamber I of the International Criminal Court (2012), pp. 218–219, para. 482.

3.8 Conclusion

14, 2019, to proceed investigating the alleged crimes that were within the ICC's jurisdiction in the situation in Bangladesh/Myanmar,[218] the Special Rapporteur recommended that the Security Council refer the situation to the ICC.[219] In any case, the cooperation of the international community and all parties involved is essential if ICC investigations are to be genuinely effective. In this sense, the OTP will need to be proactive in dealing with the present problem and willingly accept the cooperation the NUG.

Although public attention shifted to Ukraine in 2022, the international attitude toward Myanmar began to show some improvement by year's end. On December 21, the UN Security Council issued its first resolution since the February 2021 *coup*. Drafted by the UK, it reportedly expressed concern about the ruling junta, demanding a cessation of violence and the release of all arbitrarily detained prisoners, including Win Myint and Aung San Suu Kyi.[220] Some permanent Security Council members have come out in favor of referring Myanmar's situation to the ICC, in a manner consistent with the alignment of council members on measures for dealing with the country. At the very least, the U.S. government has frequently hinted at the possibility of a referral of the situation in Myanmar since December 2022,[221] while the UK government has taken the position that there is currently no consensus on a Security Council referral to the ICC because it believes that a veto of a resolution on such a referral would only give comfort to the ruling junta.[222] Unlike Ukraine, however, the permanent members of the Security Council are not actively involved in the situation in Myanmar, and thus, it may be possible for them to show a united front. The political power of the council could be a boost to any ICC investigation or prosecution, and since referral based on Security Council resolution creates an obligation on the part of concerned States Parties to cooperate with the ICC both under the UN Charter and the Rome Statute, progress in this direction is to be expected.

The key to success in international criminal justice for ongoing conflicts is ultimately said to be the prompt collection and preservation of evidence by the international community.[223] However, it is extremely difficult for international criminal justice efforts to collect evidence in an ongoing conflict, and it is usually not until long after the conflict has ended that such organized evidence collection in the field becomes possible. Hence, the international community should work together to preserve evidence to demonstrate that the ICC can function effectively even in situations involving Non-States Parties.

---

[218] *See* "Authorisation Decision" (2019).

[219] UN Doc. A/HRC/49/76 (2022), "Report of the Special Rapporteur on the Situation of Human Rights in Myanmar, Thomas H. Andrews," unedited prerelease version, p. 18, para. 94.

[220] UN Doc. S/RES/2669 (2022). *See* United Nations Meeting Coverage (2022).

[221] U.S. Mission to the United Nations (2022); U.S. Department of State (2022).

[222] Norman (2022).

[223] Meron (2021), p. 92.

References

Advisory Commission on Rakhine State (2017) Towards a peaceful, fair and prosperous future or the people of Rakhine: Final report of the advisory commission on Rakhine state

Amirfar C, Zamour R, Pickard D (2022) Representation of member states at the united nations: recent challenges. ASIL Insights 26(6). https://www.asil.org/insights/volume/26/issue/6

Aoyama R (2022) [Research Reports] China's mediation diplomacy in Myanmar. Research Group on "China" FY2021-#7. The Japan Institute of International Affairs, pp. 1–5. https://www.jiia.or.jp/en/column/2022/07/china-fy2021-07.html#sdendnote18sym

Appeals Chamber of the International Criminal Court (2020) Judgment on the Appeal against the Decision on the Authorisation of an investigation into the situation in the Islamic Republic of Afghanistan

ASEAN Leaders' Review and Decision on the Implementation of the Five-Point Consensus (2022). https://asean.org/wp-content/uploads/2022/11/06-ASEAN-Leaders-Review-and-Decision-on-the-Implementation-of-the-Five-Point-Consensus_fin.pdf

ASEAN Parliaments for Human Rights (2021) As foreign ministers meet, ASEAN urged to step up its Rakhine response. https://aseanmp.org/tag/rakhine-state/

Barber R (2022) Inching forward but a long road ahead to achieve justice for the Rohingya. Just Security. https://www.justsecurity.org/83108/rohingya-justice-inching-forward/

Barkholdt J, Winkelmann I (2019) Responsibility to protect. In: Peters A, Wolfrum R (eds) Max planck encyclopedias of public international law (MPEPIL). Oxford University Press, Oxford

Bazzar V (2022) Identification of elements of the crime against humanity of deportation into the situation in Bangladesh/Myanmar. J Int Crim Law 3(1):48–53

Becker MF (2019) The situation of the Rohingya: is there a role for the international court of justice? Cambridge University Legal Studies Research Paper Series No. 25/2019, pp 1–6

Beech H, Nang S, Simons M (2020) "Kill All You See": in a first, Myanmar soldiers tell of Rohingya slaughter. New York Times. https://www.nytimes.com/2020/09/08/world/asia/myanmar-rohingya-genocide.html

BROUK UK (2020) Press release: Argentinean judiciary moves closer to opening case against Myanmar over Rohingya genocide. https://www.brouk.org.uk/argentinean-judiciary-moves-closer-to-opening-case-against-myanmar-over-rohingya-genocide/

BROUK UK (2021) Media release: historic decision by Argentinian courts to take up genocide case against Myanmar. https://burmacampaign.org.uk/historic-decision-by-argentinian-courts-to-take-up-genocide-case-against-myanmar/

Burma Campaign UK (2019) Complaint file. https://burmacampaign.org.uk/media/Complaint-File.pdf. Last accessed 22 Sept 2022c

Cadman T, Bucklay C (2019) Filling the vacuum: Syria and the international criminal court. Justice in Conflict. https://justiceinconflict.org/2019/03/19/filling-the-vacuum-syria-and-the-international-criminal-court/

Chairman's Statement on the ASEAN Leaders' Meeting (2021) Five-point consensus. ASEAN Secretariat, Jakarta, Republic of Indonesia. https://asean.org/wp-content/uploads/Chairmans-Statement-on-ALM-Five-Point-Consensus-24-April-2021-FINAL-a-1.pdf

Delegation of the European Union for the Pacific (2017) Statement by the spokesperson on the final report of the advisory commission on Rakhine State, Myanmar. https://eeas.europa.eu/delegations/fiji/31382/statement-spokesperson-final-report-advisory-commission-rakhine-state-myanmar_nb

Dugard J, Gunness C, Thomas T, Wahyuningrum Y, Wilde R (2022) The ICC must engage with Myanmar's democratic government and hold the junta to account. The Diplomat. https://thediplomat.com/2022/08/the-icc-must-engage-with-myanmars-democratic-government-and-hold-the-junta-to-account/

European Parliament (2019) European Parliament resolution of 19 September 2019 on Myanmar, notably the situation of the Rohingya

References

European Parliament (2021) European Parliament resolution of 11 February 2021 on the situation in Myanmar

Evenson E (2022) International criminal court should reach decision on Afghanistan. Human Rights Watch News. https://www.hrw.org/news/2022/09/12/international-criminal-court-should-reach-decision-afghanistan

Fisher KJ (2020) The problem with the crime of forced migration as a loophole to ICC jurisdiction: the PTC's decision on Myanmar and the risk to vulnerable populations. J Int Humanitarian Legal Stud 11:385–409

Fortify Rights (2021) News release: Argentina: prosecute crimes against Rohingya in Myanmar. https://www.fortifyrights.org/mya-inv-2021-09-30/

Foysal QO (2022) A tale of two international law principles: ensuring justice and accountability for the Rohingya. In: Hasan M, Murshed SM, Pillai P (eds) The Rohingya crisis: humanitarian and legal approaches. Routledge, London, pp 73–95.2

Freuden S (2019) Decision on the "Prosecution's Request for a Ruling on Jurisdiction Under Article 19(3) of the Statute." Int Leg Mater 58(1):120–159

Gallant KS (2022) International criminal jurisdiction: whose law must we obey. Oxford University Press, Oxford

Gepp MGM (2021) The road not taken: failure to protect from atrocity crimes in Myanmar'. Groningen J Int Law 9(1):78–100

Gomez CE (2019) The international criminal court's decision on the Rohingya crisis: the need for a critical redefinition of trans-border jurisdiction to address human rights. California Western Int Law J 50(1):177–205

Government of the Republic of the Union of Myanmar (2018) Statement by H. E. U. Kyaw Tint Swe: Union Minister for the Office of the State Counsellor and Chairman of the Delegation of the Republic of the Union of Myanmar at the General Debate of the 73rd Session of the United Nations General Assembly. https://gadebate.un.org/sites/default/files/gastatements/73/mm_en.pdf

Government of the Republic of the Gambia (2019) Application instituting proceedings and request for provisional measures. Application of the convention on the prevention and punishment of the crime of genocide (the Gambia v. Myanmar), the international court of justice.

Government of the Republic of the Union of Myanmar, Ministry of the Office of the State Counsellor (2018) Press release, reprinted in Annex E to the prosecution notice of documents for use in status conference. ICC-RoC46(3)-01/18-27-AnxE

Guilfoyle D (2019) The ICC pre-trial chamber decision on jurisdiction over the situation in Myanmar. Aust J Int Aff 73(1):2–8

Hale K, Rankin M (2019) Extending the 'System' of international criminal law? The ICC's decision on jurisdiction over alleged deportations of Rohingya people. Aust J Int Aff 73(1):22–28

Hannah Ellis-Petersen (2020) Myanmar soldiers tell of Rohingya killings, rapes and mass burials reported video confessions could be used as evidence in international criminal court. Guardian. https://www.theguardian.com/world/2020/sep/08/myanmar-soldiers-tell-of-rohingya-killings-rapes-and-mass-burials?CMP=share_btn_link

Haque STM, Nower T (2021) The Rohingya crisis and geopolitics. In: Swazo NK, Haque STM, Haque MM, Nower T (eds) The Rohingya crisis: a moral, ethnographic, and policy assessment. Routledge, London

Hillebrecht C (2021) Saving the international justice regime: beyond backlash against international courts. Cambridge University Press, Cambridge

Hirano K (2022) Ex-Myanmar diplomat urges barring junta envoy from Abe funeral. The Japan Times. https://www.japantimes.co.jp/news/2022/09/25/national/myanmar-diplomat-junta-abe-funeral/

International Criminal Court (2019) Questions and answers: situation in the People's Republic of Bangladesh/Republic of the Union of Myanmar. "Questions and Answers." https://www.icc-cpi.int/itemsDocuments/QandA-bangladesh-myanmar-eng.pdf

International Court of Justice (2020) Order. Application of the convention on the prevention and punishment of the crime of Genocide (the Gambia v. Myanmar)

International Criminal Court (2022) Press Release: ICC Prosecutor, Karim A. A. Khan QC, concludes first visit to Bangladesh, underlines commitment to advance investigations into alleged atrocity crimes against the Rohingya. https://www.icc-cpi.int/news/icc-prosecutor-karim-khan-qc-concludes-first-visit-bangladesh-underlines-commitment-advance

International Criminal Court Press Release (2022) ICC Prosecutor, Karim A. A. Khan QC, concludes first visit to Bangladesh, underlines commitment to advance investigations into alleged atrocity crimes against the Rohingya. https://www.icc-cpi.int/Pages/item.aspx?name=20220301-otp-press-release-banglades

Islam MdR (2019) Gambia's genocide case against Myanmar: a legal review. The Diplomat. https://thediplomat.com/2019/11/gambias-genocide-case-against-myanmar-a-legal-review/

Joint Statement of Canada and the Kingdom of the Netherlands regarding Intention to Intervene in The Gambia v. Myanmar case at the International Court of Justice (2020). https://www.government.nl/documents/diplomatic-statements/2020/09/02/joint-statement-of-canada-and-the-kingdom-of-the-netherlands-regarding-intention-to-intervene-in-the-gambia-v.-myanmar-case-at-the-international-court-of-justice

Khan MZI (2019) Pathways to justice for 'Atrocity Crimes' in Myanmar: is there political will? Glob Responsib Protect 11(1):3–41

Khin T (2020) Universal jurisdiction, the international criminal court, and the Rohingya Genocide. Opinio Juris. http://opiniojuris.org/2020/10/23/universal-jurisdiction-the-international-criminal-court-and-the-rohingya-genocide/

Kieldgaard-Pedersen A (2021) Is the quality of the ICC's legal reasoning an obstacle to its ability to deter international crimes? J Int Crim Justice 19(4):939–957

Kittichaisaree K (2022) The Rohingya, justice and international law. Routledge, London

Legal Action World Wide (2021) Press release: more than 500 Rohingya request ICC prosecutor accept NUG declaration. https://www.legalactionworldwide.org/accountability-rule-of-law/law-icc-victim-submission-for-rohingya-clients-following-nug-declaration/

Magnusson A, Pedersen MB (2012) A good office? Twenty years of UN mediation in Myanmar. International Peace Institute, New York

Mahaseth H, Tulsyan A (2022) The Myanmar coup and the role of ASEAN. https://ssrn.com/abstract=4021075. https://doi.org/10.2139/ssrn.4021075

Mascarenhas V, Jacobi B, O'Connell C, Martin IS (2019) The Rohingyas' plight: what options under international law? The Diplomat. https://thediplomat.com/2019/01/the-plight-of-the-rohingya-what-options-under-international-law/

McIntyre G (2021) The ICC, self-created challenges and missed opportunities to legitimize authority over non-states parties. J Int Crim Justice 19(3):511–541

Meron T (2021) Standing up for justice: the challenges of trying atrocity crimes. Oxford University Press, Oxford

Min AM (2021) Twitter. The Minister of Human Rights for the National Unity Government of Myanmar. https://twitter.com/aung_myo_minn/status/1428680811574972416

Ministry of Foreign Affairs of Myanmar Nay Pyi Taw (2022) Myanmar rejects ASEAN leaders' review and decision on implementation of five-point consensus which was issued after 40th and 41st ASEAN summits. Infonews. https://infosheet.org/node/3628

Mulvey A (2021) 'Symposium on the current crisis in Myanmar: new communication to the international criminal court calls for justice for victims and survivors of crimes committed by Myanmar's military over past two decades. Opinio Juris. http://opiniojuris.org/2021/09/29/symposium-on-the-current-crisis-in-myanmar-new-communication-to-the-international-criminal-court-calls-for-justice-for-victims-and-survivors-of-crimes-committed-by-myanmars-military-over-pas/

Myanmar, Information Sheet (2022) 2(3)

Nagakoshi Y (2021) The scope and implications of the international criminal court's jurisdictional decision over the Rohingya crisis. Hum Rights Q 43(2):259–289

References

Nitta Y, Hlahtway T (2018) Two ethnic groups in Myanmar sign ceasefire: political dialogue still a challenge for Suu Kyi's government. Nikkei Asia. https://asia.nikkei.com/Politics/Two-ethnic-groups-in-Myanmar-sign-ceasefire

Norman J (2022) Answer to the question for foreign, commonwealth and development office by Rushanara Ali: Myanmar: International Criminal Court. https://questions-statements.parliament.uk/written-questions/detail/2022-09-05/47539

Netherlands (2020) Objection made on 23.09.2020 to the interpretative declaration made by Myanmar upon ratification

Nuclear Threat Initiative (2015) Country Spotlight 'Myanmar.' https://www.nti.org/countries/myanmar/

Ochi M, Matsuyama S (2019) Ethnic conflicts in Myanmar: the application of the law of non-international armed conflict. In: Linton S, McCormack T, Sivakumaran S (eds) Asia-Pacific perspectives on international humanitarian law. Cambridge University Press, Cambridge, pp 338–355

Office of the Prosecutor of the International Criminal Court (2018) Prosecution's Request for a Ruling on Jurisdiction under Article 19(3) of the Statute

Office of the Prosecutor of the International Criminal Court (2019) Request for Authorisation of an Investigation pursuant to Article 15

Office of the Prosecutor of the International Criminal Court (2021) Request to Authorise Resumption of Investigation under Article 18(2) of the Statute', Office of the Prosecutor. ICC-02/17-161

Office of the Prosecutor of the International Criminal Court (2022) Prosecution's Communication of Materials and Further Observations Pursuant to Article 18(2) and Rule 54(1)

Organisation for the Prohibition of Chemical Weapons (2015) Myanmar joins chemical weapons convention. https://www.opcw.org/media-centre/news/2015/07/myanmar-joins-chemical-weapons-convention

Pérez-León-Acevedo J, Pinto TA (2021) Disentangling law and religion in the Rohingya case at the international criminal court. Nordic J Human Rights 39(4):458–480

Portugal (2020) Objection made on 25.09.2020 to the interpretative declaration made by Myanmar upon ratification. https://treaties.un.org/doc/Publication/UNTS/No%20Volume/27531/A-27531-Portugal-0800000280589c6b.pdf

Pre-Trial Chamber I of the International Criminal Court (2018) Decision on the "Prosecution's Request for a Ruling on Jurisdiction under Article 19(3) of the Statute." ICC-RoC46(3)-01/18-37. "Jurisdiction Decision"

Pre-Trial Chamber I of the International Criminal Court (2018) Partially Dissenting Opinion of Judge Marc Perrin de Brichambaut. ICC-RoC46(3)-01/18-37-Anx. "Partially Dissenting Opinion"

Pre-Trial Chamber II of the International Criminal Court (2021) Decision Setting the Procedure pursuant to Rule 55(1) of the Rules of Procedure and Evidence following the Prosecutor's "Request to Authorise Resumption of Investigation under Article 18(2) of the Statute." ICC-02/17-165

Pre-Trial Chamber II of the International Criminal Court (2022a) Order Instructing the Prosecution to Submit Observations and Relevant Materials Pursuant to Article 18(2) of the Rome Statute and 54(1) of the Rules of Procedure and Evidence. ICC-02/17-194

Pre-Trial Chamber II (2022b) Decision Pursuant to Article 18(2) of the Statute Authorising the Prosecution to Resume Investigation. ICC 02/17 196

Pre-Trial Chamber III of the International Criminal Court (2019) Decision Pursuant to Article 15 of the Rome Statute on the Authorisation of an Investigation into the Situation in the People's Republic of Bangladesh/Republic of the Union of Myanmar. ICC-01/19-27

Pre-Trial Chamber III of the International Criminal Court (2020) Order on Information and Outreach for the Victims of the Situation. ICC-01/19-28

Registry of the International Criminal Court (2021) Annex II to the Transmission of Communications Submitted by the United Nations and the Bureau of the Assembly of States Parties pursuant to Pre-Trial Chamber II's Decision ICC-02/17-165 of 8 October 2021. ICC-02/17-169-AnxII

Registry of the International Criminal Court (2022) Public redacted version of "Fifth Registry Report on Information and Outreach Activities. ICC-01/19-47-Red

ReliefWeb (2020) Executive summary of independent commission of enquiry-ICOE. https://relief web.int/sites/reliefweb.int/files/resources/BM.pdf

Romania (2020) Objection made on 27.09.2020 to the interpretative declaration made by Myanmar upon ratification

Rosenthal G (2019) A brief and independent inquiry into the involvement of the united nations in Myanmar from 2010 to 2018. https://www.un.org/sg/sites/www.un.org.sg/files/atoms/files/Mya nmar%20Report%20-%20May%202019.pdf

Ross A (2019) With memories of Rwanda: the Gambian minister taking on Suu Kyi. Reuters. https://jp.reuters.com/article/us-myanmar-rohingya-world-court-gambia/with-memories-of-rwanda-the-gambian-minister-taking-on-suu-kyi-idUSKBN1Y91HA

Saleh M (2019) Syrian refugees use precedent set in Rohingya case to try to bring government officials before the international criminal court. The Intercept. https://theintercept.com/2019/03/16/syria-conflict-internation-criminal-court/

Schabas WA (2020) An introduction to the international criminal court, 6th edn. Cambridge University Press, Cambridge

Scheffer DJ (2001) A negotiators perspective on the international criminal court. Military Law Rev 167:1–19

Spadaro A (2020) The situation in the People's Republic of Bangladesh/Republic of the Union of Myanmar decision to authorize investigation (I.C.C.) and the Gambia V. Myanmar order for provisional measures (I.C.J.). Int Legal Mater 59(4):616–693

Special Advocacy Council for Myanmar (2022) ICJ judgment on preliminary objections welcome, but court must rectify Myanmar's representation and more states must intervene in the case. https://specialadvisorycouncil.org/2022/07/icj-judgement-un/

Stahn C (2015) The law and practice of the international criminal court. Oxford University Press, Oxford

The International Committee of the Red Cross (2021) Commentary on the third Geneva convention: convention (III) relative to the treatment of prisoners of war. Cambridge University Press, Cambridge

Tiezzi S (2022) How did Asian countries vote on the UN's Ukraine resolution? The Diplomat. https://thediplomat.com/2022/03/how-did-asian-countries-vote-on-the-uns-ukraine-resolution/

Trial Chamber I of the International Criminal Court (2012) Judgment pursuant to Article 74 of the Statute. ICC-01/04-01/06-2842

TRIAL International (2021) Universal jurisdiction case in Argentina: an important decision for Rohingyas. https://trialinternational.org/latest-post/universal-jurisdiction-case-in-argentina-an-important-decision-for-the-rohingyas/

UN Doc. A/RES/396(V) (1951)

UN Doc. E/CN.4/1992/58 (1992)

UN Doc. A/RES/48/150 (1994)

UN Doc. A/HRC/RES/13/25 (2010)

UN Doc. A/HRC/23/L.26 (2013)

UN Doc. A/HRC/31/13 (2015)

UN Doc. A/HRC/RES/34/22 (2017)

UN Doc. A/72/PV. 76 (2017)

UN Doc. A/HRC/RES/39/2 (2018)

UN Doc. A/HRC/39/64 (2018)

UN Doc. A/RES/72/248 (2018)

UN Doc. S/2018/507 (2018)

UN Doc. S/2018/748 (2018)

UN Doc. S/PV.8381 (2018)

UN Doc. A/HRC/42/CRP.3 (2019)

UN Doc. A/HRC/42/CRP.5 (2019)

References

UN Doc. S/2019/676 (2019)

UN Doc. S/PV.8477 (2019)

UN Doc. A/RES76/15 (2021)

UN Doc. A76/550 (2021)

UN Doc. A/HRC/50/L.21 (2022)

UN Doc. S/RES/2669 (2022)

UN Doc. A/HRC/49/76 (2022)

UN Independent Investigative Mechanism for Myanmar (2022) Bulletin 6

United Nations Meeting Coverage (2022) Security Council demands immediate end to violence in Myanmar, urges restraint, release of arbitrarily detained prisoners, adopting Resolution 2669. https://press.un.org/en/2022/sc15159.doc.htm

UN News (2017) Myanmar: UN welcomes final assessment of independent advisory panel on Rakhine state. https://news.un.org/en/story/2017/08/563812-myanmar-un-welcomes-final-assessment-independent-advisory-panel-rakhine-state

UN News (27 October 2021) Rohingya refugee crisis. https://news.un.org/en/focus/rohingya-refugee-crisis

UN News (18 June 2021) Myanmar: timely support and action by security council "Really Paramount," says UN special envoy. https://news.un.org/en/story/2021/06/1094322

UN Office for Disarmament Affairs (2022) Myanmar: signature of biological weapons convention. https://treaties.unoda.org/a/bwc/myanmar/SIG/moscow

UN Secretary General Press Release (2018) Secretary-general appoints Christine Schraner Burgener of Switzerland as special envoy on Myanmar

UN Secretary General Statements (2021) Ms. Noeleen Heyzer of Singapore—special envoy on Myanmar. https://www.un.org/sg/en/content/sg/personnel-appointments/2021-10-25/ms-noeleen-heyzer-of-singapore-special-envoy-myanmar; https://press.un.org/en/2018/sga1802.doc.htm

Vagias M (2019) Case No. ICC-RoC46(3)-01/18. Am J Int Law 113(2):368–375

U.S. Department of State (2019) Finding of non-compliance with the chemical weapons convention

U.S. Department of State (2022) Briefing with ambassador-at-large for global criminal justice Beth

U.S. Mission to the United Nations (2022) Remarks by Ambassador Chris Lu, U.S. Representative of the United States of America to the United Nations for U.N. Management and Reform, at a Georgetown University Event on Burma. https://usun.usmission.gov/remarks-by-ambassador-chris-lu-at-a-georgetown-university-event-on-burma/

U.S. President William J. Clinton, Statement by the President (2000) Signature of the international criminal court treaty. https://www.govinfo.gov/content/pkg/WCPD-2001-01-08/pdf/WCPD-2001-01-08-Pg4.pdf

U.S. President Donald J. Trump (2020) Executive Order 13928 of June 11, 2020: blocking property of certain persons associated with the international criminal court. Fed Reg 85(115):36139–36142

U.S. President Joseph R. Biden Jr. (2021) Executive Order 14022 of April 1, 2021: termination of emergency with respect to the international criminal court. Fed Reg 86(65):17895–17896

Van den Berg S (2019) Gambia files Rohingya genocide case against Myanmar at world court: justice minister. Reuter. https://www.reuters.com/article/us-myanmar-rohingya-world-court-idUSKBN1XL18S

Van Schaack: Building justice: criminal accountability and the road to peace, questions on justice in Libya and Beyond. https://www.state.gov/building-justice-criminal-accountability-and-the-road-to-peace-questions-on-justice-in-libya-and-beyond/

Verbatim Record of the International Court of Justice (2022) CR 2022/1

Ware A, Laoutides C (2019) Myanmar's 'Rohingya' conflict, New York

Williams P, Buchwald TF, Domino J, Hamilton R, Scharf MP (2020) The Rohingya genocide. Case Western Reserve J Int Law 52(1–2):543–571

Chapter 4
The Relationship Between the Rohingya Case Before the International Court of Justice and the Bangladesh-Myanmar Situation Before the International Criminal Court

Abstract With regard to the Rohingya crisis, for the first time in history, the International Court of Justice (ICJ) and the International Criminal Court (ICC) are dealing with the same case at the same time. The ICJ is the principal judicial body of the United Nations and adjudicates state responsibility for interstate disputes. As the United Nations fact-finding mission has stated, there is a growing consensus that Myanmar's armed forces and authorities are suspected of committing crimes comparable to genocide, and the ICJ is on the verge of holding the state accountable for genocide, a crime within a crime, in addition to the criminal responsibility of individuals under international law. On November 11, 2019, three days before the Pre-Trial Division of the ICC authorized the opening of an investigation into the Bangladesh/ Myanmar situation, The Gambia filed a complaint with the ICJ against Myanmar under the Genocide Convention. The application includes a request of provisional measures against Myanmar. On January 23, 2020, the ICJ issued its order for provisional measures to preserve certain rights asserted by The Gambia for the protection of the Rohingya in Myanmar. The evidentiary hurdle for the ICJ to find genocide is extremely high. It is also noteworthy that neither The Gambia, which brought the suit before the ICJ, nor Canada nor the Netherlands, which have announced their intention to intervene in the case, are directly affected parties in the matter. All of which suggests that there may be yet more plaintiffs going forward with respect to issues surrounding similar breaches of the obligation *erga omnes*.

4.1 Proceedings Before the International Court of Justice

4.1.1 Institution of Proceedings by the Gambia

The Universal Periodic Review of Myanmar of 2015 revealed many states' recommendations for Myanmar to combat and end legal impunity for those who committed crimes amounting to significant human rights violations.[1] In light of the intensified

---

[1] "Report of the Working Group on the Universal Periodic Review," UN Doc. A/HRC/31/13 (2015).

© The Author(s), under exclusive license to Springer Nature Singapore Pte Ltd. 2023
H. Takemura, *The Rohingya Crisis and the International Criminal Court*,
https://doi.org/10.1007/978-981-99-2734-0_4

clearance operations against the Rohingya by Tatmadaw, particularly after October 2016, and the emphasis by multiple UN investigations on the genocidal intent of those acts,[2] The Gambia filed a case against Myanmar at the ICJ on November 11, 2019.[3] Besides the fact that The Gambia and Myanmar are both parties to the Genocide Convention, The Gambia has no stake in human rights violations against the Rohingya, and hence Gambia's complaint is also seen as a Good Samaritan act.[4] These proceedings are also considered to be set against the background of the *erga omnes* and *erga omnes partes* character of the obligations of the Genocide Convention.[5] In this regard, The Gambia claims as follows in its application to institute proceedings and request provisional measures:

> The Gambia, mindful of the *jus cogens* character of the prohibition of genocide and the *erga omnes* and *erga omnes partes* character of the obligations that are owed under the Genocide Convention, institutes the present proceedings to establish Myanmar's responsibility for violations of the Genocide Convention, to hold it fully accountable under international law for its genocidal acts against the Rohingya group, and to have recourse to this Court to ensure the fullest possible protection for those who remain at grave risk from future acts of genocide.[6]

The Gambia accordingly justifies its claim to jurisdiction as follows: (1) Both The Gambia and Myanmar are member states of the United Nations, and as such are bound by the ICJ Statute, including Article 36(1) thereof, which states that the Court's jurisdiction comprises all cases which the parties refer to it and all matters specially provided for in the Charter of the United Nations or in treaties and conventions in force[7]; and (2) Both The Gambia and Myanmar are parties to the Genocide Convention, and the Convention is applicable between these states after the date of accession of the instrument by The Gambia on December 29, 1978.[8] Article IX of the Genocide Convention obligates its States Parties such that "[d]isputes between the Contracting Parties relating to the interpretation, application or fulfilment of the present Convention, including those relating to the responsibility of a State for genocide or for any of the other acts enumerated in Article III, shall be submitted to the ICJ at the request of any of the parties to the dispute." According to The Gambia, a dispute therefore exists between The Gambia and Myanmar relating to the interpretation and application of the Genocide Convention and the fulfilment by Myanmar of its obligations to prevent genocide and to desist from its own acts of genocide, as well as Myanmar's obligation to make reparations to victims and offer assurances and guarantees of non-repetition.[9]

---

[2] Government of the Republic of the Gambia (2019), para. 7.

[3] Ibid.

[4] Islam and Muquim (2020), p. 79.

[5] Pillai (2019).

[6] Government of the Republic of The Gambia (2019), paras.15, 20.

[7] Ibid., para. 16.

[8] Ibid., para. 17.

[9] Ibid., para. 23.

4.1 Proceedings Before the International Court of Justice

It is well established that in this case, The Gambia acted not only to reinforce binding obligations existing between the countries based on the Genocide Convention, but also as a member of the Organization of Islamic Cooperation (OIC). As the Rohingya are perceived as an ethnic minority in Myanmar, it should come as no surprise that the OIC feels sympathy for them. Indeed, on March 1–2, 2019, The Gambia, as a member state of the OIS, demanded that Myanmar was '[t]o honor its obligations under International Law and Human Rights covenants, and to take all measures to immediately halt all vestiges and manifestations of the practice of [...] genocide [...] against Rohingya Muslims."[10]

4.1.2 Desired Relief

The Gambia requested that the ICJ adjudicate and rule on the following: (1) Myanmar has breached and continues to breach its obligations under the Genocide Convention, particularly Articles I, III(a), III(b), III(c), III(d), III(e), IV, V and VI; (2) Myanmar must cease any ongoing internationally wrongful act and fully respect its obligations under the Genocide Convention, especially Articles I, III(a), III(b), III(c), III(d), III(e), IV, V and VI; (3) The Gambia must ensure that persons committing genocide are punished by a competent tribunal, including before an international criminal tribunal, as required by Articles I and VI; (4) Myanmar must perform the obligations of reparation in the interest of the victims of genocidal acts, the Rohingya, including allowing their safe and dignified return and respect for their full citizenship and human rights and other related acts, consistent with the obligation to prevent genocide under Article I of the Genocide Convention; and (5) Myanmar must offer assurances and guarantees of non-repetition of violations of the Genocide Convention, in particular the obligations provided under Articles I, III(a), III(b), III(c), III(d), III(e), IV, V and VI.[11]

4.1.3 Myanmar's Counterargument

In December 2019, at public hearings for oral arguments of the parties on the request for the order of provisional measures submitted by The Gambia, Myanmar disputed the Court's jurisdiction on various grounds, chiefly that of invalid *locus standi* and lack of dispute. Myanmar argued that The Gambia, which said it would file the suit on behalf of the OIC initiative, did not have standing to sue because Article 34(1) of the ICJ Statute stipulates that only states may be parties in cases before the Court.[12] The

---

[10] *See* ibid., para. 20, fn. 30, OIC Resolution No. 4/46-MM on the Situation of the Muslim Community in Myanmar, OIC doc. OIC/CFM-46/2019/MM/RES/FINAL (1–2 March 2019).

[11] Ibid., para. 112.

[12] Verbatim Record (2019b), p. 46, para. 25.

66   4 The Relationship Between the Rohingya Case Before the International ...

counsel for Myanmar also pointed out that Bangladesh made reservations to Article IX of the Genocide Convention that prevented it from bringing proceedings against Myanmar under that selfsame Article IX,[13] asserting that that alone was sufficient to show lack of jurisdiction.[14] Myanmar asserted that the *erga omnes* character of obligations under the Genocide Convention and the existence of a dispute between the two parties necessary for jurisdictional basis were different issues. Accordingly, Myanmar demanded the existence of a dispute which was specifically between The Gambia and Myanmar, and which concerned the interpretation, application, or fulfillment of the Genocide Convention.[15] Myanmar asserted that as The Gambia brought suit on behalf of the OIC, then if anyone was party to the suit, it was the OIC, not The Gambia.[16] Myanmar contended that the lack of jurisdiction was manifest on these grounds,[17] and emphasized that there was no imminent risk of genocide in Myanmar, because at that time Myanmar was engaged in repatriation initiatives to facilitate the return of displaced persons from Bangladesh.[18]

4.1.4   Third-Party Intervention Before the ICJ

This is not an instance of typical bilateral State-to-State dispute at the ICJ. Rather, The Gambia, which, as mentioned above, is not a direct state victim of Myanmars alleged violations of the Genocide Convention, is instead pursuing Myanmar's treaty violations based on the concept of common interest. Therefore, it is expected that this Tribunal will be concerned with the interests of states other than those involved in the proceedings, i.e., with the interests of third states as well. In international dispute resolution proceedings, it is common for third parties other than litigants to be permitted to participate in litigation concerning the interests of third parties.[19] As also indicated above, however, the actual participation of third parties in proceedings before the ICJ is unusual, as the Court functions primarily to resolve more traditional inter-state disputes.[20]

---

[13] ibid., p. 46, para. 26.

[14] ibid.

[15] ibid., p. 48, para. 30.

[16] ibid., p. 48, para. 31.

[17] ibid., p. 52, para. 48.

[18] ibid., p. 64, para. 3.

[19] *See* Articles 31, 32 of the Statute of the International Tribunal for the Law of the Sea, 2167 UNTS 271, Annex VI of the United Nations Convention on the Law of the Sea, Articles 10, 17 of the Understanding on Rules and Procedures governing the Settlement of Disputes, and Annex 2 of the Agreement Establishing the World Trade Organization, 1867 UNTS 154.

[20] *Land, Island and Maritime Frontier Dispute (El Salvador/Honduras: Nicaragua intervening)* (1992); *Land and Maritime Boundary between Cameroon and Nigeria (Cameroon v. Nigeria: Equatorial Guinea intervening)*, the International Court of Justice (2002); *Application for Revision of the Judgment of 11 September 1992 in the Case concerning the Land, Island and Maritime Frontier Dispute (El Salvador/Honduras: Nicaragua intervening) (El Salvador v. Honduras)*, the

4.1 Proceedings Before the International Court of Justice

Third party interventions in ICJ proceedings are permitted pursuant to Articles 62 and 63 of the Statute of the Court, and as supplemented by Articles 81–85 of the Statute.[21] Article 62(1) provides that "Should a state consider that it has an interest of a legal nature which may be affected by the decision in the case, it may submit a request to the Court to be permitted to intervene." If a state requests such an intervention, then "[i]t shall be for the Court to decide upon this request" under Article 62(2). Article 63(1) stipulates that "[w]henever the construction of a convention to which states other than those concerned in the case are parties is in question, the Registrar shall notify all such states forthwith," and Article 63(2) adds that "[E]very state so notified has the right to intervene in the proceedings; but if it uses this right, the construction given by the judgment will be equally binding upon it." This provision is understood as intervention as of right by other parties, and the consequences of the intervention are binding on any and all intervening parties.,[22] While consent of the litigants is not required in such cases of intervention described herein, permission must still be obtained from the ICJ under Article 84(1) of the Rules of Court.

While the Republic of Maldives, Canada, the Netherlands, Germany, and the United Kingdom have all announced they intent to intervene in this case, as of October 2022, it is unclear whether any of them have taken the formal steps to do so under either Article 62 or 63 of the ICJ Statute. Maldives was the first country to announce its intent to intervene in this case,[23] when the Maldivian Foreign Minister expressed its willingness to do so at the 43rd session of the UNHRC in February 2020.[24] It is also reported that Maldives hired Amal Clooney, a prominent British human rights lawyer, for that purpose at that time.[25] The following September, the Netherlands and Canada announced their intent to intervene as well,[26] following statements on August 25, 2022 by Amanda Milling, UK Minister for Asia, confirming the UK's own intent to intervene,[27] and a German Federal Foreign Office spokesperson, expressing Germany's intent to intervene as well.[28] Should any of these parties request intervention under Article 62(1) of the ICJ Statute, then, in accordance with Article 81(2) of the Rules of the Court, these states shall specify (a) the interest of a legal nature which the state applying to intervene considers may be affected by the decision in that case; (b) the precise object of the intervention; and (c) any basis of jurisdiction which is claimed to exist as between the state applying to intervene and the parties to the case.

International Court of Justice (2003); *Jurisdictional Immunities of the State (Germany v. Italy: Greece intervening)*, the International Court of Justice (2012); *Whaling in the Antarctic (Australia v. Japan: New Zealand intervening)*, the International Court of Justice (2014).

[21] Chinkin (1986), p. 496.

[22] Ibid.

[23] Ministry of Foreign Affairs of the Maldives (2020).

[24] Government of the Maldives (2020).

[25] Ractcliffe (2020).

[26] Governments of Canada & the Netherlands (2020).

[27] Government of the United Kingdom (2022).

[28] Federal Foreign Office of Germany (2022).

In connection with the Russian invasion of Ukraine in 2022, Ukraine filed an application before the ICJ on February 26, instituting proceedings against the Russian Federation.[29] As of December 31, 2022, 33 states,[30] mostly Western European countries, but including the US and Australia, have formally declared their willingness to intervene in these proceedings under Article 63(2), in contrast to the mere announcement of participation as a gesture in The Gambia v. Myanmar, and inevitably drawing charges of Eurocentrism.[31] It is particularly noteworthy in this regard that the UK has not taken concrete steps to intervene in the latter case, despite the fact that its former ambassador to Myanmar and her husband, a Myanmarese national, were sentenced to a year of imprisonment by a Myanmar court in 2022, giving the UK immediate reason for concern about the human rights situation there.[32]

In the Ukraine v. Russia case, the interested states expressed intent to intervene before the preliminary objections phase. Therefore, an interesting question thus emerges: that of "whether States can intervene in a case pursuant to Article 63 before the Court has concluded that it has jurisdiction to proceed to the merits."[33] However, the ICJ had previously addressed this issue in the Nicaragua case, dismissing as premature El Salvador's request to intervene at the jurisdictional stage.[34]

4.2 Provisional Measures

Since it usually takes a long time to conclude a case before the ICJ, a state may request the Court to issue an order for provisional measures under Article 41(1) of the ICJ Statute. Such a request shall have priority over all other cases in accordance with rule 74(1) of the ICJ Rules. The orders and decisions given in provisional measures proceedings do not prejudge the question of ICJ jurisdiction on the merits or any questions relating to the admissibility of the Application or the merits themselves.[35] The Court may issues provisional measures orders only if the provisions relied on by the Applicant appear, *prima facie*, to afford a basis on which the Court could be found to have jurisdiction.[36] More precisely, the Court may exercise its power to

---

[29] Government of Ukraine (2022).

[30] These States are Latvia, Lithuania, New Zealand, the United Kingdom, Germany, the USA, Sweden, Romania, France. Poland, Italy, Denmark, Ireland, Finland, Estonia, Spain, Australia, Portugal, Austria, Luxembourg, Greece, Croatia, the Czech Republic, Bulgaria, Norway, Malta, Belgium, Slovenia, Slovakia, Canada and the Netherlands, Cyprus, Liechtenstein.

[31] *See* Simpson (2022).

[32] Ibid.

[33] Mcintyre (2022).

[34] Ibid. International Court of Justice (1984).

[35] International Court of Justice (2020), para. 85.

[36] Ibid., p. 9, para.16.

4.2 Provisional Measures

order provisional measures only if it is satisfied that the rights asserted by the party requesting such measures are "at least plausible."[37]

The Gambia has accordingly requested an order for provisional measures on the following points: (1) Myanmar shall immediately take all measures within its powers to prevent all acts that amount to or contribute to the crime of genocide; (2) Myanmar shall ensure that any military, paramilitary or irregular armed units which may be directed or supported by it do not commit any act of genocide, of conspiracy to commit genocide, or direct and public incitement to commit genocide, or complicity in genocide, against the Rohingya group; (3) Myanmar shall not destroy or render inaccessible any evidence related to the events described in the Application; (4) Myanmar and the Gambia shall not take any action and shall assure that not action is taken which may aggravate or extend the existing dispute that is the subject of this Application, or render it more difficult of solution; and (5) Myanmar and The Gambia shall each provide a report to the ICJ on all measures taken to give effect to this Order for provisional measures, no later than four months from its issuance.[38]

As mentioned above, the ICJ heard oral arguments of the parties on the request for the order of provisional measures on December 10–12, 2019. At that time, the Myanmar government led by Aung San Suu Kyi was forming its defense team. Neither The Gambia it nor Myanmar were represented on the Bench of the ICJ when the former instituted the proceedings in question. Article 31(3) of the ICJ Statute provides that "[i]f the Court includes upon the Bench no judge of the nationality of the parties, each of these parties may proceed to choose a judge as provided in paragraph 2 of this Article." The Gambia accordingly chose Navanethem Pillay, and Myanmar Claus Kress, reputable experts in international criminal law. Kress continues to serve as judge *ad hoc* even after the military seized power in Myanmar in the *coup* of February 2021.

At argument, The Gambia stressed the existence of the dispute and justified its *locus standi* by holding that "[The Gambia] seek[s] to protect not only the rights of the Rohingya, but our own rights as a State party to the Genocide Convention by holding Myanmar to its *erga omnes partes* obligations not to commit genocide, not to incite genocide, and to prevent and punish genocide."[39]

On January 23 2020, the ICJ issued its order for provisional measures, with some changes to the content of the order requested by The Gambian government.[40] The Court was satisfied that the existence of a dispute between the Parties relating to the interpretation, application or fulfilment of the Genocide Convention had been established *prima facie*.[41] In finding that conflict existed, the Court attached importance to the disagreement between The Gambia and Myanmar as to what took place in Rakhine State with regard to the Rohingya, and the lack of a response by Myanmar

---

[37] Ibid., p. 18, para. 43.

[38] Government of the Republic of the Gambia (2019), para. 132.

[39] Verbatim Record (2019a), p. 19, §15.

[40] International Court of Justice (2020).

[41] Ibid., para. 31.

70   4 The Relationship Between the Rohingya Case Before the International ...

to The Gambias petition against Myanmar for violation of the Genocide Convention filed on October 11, 2019.[42]

Having recognized the existence of the dispute, the Court concludes the that Court has *prima facie* jurisdiction pursuant to Article IX of the Genocide Convention.[43] As described previously, when Myanmar ratified the Genocide Convention, it attached a reservation to Article VIII, which stipulates that "Any Contracting Party may call upon the competent organs of the United Nations to take such action under the Charter of the United Nations as they consider appropriate for the prevention and suppression of acts of genocide or any of the other acts enumerated in Article III." Also as described previously, this reservation prevents the application of that Article to Myanmar. However, the Court held that this reservation does not interfere with the Court's *prima facie* jurisdiction. Although the terms "competent organs of the United Nations" under Article VIII may encompass the ICJ, the Court held that Article VIII does not refer to the submission of disputes between contracting parties to the convention to the Court for adjudication.[44] The Court observed that Myanmars reservation to Article VIII of the Genocide Convention does not appear to deprive The Gambia of the right to bring its dispute with Myanmar under Article IX of the convention before the Court.[45]

The Court then considered the *locus standi* of The Gambia, which Myanmar disputes. Myanmar claimed that Bangladesh was entitled to hold Myanmar accountable but was unable to do so due to its declaration with regard to Article IX of the convention.[46] In response, the Court affirmed The Gambias standing as follows: "In view of their shared values, all the States parties to the Genocide Convention have a common interest to ensure that acts of genocide are prevented and that, if they occur, their authors do not enjoy impunity. That common interest implies that the obligations in question are owed by any State party to all the other States parties to the Convention. [...] It follows that any State party to the Genocide Convention, and not only a specially affected State, may invoke the responsibility of another State party with a view to ascertaining the alleged failure to comply with its obligations *erga omnes partes*, and to bring that failure to an end."[47]

The next question is whether the Rohingya are a protected group under the Genocide Convention. If not, then The Gambias claim should be rejected. The Court held that the Rohingya in Myanmar do appear to constitute a protected group within the meaning of Article II of the Convention.[48]

Next, the Court examined the relationship between the right to be protected and the measures for which the provisional measures order is being requested. The Gambia sought to protect the rights of all members of the Rohingya group in Myanmar, as

---

[42] Ibid., paras. 27–28.

[43] Ibid., para. 37.

[44] Ibid., para. 35.

[45] Ibid., para. 36.

[46] Ibid., para. 39.

[47] Ibid., para. 41.

[48] Ibid., para. 52.

4.2 Provisional Measures

members of a protected group under the Genocide Convention, from genocidal acts prohibited under the convention.[49] While The Gambia contended that the rights it asserted in the present case are plausible,[50] Myanmar did not specifically address the question, for the purposes of the order of provisional measures.[51] The ICJ focused on the plausibility of the rights claimed by The Gambia,[52] and concluded that the rights claimed by The Gambia and for which it is seeking protection were indeed plausible.[53]

While two separate opinions[54] and a declaration by the aforementioned *ad hoc* judge were attached to the Court's ruling,[55] which discussed the plausibility issue among other matters, in the end the Court unanimously issued the following provisional measures order: (1) Myanmar shall, in accordance with its obligations under the Convention on the Prevention and Punishment of the Crime of Genocide, in relation to the members of the Rohingya group in its territory, take all measures within its power to prevent the commission of all acts within the scope of Article II of this Convention, in particular: (a) killing members of the group; (b) causing serious bodily or mental harm to the members of the group; (c) deliberately inflicting on the group conditions of life calculated to bring about its physical destruction in whole or in part; and (d) imposing measures intended to prevent births within the group; (2) Myanmar shall, in relation to the members of the Rohingya group in its territory, ensure that its military, as well as any irregular armed units which may be directed or supported by it and any organizations and persons which may be subject to its control, direction or influence, do not commit any acts described in point (1) above, or of conspiracy to commit genocide, of direct and public incitement to commit genocide, of attempt to commit genocide, or of complicity in genocide; (3) Myanmar shall take effective measures to prevent the destruction and ensure the preservation of evidence related to allegations of acts within the scope of Article II of the Convention on the Prevention and Punishment of the Crime of Genocide; and (4) Myanmar shall submit a report to the Court on all measures taken to give effect to this Order within four months, as from the date of this Order, and thereafter every six months, until a final decision on the case is rendered by the Court.[56]

Following the order by the ICJ, the UN Secretary-General issued a statement that he welcomes the Order from the Court and trusts that Myanmar will duly comply with same.[57] A joint statement issued by the High Representative on behalf of the European Union (EU), and the Foreign Ministers of Australia, Canada, New Zealand,

---

[49] Government of the Republic of the Gambia (2019), para. 126.

[50] International Court of Justice (2020), para. 46.

[51] Ibid., para. 47.

[52] Spadaro (2020), p. 617.

[53] International Court of Justice (2020), para. 56.

[54] Separate Opinion of Vice-President Judge Xue (2020); Separate Opinion of Judge Cançado Trindade (2020).

[55] Declaration of Judge Ad Hoc Kress (2020).

[56] International Court of Justice (2020), para. 86.

[57] Spokesman for the UN Secretary General (2020).

Norway, the UK, and the US urges that "Myanmar must comply with the International Court of Justices provisional measures order."[58]

The provisional measures ordered under Article 41 of the ICJ Statute are binding,[59] and Myanmar accordingly submitted its first ordered report on May 22, 2020 and its second report on November 23, 2020.[60] However, criticism has been leveled that it is not possible to ascertain whether the objectives of the provisional measures have been met because these reports have not been made public.[61] Nevertheless, the order is said to be important in the following respects: First, imposing the semiannual reporting requirement on Myanmar brings the Rohingya issue to international attention every six months, even if the report are not made public.[62] Second, if Myanmar were to disobey the reporting requirement to the ICJ, it would be in violation of Article 94 of the UN Charter and thus subject to further international reprimand, even if it is unlikely that the Security Council would take any action against it.[63] And third, the measures could represent "the group's first taste of justice since Burma's military *coup* in the 1960s."[64]

4.3 Preliminary Objections

4.3.1 Myanmar's Preliminary Objections

On January 20, 2021, Myanmar raised preliminary objections to the jurisdiction of the Court and the admissibility of the Application.[65] Accordingly, the Court held public hearings on Myanmars preliminary objections on February 21–28, 2022. It should go without saying these hearings took place after the February 2021 *coup*, and thus, while the written submission of the objections was prepared by the former civilian government under Aung San Suu Kyi, it was the military junta that was represented at the hearings.

The objections raised by Myanmar are as follows. The first is that the ICJ lacks jurisdiction, or alternatively that the application is inadmissible, on the ground that the real applicant in these proceedings is the OIC.[66] For Myanmar, Article 34, paragraph 1 of the Statute of the Court provides that "[o]nly States may be parties in cases before the Court," and thus, the Court cannot entertain a case that is in reality brought

---

[58] European Union (2022).

[59] LaGrand Case (2001), p. 506, para. 109.

[60] Republic of the Union of Myanmar (2021), p.1, para. 4.

[61] Kapucu (2022), p. 235.

[62] Ramsde (2021), p. 179.

[63] Ibid., pp. 179–180.

[64] Lee (2021), p. 101.

[65] Kapucu (2022), p. 235.

[66] Republic of the Union of Myanmar (2021), p. 7, para. 25.

4.3 Preliminary Objections

by an international organization.[67] Additionally, the Genocide Convention allows only states to become signatories, and thus, the OIC is in no position to invoke the compromissory clause in Article 9 of the convention.[68]

The second objection concerns lack of standing on the part of The Gambia as a state, because it is a non-injured State Party to the Genocide Convention, which does not provide for the concept of *actio popularis*.[69] According to Myanmar, while Bangladesh is specifically affected by the alleged violations of the Genocide Convention, when Bangladesh ratified the convention it entered a reservation to the aforementioned Article 9, thereby waiving its right to settle disputes relating to the interpretation, application, or fulfillment of the Convention by bringing a case before the Court under that provision.[70]

The third objection relates to Myanmar's own aforementioned reservation of Article 8 of the Genocide Convention, which stipulates that "Any Contracting Party may call upon the competent organs of the United Nations to take such action under the Charter of the United Nations as they consider appropriate for the prevention and suppression of acts of genocide or any of the other acts enumerated in Article III."[71] Myanmar asserts that this reservation prevents The Gambia, a non-injured state, from calling upon the ICJ, especially when taken in conjunction with Article 9.[72]

The fourth objection is an absence of dispute between The Gambia and Myanmar on the date of the filing of the application instituting proceedings. Myanmar argues that its failure to respond within a month to a note verbale sent by The Gambia to Myanmar on October 11, 2019 may not lead to a presumption that a legal dispute existed between The Gambia and Myanmar on November 11, 2019, the date of The Gambia's application to the ICJ.[73] Myanmar recommends that, in order to maintain the Court's proper functioning, it should strictly interpret claims of pre-existing disputes,[74] such that there must be "mutual awareness" of positively opposed views by the parties in relation to legal claims to establish that a dispute exists.[75]

4.3.2 Rulings

The Court delivered its judgment on Myanmar's preliminary objections on July 22, 2022. In summary, it rejected the first, third and fourth objections unanimously, and

---

[67] Ibid.

[68] Ibid.

[69] Ibid., p. 8, para. 27.

[70] Ibid.

[71] Ibid., p. 8, para. 28.

[72] Ibid.

[73] Ibid., p. 9, para. 31.

[74] Ibid., p. 150, para. 491.

[75] Ibid., p. 183, para. 575.

the second objection 15 to 1, with Judge Xue Hanquin dissenting. The Court further found that it has jurisdiction and that the application was admissible, with Judge Xue again the lone dissent, and Judge *ad hoc* Kress appending a declaration.

The Court began with the objection relating to the "real applicant" in the case (first preliminary objection), before turning to the existence of a dispute (fourth preliminary objection) and Myanmar's reservation to Article VIII of the Genocide Convention (third preliminary objection),[76] and finally the standing of The Gambia (second preliminary objection).[77] To the contrary, Myanmar argued that if the Court were to accept jurisdiction, Gambia's application on behalf of a state or an entity would constitute an abuse of process and eventually deny admissibility.[78] Particulars of the Court's findings are as follows.

As described above, the first preliminary objection concerns whether The Gambia is the "real applicant" in this case. That is to say, Myanmar regards the OIC, not The Gambia, as the true applicant. However, the Court found that "The Gambia instituted the present proceedings in its own name, as a State party to the Statute of the Court and to the Genocide Convention."[79] Moreover, the Court "observes that the fact that a State may have accepted the proposal of an intergovernmental organization [...] does not detract from its status as the applicant before the Court."[80] Consequently, the ICJ "sees no reason why it should look beyond the fact that The Gambia has instituted proceedings against Myanmar in its own name. The Court is therefore satisfied that the Applicant in this case is The Gambia."[81] Thus, the Court rejected this objection, reiterating its position[82] that it is only in exceptional circumstances that the Court should reject a claim based on a valid title of jurisdiction on the ground of abuse of process.[83] Having found that no evidence has been presented to it showing that the conduct of The Gambia amounts to an abuse of process,[84] Myanmars first preliminary objection is rejected.[85]

Also as previously described, the fourth preliminary objection concerned lack of dispute between the parties on the date of filing of the application instituting proceedings.[86] The Court reiterated the requirements for the existence of a dispute between parties under Article 9 of the Genocide Convention.[87] The ICJ recognized that, in its established jurisprudence, a dispute is "a disagreement on a point of law or

---

[76] International Court of Justice (2022), p. 19, para. 33.

[77] Ibid.

[78] Ibid., p. 20, para. 47.

[79] Ibid., p. 19, para. 44.

[80] Ibid., pp. 19–20, para. 44.

[81] Ibid., p. 20, para. 45.

[82] International Court of Justice (2019), pp.42–43, para.113.

[83] International Court of Justice (2022), p. 20, para. 49.

[84] Ibid.

[85] Ibid., p. 20, para. 50.

[86] Ibid., p. 20, para. 51.

[87] Ibid., p. 25, para. 63.

4.3 Preliminary Objections

fact, a conflict of legal views or of interests" between parties.[88] At the same time, in order to prove the dispute, the claim of one party is positively opposed by the other.[89] Said jurisprudence shows that the Court takes particular account of any statements or documents exchanged between the parties in determining the existence of a dispute.[90] The Court noted that in the present case there are four relevant statements made by representatives of the parties before the United Nations General Assembly in September 2018 and September 2019, and one note verbale that The Gambia sent to the Permanent Mission of Myanmar to the United Nations on October 11, 2019.[91]

In the Court's opinion, the IIFFMM reports of 2018 and 2019 enabled Myanmar to be informed of the allegations made against it concerning violations of the Genocide Convention.[92] According to the Court, Myanmar could not have failed to notice that during its speech to the UN General Assembly General Debate of September 2019, The Gambia stated that it intended to lead concerted efforts to take the case to the ICJ.[93] The statements that Myanmar's representative made before the General Assembly in 2018 and 2019 indicated the views of his Government, which are opposed to those of The Gambia's government and clearly reject the reports and findings of the IFFMM.[94] The Court accordingly concluded that the note verbale did not constitute the first time that these allegations were made known to Myanmar.[95]

The Court also denied the requirement of "mutual awareness" of two explicitly opposing views suggested by Myanmar for establishing the existence of a dispute. The Court clarified that "the conclusion that the parties hold clearly opposite views concerning the performance or non-performance of legal obligations does not require that the respondent must expressly oppose the claims of the applicant."[96] That is to say, if an applicant has to prove that a respondent is required to expressly oppose the applicant's claims, then "a respondent could prevent a finding that a dispute exists by remaining silent in the face of an applicant's legal claims."[97] Therefore, the Court held that, if the respondent has failed to reply to the applicant's claims, then it may be inferred from this silence, in certain circumstances, that the respondent rejects those claims and that, therefore, a dispute exists at the time of the application.[98] The Court further notes that the possibility of drawing such an inference depends on the particular circumstances of a given case.[99] Myanmar's fourth preliminary objection was thus rejected by the Court, as the Court accordingly concluded that a dispute

---

[88] Ibid.

[89] Ibid.

[90] Ibid., p. 25, para. 64.

[91] Ibid., p. 25, para. 65.

[92] Ibid., p. 29, para. 76.

[93] Ibid., p. 28, para. 73.

[94] Ibid., p. 28, para. 73.

[95] Ibid., p. 29, para. 76.

[96] Ibid., p. 27, para. 71.

[97] Ibid.

[98] Ibid.

[99] Ibid., p. 29, para. 75.

relating to the interpretation, application, and fulfillment of the Genocide Convention existed between the Parties at the time of the filing of the Application by The Gambia on November 11, 2019.[100] As described above, the Court again referred to its own jurisprudence that "the existence of a dispute may be inferred from the failure of a State to respond to a claim in circumstances where a response is called for."[101] Taking into account the nature and gravity of the allegations made in The Gambia's note verbale and Myanmar's prior knowledge of their existence, the Court was of the view that Myanmar's rejection of the allegations made by the Gambia could also be inferred from its failure to respond to the note verbale within the one-month period preceding the filing of the Application.[102]

The third preliminary objection was Myanmars contention that reservation to Article 8 of the Genocide Convention negates the jurisdiction or admissibility of the Court.[103] The Court interpreted Article 8 as "addressing the prevention and suppression of genocide 'at the political level rather than as a matter of legal responsibility."[104] Moreover, the Court clarified that Articles 8 and 9 of the convention have distinct areas of application.[105] While Article 9 provides the conditions for recourse to the principal judicial organ of the United Nations in the context of a dispute between Contracting Parties, Article 8 allows any Contracting Party to appeal to other competent organs of the United Nations with or without a dispute with another Contracting Party.[106]The Court ruled that Article 8 does not relate to filing suit with the Court, and thus, that Myanmar's reservation to that provision was irrelevant for the above-mentioned purposes of determining the Court's jurisdiction or admissibility.[107] In this manner, this objection was also rejected.[108]

The last preliminary objection the Court considered in its ruling was the second objection raised by Myanmar. The Court defines the question to be answered by the Court in this instance as whether The Gambia is entitled to hold Myanmar to account before the Court for alleged breaches of Myanmar's obligations under the Genocide Convention.[109] The Court notes that all the States Parties to the Genocide Convention share a common interest in ensuring the prevention, suppression, and punishment of genocide.[110] The Court found that such *erga omnes partes* obligation derives from the common interests of the parties to the convention. Thus, the Court held that "such a common interest implies that the obligations in question are owed by any State party to all the other States parties to the relevant convention; they are obligations

---

[100] Ibid., p. 71, para. 29.

[101] International Court of Justice (2022); International Court of Justice (2011), p. 84, para. 30.

[102] International Court of Justice (2022), p. 29, para. 76.

[103] Ibid., p. 29, para. 78.

[104] Ibid., p. 31, para. 88. International Court of Justice (2007), p. 109, para. 159.

[105] International Court of Justice (2022), p. 32, para. 89.

[106] Ibid.

[107] Ibid., p. 32, para. 91.

[108] Ibid., p. 32, para. 92.

[109] Ibid., p. 35, para. 106.

[110] Ibid., p. 35, para. 107.

4.3 Preliminary Objections 77

erga omnes partes, in the sense that each State party has an interest in compliance with them in any given case."[111] The Court found that pursuing "[r]esponsibility for an alleged breach of obligations *erga omnes partes* under the Genocide Convention may be invoked through the institution of proceedings before the Court, regardless of whether a special interest can be demonstrated."[112] With regard to human rights treaties, it is assumed that the nationals of the state concerned are most affected by a state's failure to fulfill its obligations, and in such a case, the territorial state is likely to be indifferent to improve the situation by itself.[113] Therefore, the Court may allow the pursuit of responsibility for nonfulfillment of obligations by a State Party that is not directly affected by such nonfulfillment. In the words of the Court, "a State does not need to demonstrate that any victims of an alleged breach of obligations *erga omnes partes* under the Genocide Convention are its nationals."[114] The Court found that even though Bangladesh is directly affected by the influx of Rohingya refugees, this fact does not affect the right of all other States Parties to the Genocide Convention to call for performance of obligations based on common interests.[115] Accordingly, "the Court concludes that The Gambia, as a State party to the Genocide Convention, has standing to invoke the responsibility of Myanmar for the alleged breaches of its obligations under Articles I, III, IV and V of the Convention."[116]

Once The Gambia received permission to carry on with proceedings before the ICJ, the governments of Canada and the Netherlands released a joint statement on July 22, 2022, the same day as the Court's ruling,[117] in which they welcomed the Court's findings in the matter and reaffirmed their intent to intervene.

Myanmars military junta also issued a statement in response to the ruling on July 23, in which it that "Myanmar takes note of the decision by the International Court of Justice to reject the preliminary objections raised by Myanmar. [...] Myanmar is disappointed that its preliminary objections were rejected, while it notes that the Court has now determined the matter. Myanmar noted that this judgement will become not only a source of international law but also set a precedent for future cases."[118]

In her dissent, Judge Xue denied The Gambia's standing.[119] For Judge Xue, the institution of proceedings against Myanmar by The Gambia was essentially a collective lawsuit[120] and public-interest litigation.[121] She redefined the issue before the Court as "whether the Court has jurisdiction ratione personae to entertain the case

---

[111] Ibid.

[112] Ibid., p. 35, para. 108.

[113] Ibid., p. 36, para. 109.

[114] Ibid., p. 35, para. 109.

[115] Ibid., p. 37, para. 113.

[116] Ibid., p. 38, para. 114.

[117] Governments of Canada & Netherlands (2022).

[118] Ministry of International Cooperation of the Government of Republic of the Myanmar (2022).

[119] Dissenting Opinion of Judge Xue (2022).

[120] Ibid., p. 1, para. 2.

[121] Ibid., p. 2, para. 5.

instituted by a non-injured State."[122] On this basis, Judge Xue examined the *travaux préparatoires* of the Genocide Convention and concluded that there was no indication that the States Parties to the convention thought that the principle that no action could be instituted save by a party concerned in a case would not apply to cases that are filed under Article IX.[123] Therefore, Judge Xue found that the Court had never considered or even implied that a State Party may invoke international responsibility of another State Party solely on the basis of the convention's *raison d'être*,[124] and she warned that the majority ruling's "innovative interpretation has extended well beyond the reasonable expectations of the States parties, inconducive to the security and stability of treaty relations."[125]

Judge Xue recalled her dissent in the ICJ ruling on *the Questions relating to the Obligation to Prosecute or Extradite (Belgium v. Senegal)* case, and emphasized the Court's position in the *East Timor* case that the *erga omnes* character of a norm and the rule of consent to jurisdiction are two different things.[126] While noting that the devastation the Rohingya have experienced deserves the attention of the international community, she further emphasized that the UN is in the process of addressing the issue without waiting for the exercise of Article 8 rights of the Genocide Convention, as UN member states are authorized by various UN agencies to so act.[127]

Judge *ad hoc* Kress's declaration began with the change in Myanmar's representation and The Gambia's eligibility as a plaintiff.[128] Judge Kress found the fact that the ruling did not address the former matter to be less than satisfactory,[129] pondering whether it might be appropriate for the Court to reflect on how it deals with factual and legal difficulties in identifying the government of a given state for the purposes of representation in proceedings before the Court.[130]

As described above, the issue of the representation of the Myanmar government before the Court stems from the *coup d'etat* that took place in Myanmar during the preliminary objection phase of this case. Recall that the Republic of the Union of Myanmar filed preliminary objections to the jurisdiction of the Court and the admissibility of the Application on January 20, 2021, that Tatmadaw staged the *coup* the following February 1, and that the NUG continued to issue communiques regarding the Court proceedings even after the junta had taken over. For example, in its press release of May 30, 2021, the NUG asserted that "[t]he National Unity Government is taking every step to cooperate with the International Court of Justice, the world's highest court, and, by that, to ensure that we comply with Myanmar's international legal obligations. We are very concerned about the difficult situation of the Rohingya

---

[122] Ibid., p. 4, para. 14.

[123] Ibid., p. 6, para. 22.

[124] Ibid., p. 6, para. 24.

[125] Ibid., p. 6, para. 25.

[126] Ibid., p. 12, para. 38.

[127] Ibid., pp. 12–13, para. 40.

[128] Declaration of Judge Ad Hoc Kress (2022), p. 1, para. 1.

[129] Ibid., p. 3, para. 5.

[130] Ibid.

4.3 Preliminary Objections

especially who fled to Bangladesh in 2016–17."[131] In emphasizing its continuity, the NUG held in the same statement that "It is amongst the duties of the National Unity Government, as the lawful government of Myanmar, to ensure continuity of representation before the Court, and to be mindful of the timetable established by the Court."[132] It further asserted that "[t]he National Unity Government of Myanmar is also actively considering accepting the exercise of jurisdiction by the International Criminal Court over the killings, torture and other crimes against civilians that have occurred since the attempted *coup* started on 1 February 2021."[133]

Judge Kress went on to point out that the terms an "injured State" and a "State other than an injured State" are distinguished under the International Law Commission's Articles on Responsibility of States for Internationally Wrongful Acts, and that a "State other than an injured State" is entitled to invoke the responsibility of another state resulting from that state's violation of an obligation *erga omnes partes*.[134] Therefore, Judge Kress suggested that The Gambia is a non-injured state as designated by Myanmar.[135] However, given that the jurisprudence of the Court has not adopted such distinction between injured and non-injured states as proposed by the ILC, the Court instead uses the concept of legal interest covering all situations covered by Articles 42 and 48 of the ILC Articles on State Responsibility.[136] Judge Kress then noted that in an unorganized international community, it is difficult to make as strict a distinction between individual and collective interests as Myanmar suggests.[137] In his view, with respect to treaties designed to protect collective interests, such as the Genocide Convention, it is not necessary for a State Party to prove its individual interests in justifying standing in the ICJ; rather, the collective interests of each State Party must be presumed in such cases unless otherwise specified.[138] For Judge Kress, however, no state is in a position to dispose of the relevant collective interest, because the collective interest in the existence of the protected group under genocidal attack and the human beings composing that group is not mediated through the special legal interest of any state. In this sense, The Gambia's standing in this case does not depend on the standing of Bangladesh or its reservation on the compromissory clause that constitutes Article 9 of the convention.[139] Judge Kress also explained the need to distinguish between the obligation *erga omnes partes* versus secular obligations and *actio popularis* in the full meaning of the term, as international law generally does not recognize the latter.[140]

---

[131] National Unity Government (2021).

[132] Ibid., para. 2.

[133] Ibid., para. 3.

[134] Declaration of Judge Ad Hoc Kress (2020), p. 3, para. 7.

[135] Ibid., p. 3, para. 8.

[136] Ibid., p. 4, para. 10.

[137] Ibid., p. 5, para. 14.

[138] Ibid., p. 6, para. 15.

[139] Ibid., pp. 12–13, para. 29.

[140] Ibid., pp. 13–14, para. 32.

One further development following this ruling was the declaration of intervention in the proceedings by the UK, which was and filed in the Registry of the ICJ pursuant to Article 63 of the ICJ Statute,[141] which, as described above, is also the basis for intervention in Ukraine's suit against Russia, as it states that whenever the construction of a convention to which states other than those concerned in the case are parties is in question, each of these states has the right to intervene in the proceedings.[142]

4.4 Related Developments

On June 8, 2020, The Gambia filed a request for discovery before the District Court of Columbia to compel Facebook to provide data on "suspended or terminated" accounts of Myanmar military institutions and personnel,[143] because Facebook has offices in Washington, D.C. On September 22 2021, more than a year after the request was filed, US Magistrate Judge Zia M. Farqui ordered Facebook to disclose the requested content for use in The Gambia's litigation against Myanmar at the ICJ.[144] The judge made a strong argument for Facebook's cooperation in revealing the plight of the Rohingya: "Facebook can act now. It took the first step by deleting the content that fueled a genocide. Yet it has stumbled at the next step, sharing that content. Failing to do so here would compound the tragedy that has befallen the Rohingya. A surgeon that excises a tumor does not merely throw it in the trash. She seeks a pathology report to *identify* the disease. Locking away the requested content would be throwing away the opportunity to understand how disinformation begat genocide of the Rohingya and would foreclose a reckoning at the ICJ." Facebook filed an appeal on October 13.[145] Additionally, on December 6, 2021 Facebook's parent company Meta was also sued in California for over $150 billion in damages in a proposed class action alleging that the company failed to stop hate speech and misinformation resulting in violence against the Rohingya.[146]

As described above, on September 2, 2020, the Ministers of Foreign Affairs of Canada and the Netherlands issued a joint statement regarding their intent to intervene in *the Gambia v. Myanmar* case before the ICJ.[147] In May and November 2020, Myanmar submitted the previously mentioned reports[148] pursuant to the provisional measures order, which, as also indicated above, are available only to the Court and The Gambia. However, this wave of international calls for responsibility arguably constitutes one of the causes for the *coup d'etat* by the Myanmar military on February

---

[141] International Court of Justice Press Release (2022b).

[142] Ibid.

[143] Domino (2020).

[144] U.S. District Court, District of Columbia (2021).

[145] Towey (2021).

[146] Messmer (2021).

[147] Governments of Canada and the Netherlands (2020c).

[148] Global Justice Center (2020).

4.4 Related Developments

1, 2021,[149] whereafter the pursuit of responsibility at the ICJ and the ICC lapsed into uncertainty. In the course of the *coup*, Tatmadaw suppressed peacefully protesting civilians as a prelude to and the human rights violations against not only the Rohingya but also all those who oppose the ruling junta, including the unforeseen situation of Aung San Suu Kyi being taken into custody.

Immediately following the *coup*, ASEAN published the "Chairman's Statement on the Developments in the Republic of the Union of Myanmar, in which member states recall the purposes and the principles enshrined in the ASEAN Charter, including adherence to the principles of democracy, the rule of law, and good governance. The UN is also urging restraint on Myanmar's military junta, in cooperation with ASEAN. On February 4, 2021, the Security Council issued a statement[150] expressing concern at the state of emergency imposed in Myanmar by the military and the arbitrary detention of members of the Government, including State Counsellor Aung San Suu Kyi.[151] In March 2021, the President of the Security Council issued a further statement that "[t]he Security Council strongly condemns the violence against peaceful protestors, including against women, youth and children."[152] The UNHRC adopted its own similarly worded resolution on February 12, 2021[153] which, while not referring specifically to impunity for human rights violations against the Rohingya, notes nonetheless "the ongoing processes to ensure justice and accountability in respect of alleged crimes committed against Rohingya Muslims and other minorities in Myanmar."[154]

On 18 June 2021, the General Assembly adopted a draft resolution on the situation in Myanmar[155] by a recorded vote of 119 for to 1 against (Belarus), with 36 abstentions,[156] by which the member states expressed concern over "the persistent impunity."[157] In this regard, the resolution makes reference to the aforementioned opening of the investigation of the situation in Bangladesh and Myanmar by the ICC Prosecutor, as well as the order of the provisional measures by the ICJ of January 23, 2020 in the case lodged by The Gambia against Myanmar.[158] In describing the resolution as "a rare and significant expression of the General Assembly condemnation in the face of a gross violation of fundamental democratic norms and neglecting the clearly expressed wish of a people,"[159] the EU also reiterates its support for the work

---

[149] Renshaw (2021).

[150] UN Doc. SC/14430 (4 February 2021).

[151] Ibid.

[152] UN Doc. S/PRST/2021/5 (10 March 2021).

[153] UN Doc. A/HRC/S-29/L.1 (12 February 2021).

[154] ibid., preambular para. 8.

[155] UN Doc. A/75/L.85/Rev.1 (14 June 2021).

[156] UN Doc. A/RES/75/287 (18 June 2021).

[157] ibid., preambular para. 15.

[158] Ibid., preambular para. 19.

[159] Delegation of the European Union to the United Nations in New York (2021).

of the IIMM and the ICC, and calls on the Myanmar authorities to fully implement the aforementioned ICJ provisional measures order.[160]

On November 17, 2021, the seventy-sixth session of the United Nations General Assembly Third Committee unanimously adopted a resolution on "the situation of human rights of Rohingya Muslims and other minorities in Myanmar,"[161] which was co-sponsored by the EU and the OIC with endorsement chiefly provided by the US, Canada, Mexico, Argentina, Australia, New Zealand, Switzerland, Japan, and the Republic of Korea.[162] The resolution noted that the ICC has authorized its Prosecutor to investigate alleged crimes within the Court's jurisdiction related to the situation in Bangladesh/Myanmar, as described above. It also welcomed the ICJ's provisional measures order on the application by The Gambia of its Genocide Convention case against Myanmar. It also emphasizes "the importance of conducting international, independent, fair and transparent investigations into the gross human rights violations in Myanmar, including sexual and gender-based violence and violations and abuses against women and children, and of holding accountable all those responsible for brutal acts and crimes against all persons, including Rohingya, in order to deliver justice to victims using all legal instruments and domestic, regional and international judicial mechanisms, including the International Court of Justice and the International Criminal Court."[163]

All of these measures show that the international community remains dedicated, despite the *coup*, to the pursuit of accountability for the persecution of the Rohingya. Notwithstanding, there are those who believe that if the international community insists on so doing, it will create more victims of Myanmarese military oppression and make the road to democracy that much longer,[164] in contrast to still others who argue that international efforts to hold the junta accountable must continue, with the Security Council leading the way in resolving the matter by imposing non-military sanctions in conjunction with the existing ICC referral.[165]

As no self-evident causal connection can be readily drawn between the *coup* and the international pursuit of responsibility, the ICJ and the ICC will have no choice but to proceed carefully independent of world politics in this regard. This does not rule out a possible degree of intervention by the Security Council, however, under Article 16 of the ICC Statute, which addresses just such pursuit of responsibility in the face of political considerations.

---

[160] Ibid.

[161] UN Doc. A/C.3/76/L.30 Rev.1 (11 November 2021).

[162] Zaman (2021).

[163] Ibid., para. 2.

[164] Renshaw (2021).

[165] Shubin and Radhakrishnan (2021).

4.5 Prospects for Establishing Genocide

At the provisional measures order stage of its proceedings, the ICJ did not take a clear position on the Myanmar government's intent to commit genocide.[166] Nor did the Court address the merits when it ruled on Myanmar's preliminary objections.[167] The case before the ICJ is concerned with state responsibility. The Gambia must prove Myanmar has breached the relevant provisions of the Genocide Convention, meaning that The Gambia must show that acts of genocide prohibited under Articles II and III of the convention were committed by certain individuals or groups, and that these acts are attributable to Myanmar.[168]

We return to the definition of genocide, which is provided in Article II of the Genocide Convention as any of the following acts committed with the intent to destroy, in whole or in part, a national, ethnical, racial or religious group, as such: (a) killing members of the group; (b) causing serious bodily or mental harm to members of the group; (c) deliberately inflicting on the group conditions of life calculated to bring about its physical destruction in whole or in part; (d) imposing measures intended to prevent births within the group; (e) forcibly transferring children of the group to another group. In accordance with this definition, in order to establish genocide, it is required to consider (i) whether there is a protected group, (ii) whether acts in one or more of the specified categories have been committed, and (iii) whether the acts were committed with genocidal intent.[169]

The IIFFMM determined in its aforementioned September 2018 report that all of these requirements were met, as follows.[170] It found that the Rohingya, who predominantly live in Myanmar's Rakhine State, constitute a protected group, because the Rohingya could be seen as an ethnic ("members share a common language or culture"), racial ("based on hereditary physical traits often identified with a geographical region, irrespective of linguistic, cultural, national or religious factors"), or religious ("members share the same religion, denomination or mode of worship") group, or a combination thereof.[171] It concluded that "the differential treatment of the Rohingya, through the adoption of specific laws, policies and practices, supports the conclusion that they are a protected group as defined by the Genocide Convention."[172] Outside researchers relied on these findings in determining that the Rohingya are in fact a protected group,[173] as well as that intersectionality in their persecution

---

[166] Manti and Islam (2022), p. 24.

[167] International Court of Justice (2022).

[168] Kittichaisaree (2022), p. 91.

[169] *Report of the detailed findings of the Independent International Fact-Finding Mission on Myanmar*, UN Doc. A/HRC/39/CRP.2 (17 September 2018) pp. 351–352, para. 1389.

[170] Ibid., p. 364, paras. 1439–1441.

[171] Ibid., p. 352, paras. 1391.

[172] Ibid.

[173] Kittichaisaree (2022), p. 96; Manti, Islam (2022), p. 24.

84   4 The Relationship Between the Rohingya Case Before the International …

is clearly demonstrated, said persecution being on religiously as well as ethnically based as described above.[174]

With respect to physical acts, the IIFFMM report includes conduct that falls within four of the five categories of prohibited acts cited in the definition of the Genocide Convention.[175] To wit, "[p]erpetrators have killed Rohingya, caused serious bodily and mental harm to Rohingya, deliberately inflicted conditions of life calculated to bring about the physical destruction of Rohingya, and imposed measures intended to prevent births of Rohingya."[176]

Finally, to satisfy the specific intent requirement, it must also be shown that the acts were committed with specific intent (*dolus specialis*), being the intent to destroy in whole or in part a protected group as such, in addition to demonstrating that the perpetrators had intent to commit the underlying acts. To this end, the IIFFMM assessed the available information in light of relevant international tribunal jurisprudence, and considered whether factors are present in the case of the Rohingya in Rakhine State that have allowed for the reasonable inference of genocidal intent in other contexts and cases. The IIFFMM accordingly applied the criminal standard of "beyond reasonable doubt" for genocidal intent to be established and noted that "any inference drawn from circumstantial evidence must be the only inference that could reasonably follow from the acts in question"[177] in line with the aforementioned jurisprudence of the ICJ[178] and the International Criminal Tribunal for the Former Yugoslavia (ICTY).[179] It determined that the actions taken against the Rohingya, including the systematic stripping of human rights, dehumanizing narratives and rhetoric, methodical planning, mass killing, mass displacement, mass fear, and overwhelming levels of brutality, combined with the physical destruction of the home of the targeted population, in every sense and on every level, allow the inference of genocidal intent.[180]

For their part, Manti and Islam identify five main factors in delineating this selfsame genocidal intent on the part of the Myanmar government.[181] The first is widespread propaganda spread by reason of dislike and contempt of the Rohingya.[182] The second is specific statements given by Myanmar authorities, politicians, religious authorities, and military commanders prior to during, and after the brutality.[183] The third concerns the government's policies and plans to alter the demography of the area.[184] The fourth is organized plan and policy by Myanmar authorities to erase the

---

[174] Pérez-León-Acevedo and Pinto (2021), p. 459.

[175] UN Doc. A/HRC/39/CRP.2 (2018) p. 352, paras. 1392.

[176] Ibid.

[177] Ibid., p. 357, paras. 1415.

[178] International Court of Justice (2007), p. 196, para. 373.

[179] International Criminal Tribunal for the Former Yugoslavia (2016), pp. 1001–1002, para. 2592.

[180] UN Doc. A/HRC/39/CRP.2 (2018), p. 364, paras. 1440–1441.

[181] Manti, Islam (2022), p. 28.

[182] Ibid., p. 28.

[183] Ibid., p. 29.

[184] Ibid., p. 31.

4.5 Prospects for Establishing Genocide

Rohingya identity from Rakhine State.[185] The fifth is the extreme violence of the acts and operations against the Rohingya.[186] Accordingly, Manti and Islam concur with the aforementioned IIFFMM observations that these acts were indeed committed with genocidal intent.[187]

Others see it as easy to prove Tatmadaws genocidal intent against the Rohingya through the military's long-standing rule.[188] It cannot be said, however, that the citizenry of Myanmar shared this intent. Rather, they may have merely affirmed Tatmadaws aforementioned denial of citizenship to the Rohingya.[189] By contrast, the ICTYs recognition of genocide in the Srebrenica genocide preceded the ICJs recognition of genocide therein, thereby simplifying the latter.[190] It is doubtful, however, that the ICC's case on Bangladesh/Myanmar will precede that of the ICJ, and the ICJ will thus need to recognize genocide on its own in this instance, which will draw attention to how the case is made.

In this regard, even if the intent to commit genocide against the Rohingya is not proven, the human rights violations are described as "a textbook example of ethnic cleansing,"[191] and will therefore at least be labeled as such. As ethnic cleansing is not a distinct crime under international law, however, it will be necessary to consider whether it constitutes crimes against humanity or genocide under the Rome Statute.[192] The term ethnic cleansing has been employed in practice in UNSC resolutions, UN General Assembly resolutions, and ICTY judgments and indictments.[193] As a concept, it is nonetheless relatively new, having been initially popularized through repeated citations in the context of the conflict in the former Yugoslavia.[194] It has been defined as "a purposeful policy designed by one ethnic or religious group to remove by violent and terror-inspiring means the civilian population of another ethnic or religious group from certain geographic areas."[195] Therefore, in most cases, the term ethnic cleansing has the distinction of being used when a particular ethnic group is moved from its ancestral lands in an attempt to eradicate it.[196] While ethnocide is similar to ethnic cleansing, it is distinguished from the latter by being murder committed to extinguish the culture and heritage of a specific ethnic group, and from genocide in that it is murder aimed at the extinction of a culture.[197] The actual means used for ethnic cleansing in the case of the Rohingya include detainment,

---

[185] Ibid., p. 32.

[186] Ibid., p. 33.

[187] Ibid., p. 33.

[188] Lee (2021), p. 217.

[189] Ibid.

[190] Kreß (2007) pp. 619–629.

[191] United Nations Human Rights Office of the High Commissioner (2017).

[192] *See* Khan (2022), p. XXXII.

[193] Alam and Khan (2022), p. 351.

[194] *See* United Nations Commission of Experts (1995).

[195] Ibid., p. 33, para. 130.

[196] Uddin (2022), p. 109.

[197] Ibid., p. 15.

deportation, murder, torture, arbitrary arrest and detention, rape, and other severe injury.[198] Persecution and ethnic cleansing against the Rohingya is strongly linked to Myanmarese nationalism and its nation-building process.[199] As the term "ethnic cleansing" does not currently designate a recognized crime, its labeling has only moral and political connotations. It may, however, serve as a warning that human rights violations against a group of people comparable to ethnic cleansing have been committed, even if genocide against the Rohingya is not proven. Still, some have suggested that ethnic cleansing sounds somewhat soft in light of the murder, rape, and arson committed in Rohingya villages, and that genocide is more appropriate.[200] In any event, the definition is a narrow one under the Genocide Convention, and its legal recognition depends on evidence and the findings of the ICC and ICJ.

4.6 The Gambia V. Myanmar as Strategic Human Rights Litigation

Strategic human rights litigation (SHRL) is nowadays regarded as the one of the prominent features of modern international litigation. Although there is no authoritative definition as yet, SHRL is defined as litigation that pursues goals or interests that are broader than those of the immediate parties.[201] The case of The Gambia v. Myanmar is seen as an example of how SHRL can be used "as part of a campaign for atrocity crimes accountability, set in the context of a humanitarian crisis negotiation."[202] That is to say, the OIC's strategic litigation in this case may have an impact on securing accountability for the atrocities against the Rohingya, and advancing the both diplomatic negotiation of the refugee crisis and of Myanmar's internal armed conflict.[203] There are three reasons why this case fits the definition of SHRL: First, the plaintiff is suing for interests greater than their own. Second, the case is being used to obtain judicial finding or remedies that go beyond the legal and political claims of the case. Third, it augments the campaign activities of the group that filed the case.[204] For the purpose of SHRL in respect of the Rohingya, The Gambia seems an ideal complainant, because it comes with relatively clean hands and is the one of the smallest state in the world and the smallest in Africa, and this relative size lends The Gambia a patina of sincerity.[205]

To elaborate on the foregoing, the distinguishing characteristics of such "strategic litigation" may be summarized as follows. First, the strategy deployed in the strategic

---

[198] Alam, Khan (2022), p. 355.

[199] Ibid., p. 356.

[200] Uddin (2022), p. 54.

[201] Duffy (2018), p. 3.

[202] Ramsden (2021), p. 156.

[203] Ibid., p. 157.

[204] Ibid., p. 172.

[205] Ibid., p. 173.

litigation is meant not only for solving a past dispute in the client's interest, but also to develop principles that could be of interest to others and thus have broader impact.[206] Second, the litigation advances various causes that transcend the present case, including community interests in addition to human rights activism.[207] Third, the litigation is not aimed solely at producing legal outcomes, but also to advance social causes including behavior change and political reform.[208] Fourth, the venues of such litigation are similarly in scope.[209] They may take such traditional forms as criminal, civil, administrative, or constitutional cases, but may also be filed in international venues including UN treaty monitoring bodies or the ICJ.[210]

The reason for litigants viewing the ICJ as a suitable forum for SHRL is explained as "the potential for such litigation to impact diplomacy in the principal political organs of the UN," both the Security Council and the General Assembly.[211] Additional reasons cited are the authority of the ICJ, relative lack constraint in legal and evidentiary aspects therein, and the ICJ being the UN's principal judicial organ.[212]

4.7 The Dynamic Relationship Between State and Individual Responsibility for Crimes Under International Law

4.7.1 The ICJ and the ICC

The duality of state and individual responsibility in international law is educed by the practice of international law and legal norms alike. Thus, whereas the ICJ is authorized to settle inter-state disputes, the ICC is instead authorized to determine individual responsibility. For instance, individual responsibility and state responsibility were pursued before respective the ICTY and the ICJ for the alleged genocide situations of the former Yugoslavia, as confirmed by the Trial Chamber of the ICTY in the case of *Furunzija*.[213] This is particularly true with respect to cases of genocide, as "[the] regulatory concept of the Genocide Convention combines individual responsibility for genocide with the obligation of the contracting parties of the Convention to enact the necessary legislation to make genocide a crime in their domestic criminal

---

[206] Ramsden and Gledhill (2019), p. 425.

[207] Ibid.

[208] Ibid.

[209] Ibid.

[210] Ibid.

[211] Ramsden (2021), p. 173.

[212] Ibid., pp. 159–160.

[213] International Criminal Tribunal for the Former Yugoslavia (1998), para. 42. "Under current international humanitarian law, in addition to individual criminal liability, State responsibility may ensue as a result of State officials engaging in torture or failing to prevent torture or to punish torturers.".

law codes and to prevent and punish all forms of genocide under their jurisdiction as far as that is within their power."[214] The State Party's obligation not to commit genocide under the Genocide Convention was disputed by the former Republic of Yugoslavia and Serbia and Montenegro in Bosnia v. Serbia and Montenegro on the grounds that Article I of the convention "does not *expressis verbis* require States to refrain from themselves committing genocide."[215] The ICJ concluded that said State Party's obligation not to commit genocide is indeed implied based on the established purpose of the Convention, for the following reasons[216]: First, by agreeing to a categorization of genocide as "a crime under international law," the states parties must logically be undertaking not to commit the act which constitutes a crime under international law[217]; and second, the obligation to prevent genocide necessarily implies the prohibition of the commission of genocide.[218]

This position is summarized thus[219]: (1) Any person, regardless whether such a person is a public official or a private individual, who commits genocide should be punished for the crime of genocide; (2) If a state fails to prevent or punish the genocide of the actors of genocide whose acts are attributable to that state, and the state has committed an act of international illegality and is liable to the State. When arriving at the conclusion of the State Party's responsibility to commit genocide, the Court relied on the UN General Assembly's reference 'that genocide is an international crime entailing national and international responsibility on the part of individuals and states' back in 1947.[220] In this way, the Court observed that duality of responsibility remains a constant feature of international law.[221]

Given that the ICJ thus determined that states also bear responsibility for committing genocide under the Genocide Convention, questions have arisen about the relationship between individual criminal responsibility and state responsibility, the burden of proof, and the process of proving theses under the convention. The question of whether there exists a fundamentally different burden of proof of the crime of genocide where individual versus state responsibility is concerned still seems contentious.[222] There also seems to be some dispute as to whether individual criminal responsibility, particularly conviction of individuals, of state agents for genocide is a prerequisite for state responsibility for genocide. For instance, Judge Kriangsak Kittichaisaree, a member of the International Tribunal for the Law of the Sea (ITLOS), asserts that "[o]nly after the guilt of an individual has been proved beyond

---

[214] Wolf (2016), p. 17.

[215] International Court of Justice (2007), p. 114, para. 167.
ibid., at p. 113, para. 166.

[216] Ibid.

[217] Ibid.

[218] Ibid.

[219] Wolf (2016), p. 18.

[220] "Draft Convention on Genocide," UN Doc. A/RES/180(II) (21 November 1947); International Court of Justice (2007), p. 111, para. 163.

[221] Ibid., p. 116, para. 173.

[222] Dissenting Opinion of Vice-President, Al-Khasawneh (2007), para. 42.

4.7 The Dynamic Relationship Between State and Individual ...

doubt may the ICJ proceed to determine whether the conduct of the individual is attributable to Myanmar, as a nation State, and if so determined, whether Myanmar has breached its obligations under the Genocide Convention."[223] However, the ICJ itself acknowledges that state responsibility for genocide may arise without being predicated on the conviction of any individual.[224]

While the relationship between state and individual responsibility is seen as dual and parallel, the consequences are unclear. For example, Article 58 of the 2001 Draft Articles on Responsibility of States for Internationally Wrongful Acts of the UN International Law Commission (ILC) states that "[t]hese articles are without prejudice to any question of the individual responsibility under international law of any person acting on behalf of a State."[225] Conversely, Article 25(4) of the ICC Statute stipulates that "[n]o provision in this Statute relating to individual criminal responsibility shall affect the responsibility of States under international law."[226] The importance of pursuing state responsibility in cases of aggression, genocide, crimes against humanity, and war crimes is further explained in terms of both reparatory and systemic functions.[227] The reparatory function is to remedy damage caused to injured states or other persons. These reparations may take the form of restitution, compensation, or satisfaction, in accordance with Article 34 of the aforementioned ILC Draft Articles on Responsibility of States. The systemic function is to impose aggravated responsibility on states as per Article 40 of the ILC Draft Articles, even though the legal consequence of serious breaches of international law remains under development.[228]

The proposed Draft Conclusions on peremptory norms of general international law (*jus cogens*) also prepared by the ILC raised the prohibitions of the crime of aggression, the crime of genocide, and crimes against humanity as examples of the norms in question.[229] According to Article 17(2) of the Draft Conclusions, a consequence of the violation of peremptory norms of general international law is that "[a]ny State is entitled to invoke the responsibility of another State for a breach of a peremptory norm of general international law (*jus cogens*), in accordance with the rules on the responsibility of States for internationally wrongful acts."[230]

---

[223] Kittichaisaree (2022), p. 116.

[224] International Court of Justice (2007), pp. 119–120, para. 182; International Court of Justice (2015), p. 61, para. 128.

[225] "Draft articles on Responsibility of States for Internationally Wrongful Acts, with Commentaries", *the Yearbook of the International Law Commission 2001*, UN Doc. A/CN.4/SER.A/2001/Add.1 (Part 2), p. 142; UN Doc. A/56/10 (2001), pp. 30, 142.

[226] Rome Statute of the International Criminal Court (1998) 2187 UNTS 90.

[227] Nollkaemper (2003), p. 622.

[228] Ibid., p. 627. "Draft articles on Responsibility of States for Internationally Wrongful Acts, with Commentaries", *the Yearbook of the International Law Commission 2001*, UN Doc. A/CN.4/SER.A/2001/Add.1 (Part 2), p. 116; UN Doc. A/56/10 (2001), pp. 29, 112.

[229] *Report of the International Law Commission, Seventy-first session, (29 April–7 June and 8 July–9 August 2019)*, UN Doc. A/74/10 (2019), p. 147.

[230] Ibid., p. 190.

The synergy between individual and state responsibility may be categorized into substantive and procedural aspects, with the former concerned with, for instance, emerging and developing international law relating to sovereign immunity, and the latter evidentiary matters. First, the substantive aspect of this synergy is found in the punishment of individuals who are responsible for wrongful acts as a form of remedies for state responsibility.[231] Second, this synergy is also seen in the earlier mentioned procedural aspects. For example, the ICJ 2007 ruling in Bosnia v. Serbia and Montenegro is famous both for holding that state responsibility may arise from failure to prevent or punish genocide as well an act of state genocide,[232] and for relying heavily on the findings of the ICTY,[233] although whether the burden of proof of the crime of genocide is fundamentally different for individual versus state responsibility appears to remain an open question.[234] The reason is that, while the ICJ clarified in this ruling that "State responsibility can arise under the Convention for genocide and complicity, without an individual being convicted of the crime or an associated one,"[235] it also emphasized the absence of charges brought by the Office of the Prosecutor (OTP) of the ICTY against any individual for genocide against the Croat population in the context of the armed conflict which took place in the territory of Croatia in the period 1991–95 when assessing *dolus specialis* in its of 2015 ruling in Croatia vs. Serbia.[236] Accordingly, the Court held that it "did not intend to turn the absence of charges into decisive proof that there had not been genocide, but took the view that this factor may be of significance and would be taken into consideration."[237]

Nevertheless, as far as the situation in Myanmar is concerned, it is expected that the ICJ will find it difficult to rely on the judgment and evidence of the OTP to find genocide. First, chronologically, there is currently little guarantee that a conviction by a national criminal court will occur before the ICJ issues any such ruling. While the proceedings before the ICJ are based on the Genocide Convention and involve finding whether the convention has been violated, including whether genocide has occurred, the OTP preliminary investigation has thus far determined only that there is a reasonable basis for believing that crimes against humanity have occurred.[238] In other words, the ICJs jurisdiction over the situation in Myanmar is limited to state responsibility for genocide, while the OTP is currently focusing on crimes against humanity. However, depending on how the OTP investigation goes, genocide may yet become a subject of investigation and prosecution on its part.[239]

---

[231] UN Doc. A/CN.4/SER.A/2001/Add.1 (Part 2) (2001), p. 143, fn. 840.

[232] International Court of Justice (2007), p. 114, para. 167.

[233] Ibid., pp. 155, 197, paras. 277, 374.

[234] Dissenting Opinion of Vice-President, Al-Khasawneh (2007), para. 42.

[235] International Court of Justice (2007), p. 120, para. 182.

[236] International Court of Justice (2015), p. 128, para. 440.

[237] Ibid., p. 75, para. 187.

[238] Pre-Trial Chamber III of the International Criminal Court (2019), para. 4.

[239] Ibid., § 126.

4.7.2 The ICC and Regional Human Rights Institutions

The duty to investigate and prosecute in European and Inter-American human rights law has some similarity with the principle of complementarity imposed by Article 17 of the Rome Statute.[240] In particular, both the idea and the prosecutorial policy of the positive complementarity of the ICC with States Parties encourage domestic investigation and prosecution. Additionally, the duties of States Parties to investigate and prosecute human rights violations have been established under both regional human rights treaties and the UN International Covenant on Civil and Political Rights (ICCPR).[241] Historically speaking, it was only after the 1994 Rwandan genocide that the prevention of genocide and other international crimes attracted attention,[242] while the duty to prosecute garnered attention prior to this, following democratic transitions from military rule in Latin America and communism in Eastern Europe.[243] Today, some human rights treaties request that States Parties to prevent violations of treaty obligations.[244] From the perspective of international human rights law, the positive duty to prevent human rights violations is also recognized as a state's obligation to ensure respect for the right to life and the freedom from torture.

The duty to prevent the crime of genocide was incorporated into the Genocide Convention, but its scope was ambiguous,[245] and it was contemplated in a narrow sense that such prevention would be achieved by criminal prosecution.[246] Hence, the scope of the duty to prevent genocide was not differentiated from the duty to punish genocide, because the scope of the former was not clear enough. However, it is now recognized that Article I of the Genocide Convention stipulates both the duty to prevent and to punish genocide,[247] a phenomenon that might be called fractionalization of duties, and which may also be seen to some extent in the course of the development of superior and command responsibilities. For example, the Convention against Torture also requires that States Parties prevent acts of torture in their territories under Article 2, as well as the obligation to investigate under Article 12, the criminalization of torture under Article 4, and the establishment of jurisdiction under Article 5. As of this writing, the latest such example is that Draft Article 3(2) of the ILC Draft Articles of the Proposed International Convention for the Prevention and Punishment of Crimes Against Humanity provides for duties both to prevent and

---

[240] Schabas (2011), p. 619; Lyngdorf and Wilt (2009), pp. 39–75.

[241] Roht-Arriaza (1990), pp. 449–513.

[242] Schabas (2018), p. 708.

[243] Rodman (2011), p. 284.

[244] International Convention on the Elimination of All Forms of Racial Discrimination (1969) 660 UNTS 195, Article 3; Council of Europe Convention on Preventing and Combating Violence against Women and Domestic Violence, CETS No. 210 (2014) Article 4(2). International Covenant on Civil and Political Rights (1976) 999 UNTS 171, Article 20(1).

[245] Schiffbauer (2018), p. 84.

[246] Schabas (2018), p. 707.

[247] Tams (2014), p. 42, para. 23.

92 4 The Relationship Between the Rohingya Case Before the International ...

punish crimes against humanity, which are crimes under international law, regardless of whether such crimes are committed in time of armed conflict.[248]

Today, links seems to be weakening between the ICC complementarity regime and regional human rights institutions. There is still hope, however, for the construction of a systematic international legal regime of state prevention, investigation, and prosecution obligations. On February 15, 2016, the Presidents of the ICC and the Inter-American Court of Human Rights (IACHR) signed a Memorandum of Understanding on strengthening cooperation between the two judicial institutions,[249] so as to enhance judicial dialogue and practical cooperation between these institutions.

In this regard, what would be a viable prescription for the aforementioned systematic legal regime? One suggestion is that "[t]he international tribunal could thus try the highest-ranking officers, with the rest left to the national system under a system of quasi-criminal review."[250] From the psychological point of view of the state, a direct investigation by the OTP of the ICC may have the effect of encouraging the state itself to fulfill its treaty obligations to investigate and prosecute,[251] and any steps that caused states to take such obligations seriously might at least reduce the ICC's workload.

4.7.3 Superior Responsibility

In addition to being an inter-agency issue, the synergy between state and individual responsibility also manifests itself as a substantive issue in relation to both superior and state responsibilities. Two obligations that commanders bear—to prevent and punish crimes committed by their subordinates—were said to have started out as one.[252] The development of the terms of superior responsibility is similar to the state's obligation to prevent and punish crime, in that duties to prevent and punish international crimes have likewise been subdivided, as described above.

A commander's responsibility for subordinates' grave breaches of the Geneva Conventions or Additional Protocol I is known as superior responsibility, and is regulated by Article 86(2) of the latter. It also constitutes a form of individual criminal responsibility under Article 28 of the ICC Statute, Article 7(3) of the ICTY Statute, and article 6(3) of the International Criminal Tribunal for Rwanda (ICTR) Statute. Accordingly, failure to act appropriately against alleged war crimes may give rise to a commanding officer's individual criminal responsibility for same.

This means that commanders and other superiors are criminally responsible for war crimes committed by their subordinates if they knew, or had reason to know, that said subordinates were about to commit or were committing such crimes and

---

[248] UN Doc A/74/10 (2019), p. 13.

[249] International Criminal Court Official Journal Publication (2016).

[250] Huneeus (2013), pp. 1–44, at 39.

[251] Ibid.

[252] Mettraux (2009), p. 229.

did not take all necessary and reasonable measures in their power to prevent their commission, or if such crimes had been committed, to punish the persons responsible. The duty to investigate human rights violations can also be found in the doctrine and legal norms of command responsibility. This duty is both integral and corollary to the duty to prevent and suppress alleged violations thereof.

The doctrine of superior responsibility under international humanitarian law and international criminal law may facilitate a reconciliation between state and individual responsibility for international crimes.[253] It has been pointed out that "individual criminal responsibility of military and civilian superiors necessarily implicates the responsibility of the State, because the duties that are imposed on superiors to prevent and punish the crimes of their subordinates are in turn derived from the more general obligations that are imposed on states to prevent and punish certain violations of international law by individuals."[254] However, the order in which the blame is assigned will be an issue here as well. It is easy to imagine that the finding of personal responsibility will be meaningful in the determination of state responsibility. On the other hand, it is undesirable from the perspective of the principle of presumption of innocence to rely on state responsibility when determining individual responsibility.

Interactions between international human rights law and international humanitarian law, as well as between state and individual responsibility, may be observed with regard to certain serious human rights violations. International human rights treaties also explicitly provide for a State Party's duty to investigate specific human rights violations, such as the Article 6 of the Torture Convention, Article 12 of the Enforced Disappearance Convention, Article 8 of the Inter-American Convention to Prevent and Punish Torture, and Article 6 of the Inter-American Convention on the Forced Disappearance of Persons.

At present, while it is possible to point out a theoretical overlap between state and superior responsibilities, there are many unknowns about their synergies. The simultaneous pursuit of these responsibilities can at least be expected, however, to lead to the efficient implementation of international criminal law through the proper fulfillment of state obligations under international human rights law and humanitarian law, as well the promotion of domestic trials through the domestic pursuit of individual responsibility. That is to say, both state and individual criminal responsibility accordingly may serve as pressure points toward the aforementioned implementation of international human rights law and international humanitarian law.[255]

---

[253] Reid (2005), p. 827. Bonafè (2009), p. 173, fn. 10.

[254] Ibid., (Reid), p. 798.

[255] ibid., at 806.

4.8 Responsibility to Protect and the Gambia's Application

The plight of the Rohingya in Myanmar is also discussed in the context of "the Responsibility to Protect (R2P)" of Myanmar and the international community. As officially recognized in the 2005 World Summit Outcome Document, adopted as a resolution by the UN General Assembly,[256] "[e]ach individual State has the responsibility to protect its populations from genocide, war crimes, ethnic cleansing and crimes against humanity. This responsibility entails the prevention of such crimes, including their incitement, through appropriate and necessary means."[257] Therefore, "the international community should, as appropriate, encourage and help States to exercise this responsibility and support the United Nations in establishing an early warning capability."[258] In other words, each territorial state bears the primary responsibility to protect its nationals, and the international community owes a subsidiary responsibility to protect people in the state which fails to carry out its R2P.

The UN Security Council is seen as the most effective instrument for implementing R2P, including through armed sanctions. However, as seen in protests by China and Russia over Syria and Myanmar, in many cases the Security Council either has been unable to put R2P measures on the table due to political divisions, or has been prevented from taking action due to veto power.[259] As mentioned above, exercise of the latter by China and Russia hampers UNSC action against Myanmar over the human rights abuses against the Rohingya. Following similar abovementioned Security Council paralysis over Syria, again caused by Chinese and Russian vetoes, France and Mexico proposed a code of conduct aimed at preventing further such vetoes from negating the R2P ideal.[260] Said code of conduct was subsequently elaborated in the framework of the Accountability, Coherence and Transparency (ACT), in consultation with states, civil society, and the Secretariat of the United Nations, before being presented by Liechtenstein in a letter to the Secretary-General.[261] In this letter, 107 UN member states, including France and the UK as permanent members of the Security Council, "[p]ledge in particular to not vote against a credible draft resolution before the Security Council on timely and decisive action to end the commission of genocide, crimes against humanity or war crimes, or to prevent such crimes."[262] Thus, even though the alleged genocide against the Rohingya in Myanmar has been identified as a good case for humanitarian military intervention as part of the implementation of the Genocide Convention based on the R2P concept,[263] it would be unrealistic to expect implementation thereof by Security Council authorization.

---

[256] UN Doc. A/RES/60/1 (2005).

[257] ibid., p. 30, para. 138.

[258] Ibid.

[259] Mennecke (2021), p. 339.

[260] Gepp (2021), p. 92.

[261] "Letter dated 14 December 2015 from the Permanent Representative of Liechtenstein to the United Nations addressed to the Secretary-General," UN Doc. A/70/621–S/2015/978 (2015).

[262] Ibid., para. 2.

[263] Karazsia (2018), p. 26.

Military intervention without Security Council authorization is underdeveloped in international law, and thus, there has been no R2P-based military intervention on behalf of the Rohingya.[264]

A follow-up report by Secretary-General Ban Ki-Moon on the topic of "implementing the responsibility to protect" was submitted to the General Assembly in January 2009,[265] in which the Secretary-General found that the provisions of paras 138 and 139 of the World Summit Outcome (A/RES/60/1) suggest that the responsibility to protect rests on three pillars.[266] The first is the protection responsibilities of the state, that is, "the enduring responsibility of the State to protect its populations, whether nationals or not, from genocide, war crimes, ethnic cleansing and crimes against humanity, and from their incitement."[267] The second is international assistance and capacity-building, "the commitment of the international community to assist States in meeting those obligations."[268] The third is timely and decisive response by UN member states. Namely, it is the responsibility of member states to respond collectively in a timely and decisive manner when a state is manifestly failing to provide such protection.[269] According to Secretary-General Ban Ki-Moon, a calibrated and timely response could include pacific measures under Chapter VI of the Charter, coercive ones under Chapter VII, and/or collaboration with regional and subregional arrangements under Chapter VIII.[270] It is stressed that "the key to success lies in an early and flexible response, tailored to the specific needs of each situation."[271]

International criminal justice is described by Secretary-General Ban Ki-Moon as an important tool for implementing R2P under the first and third pillars. First, for state implementation of R2P, "the four specified crimes and violations and their incitement are criminalized under domestic law and practice."[272] The crimes referred to are genocide, war crimes, ethnic cleansing, and crimes against humanity. Per the principle of complementarity, states must cooperate with efforts by the ICC and *ad hoc* tribunals to detain and prosecute core crime suspects related to their responsibility to protect.[273] Under the third pillar of timely and decisive response by the international community, if a state manifestly fails to prevent such incitement, the international community should remind the authorities of this obligation and that such acts could be referred to the ICC.[274] With regard to R2P for the Rohingya,

---

[264] Ibid., p. 27.

[265] *Implementing the responsibility to protect: Report of the Secretary-General*, UN Doc. A/63/677 (2009).

[266] Ibid.

[267] Ibid., p. 8, para. 11.

[268] Ibid., p. 9, para. 11.

[269] Ibid.

[270] Ibid.

[271] Ibid.

[272] Ibid., p. 11, para. 17.

[273] Ibid., p. 12, para. 19.

[274] Ibid., p. 23, para. 53.

the first pillar is not expected to work, owing to of the lack of Rohingya citizenship and the unwillingness and inability of Myanmar to exercise R2P on their behalf.[275] Therefore, the second and third pillars are relevant in to the present matter, as they relate to the role of the international community in responding to humanitarian crises requiring R2P action.[276] The second pillar, wherein the UN and regional organizations are expected to reach out to Myanmar, has not worked as intended, because the UN has turned a blind eye to sensitive domestic issues such as dealing with the country's ethnic minorities while vigorously addressing economic development, while ASEAN takes noninterference as a guiding principle.[277] It is also noted that under the third pillar, R2P should be sought by peaceful means,[278] meaning that "[w]hen it comes to accountability and justice, two pathways are available in the international justice system, namely, the responsibility of the State based on international humanitarian law and human rights law, and criminal responsibility of individuals based on international criminal law."[279]

In this regard, it has already been demonstrated that R2P fulfillment is indeed not limited to military intervention, but can also be achieved by bringing suit with the ICJ, as with The Gambia lawsuit, which is accordingly being hailed as a historic step for R2P, as it represents the first attempt to pursue liability under the Genocide Convention since the adoption of the aforementioned UN General Assembly resolution on R2P in 2005.[280] It has been noted that the motivation behind this lawsuit is similar to the underpinnings of the R2P concept: "the international community had to realise and act on its responsibility to protect endangered populations against atrocity crimes."[281]

While ICC membership had been considered part and parcel of R2P fulfillment by the international community, the role of the ICJ in said fulfillment has been largely ignored,[282] to the extent that there seems to be no direct R2P on the part of the ICJ because the R2P imposes obligations on states by definition.[283] However, the ICJ may contribute indirectly to R2P through its functions of resolving inter-state disputes, preventing the outbreak of armed conflict, and preventing crimes under international law.[284] On the other hand, as mentioned elsewhere, the ICJs pursuit of responsibility on the part of Myanmar may have set the *coup* in motion, as indicated chiefly by the fact that Tatmadaw launched the *coup* when the Myanmar government filed its preliminary objections. After all, it is inevitable that interference with a sovereign state that is not properly fulfilling its responsibility to protect will lead to a backlash

---

[275] *See* Kapucu, p. 228.

[276] Ibid., p. 229.

[277] Ibid., pp. 229–230.

[278] Ibid., p. 231.

[279] Ibid., p. 233.

[280] Mennecke (2021), p. 326.

[281] Ibid., p. 342.

[282] Ibid., pp. 330–331.

[283] Ibid., p. 336.

[284] Ibid.

4.8 Responsibility to Protect and the Gambia's Application

from the state in question, whether such intervention takes a non-military form, such as bringing a case before an international tribunal, or not. At the same time, it is also undeniable that indifference or inability to act on the part of the international community may be making human rights violations around the world even worse than if there had been intervention.

Doubts have been raised of late as to whether the R2P can resolve the plight of the Rohingya, and whether the very concept of a state's responsibility to protect its citizens even applies, given the aforementioned denial of citizenship to the Rohingya.[285] Such concerns have been expressed in the following criticisms: first, R2P has not been codified, meaning that no precise definition has been agreed upon; second, individual states are not actively involved; third, it is colonialism in disguise; fourth, the Security Council is paralyzed; and finally, it is not novel.[286] It has additionally pointed out that emphasizing the responsibility to protect in Myanmar strengthens the state's authority to rule, while as already stated, the Rohingya are outside the bounds of constitutional sovereignty from the outset and therefore have no prospect of protection thereunder.[287] These concerns can be attributed to the aforementioned ambiguity of the concept of R2P in international law, and can also be seen as a kind of distaste for a hegemony of Western values, restating the abovementioned colonialism argument. The use of the ICJ by African countries as a consistent means of genocide crime prevention through non-military means, as in The Gambia, would dispel such negative images.

Apart from the question of whether collective measures can be taken by the UN based on the concept of responsibility to protect, another issue that is currently the focus of attention in the Ukraine-Russia issue is whether states can use force to prevent genocide under the Genocide Convention. When Ukraine brought its case against Russia under the convention in 2022, it developed an argument that Russia may not use force against Ukraine to fulfil its obligation under the Genocide Convention to prevent genocide, an argument that could be interpreted as meaning that use of force by a state under its responsibility to protect was impermissible. Specifically, Ukraine claims that "[t]he duty to prevent and punish genocide enshrined in Article I of the Convention necessarily implies that this duty must be performed in good faith and not abused, and that one Contracting Party may not subject another Contracting Party to unlawful action, including armed attack, especially when it is based on a wholly unsubstantiated claim of preventing and punishing genocide."[288] However, "[t]his might be read as suggesting that where there is substantial evidence of genocide, Article I of the Convention might authorize a State to undertake an armed attack."[289] In oral arguments on provisional measures, Ukraine's claim was clarified: it held that nothing in the convention authorizes a state to invade the territory of

---

[285] *See* Nishikawa (2020), pp. 90–106; Alam (2021), pp. 114, 131; Kapucu (2022), p. 226.

[286] *See* Kassim (2014), p. 76.

[287] Nishikawa (2020), pp. 99–100.

[288] Government of Ukraine (2022), p. 16, para. 27.

[289] Schabas (2022).

another in order to prevent or punish the crime of genocide.[290] In any event, if the case of the application of the Genocide Convention to the Ukraine-Russia matter proceeds, the question will be whether the obligation to uphold the Genocide Convention and the scope of the use of force, in particular the violation of the peremptory norm of the prohibition of genocide by another state, can justify use of force outside the UN Charter.

4.9 Responsibility to Protect and the US Government

The US has been a State Party to the Genocide Convention since 1988. In recent times, the US administration has focused on preventing atrocities including genocide, and in this sense, it is noteworthy that it has acted to prevent such crimes against the Rohingya. Several achievements are noted on the part of the Trump administration in this regard, which, while having famously sanctioned ICC personnel in 2017, also withdrew military assistance from the Myanmar government in response to the mass displacement of Rohingya by Myanmar's armed forces and militias, and provided more than $600 million in humanitarian assistance over the following two years.[291] In addition, on December 21, 2017, the Trump administration issued an executive order that inaugurated a new targeted sanctions regime against human rights abusers and corrupt actors,[292] including Maung Maung Soe, who "oversaw the military operation in Burma's Rakhine State responsible for widespread human rights abuse against Rohingya civilians in response to attacks by the Arakan Rohingya Salvation Army."[293] The order invoked the Global Magnitsky Human Rights Accountability Act which the US Congress passed in 2016,[294] and clearly has the potential to help advance US human rights policy.[295] Since the order was issued, the sanctions list has grown to more than one hundred individuals.[296] In January 2019 President Trump also signed the Elie Wiesel Genocide and Atrocity Prevention Act, named for Holocaust survivor and Nobel laureate Elie Wiesel,[297] which aims to enhance US capacities to prevent, mitigate, and respond to atrocities.[298] It requires an annual report to Congress describing government actions in aid of preventing atrocities. Under this Act, President Trump launched a White-House-led Mass Atrocities Task Force, which was regarded as a reboot of the Atrocities Prevention Board established by the

---

[290] Verbatim Record of the International Court of Justice (2022c), p. 28, para. 44. *See* also Schabas (2022).

[291] Glanville (2021), p. 165.

[292] U.S. President Donald J. Trump (2017), pp. 60,839–60,843.

[293] Ibid., p. 60,843.

[294] Global Magnitsky Human Rights Accountability Act (S. 284) (2016).

[295] Berschinski (2018).

[296] Glanville (2021), p. 165.

[297] Elie Wiesel Genocide and Atrocity Prevention Act (S. 1158) (2018).

[298] Glanville (2021), p. 164.

4.9 Responsibility to Protect and the US Government

Obama administration in 2012.[299] The first report by President Trump to the Congress includes the statement that the US government "provided publicly available satellite imagery and pertinent information to the Independent International Fact-Finding Mission on Burma, which aided in the investigation of atrocities and human-rights violations and abuses committed by the Burmese security forces after 2011".[300] As discussed above, however, while these contributions on the part of President Trump to aiding the Rohingya may be noteworthy, the US government's focus and appetite for engaging with the Rohingya crisis does not appear to be terribly great,[301] with US policy regarding Myanmar accordingly described as "inconsistent and ambiguous" at best.[302] This makes it difficult to conceive of any US initiative to refer Myanmar to the ICC through the Security Council,[303] as epitomized by the following anecdote. In 2019, President Trump was asked by a Rohingya refugee in Bangladesh, "What is the plan to help us?" To which Trump replied, "And where is that, exactly?"[304] As will be seen in the last chapter, however, the Biden administration has certainly taken an ongoing interest in addressing the Rohingya crisis, with economic sanctions and other measures.[305] In March 2022, the US government concluded that the Burmese military has committed genocide, crimes against humanity, and ethnic cleansing against the Rohingya.[306] Nevertheless, even this administration has only recognized three genocides to-date[307]: the Ottoman Empire's genocide of the Armenians,[308] China's genocide of the Uyghurs,[309] and Myanmar's genocide of the Rohingya, out of a mere eight total recognized instances of genocide on the part of the US since the Holocaust.[310]

Even so, the US recognition of genocide against the Rohingya in Myanmar is still considered significant in terms of both policy and political significance. First, even if the US uses genocide in a political rather than a legal sense, it is certain to have a social impact. Second, the US Department of State's finding of genocide appears to include detailed analyses of relevant facts and law, making more credible than anonymous news reports.[311] It is further suggested that this finding on the part of the US also reinforces the reports of the IIFFMM and may support The Gambia's ICJ suit.[312]

---

[299] Ibid.

[300] Elie Wiesel Genocide and Atrocity Prevention Report (2019), p. 3.

[301] Glanville (2021), p. 167.

[302] Almuhana (2019), p. 75.

[303] Ibid.

[304] Ibid. *See* Murad (2019).

[305] U.S. President Joseph R. Biden Jr. (2021), pp. 9429–9432.

[306] U.S. Department of Treasury (2022).

[307] Baghdassarian (2022).

[308] White House (2021).

[309] U.S. Embassy and Consulates in China (2021).

[310] US Department of State (2022).

[311] Islam (2022), p. 5.

[312] Ibid.

4.10 Possible Effects Associated with the February 2021 *coup d'état*

Political upheaval due to the *coup d'etat* raises the issue of government recognition, and plaintiff eligibility becomes an issue in the pending ICJ case. It was reported that two of the lawyers who served on Myanmar's legal team under Aung San Suu Kii, William Schabas and Phoebe Okowa, are no longer working on the case following the *coup*.[313] *Ad hoc* Judge Claus Kress, appointed as mentioned elsewhere by the ousted government, continues to hear the case, however. The General Assembly adopted a draft resolution (A/75/L.85/Rev.1) on the situation in Myanmar on June 18, 2021,[314] which does not call on the junta to cooperate with the ICC and the ICJ, but notes that issues are pending before these courts.

Pillai points out the implications of the *coup* as follows: the continuation of appearance and representation; compliance with provisional measures; third party intervention; and evidentiary issues.[315] Regarding the first item, given that the ICJ adjudicates disputes between nations, it is expected that proceedings will continue even in cases of changes of government, such as in the present instance. If the Myanmar military junta refuses to appear in court, Article 53(1) of the ICJ Statute will apply, which stipulates that "[w]henever one of the parties does not appear before the Court, or fails to defend its case, the other party may call upon the Court to decide in favour of its claim.",[316] Article 53(2) places the following conditions on trials *in absentia* as follows: "[t]he Court must, before doing so, satisfy itself, not only that it has jurisdiction in accordance with Articles 36 and 37, but also that the claim is well founded in fact and law."[317] Pillai suggests that the timing following the ICJ ruling on Myanmar's preliminary objections is of note in this matter.[318]

Regarding whether Myanmar will comply with the ICJ order for provisional measures of January 23, 2020, it is significant that in December 2020, the Judges of the ICJ adopted "a new Article 11 of the Resolution concerning the Internal Judicial Practice of the Court. The article provides for the establishment of an *ad hoc* committee, composed of three judges, which will assist the Court in monitoring the implementation of the provisional measures that it indicates."[319] The full text of the newly adopted article is as follows:

New Article 11 of the Resolution concerning the Internal Judicial Practice of the Court

(i) Where the Court indicates provisional measures, it shall elect three judges to form an *ad hoc* committee which will assist the Court in monitoring the

---

[313] Nachemson (2021).

[314] UN Doc. A/RES/75/287 (2021).

[315] Pillai (2021).

[316] Statute of the International Court of Justice (1945), 33 UNTS 993.

[317] Ibid.

[318] Pillai (2021).

[319] International Court of Justice Press Release (2020).

4.10 Possible Effects Associated with the February 2021 *coup d'état*

implementation of provisional measures. This committee shall include neither a Member of the Court of the nationality of one of the parties nor any judges ad hoc.

(ii) The *ad hoc* committee shall examine the information supplied by the parties in relation to the implementation of provisional measures. It shall report periodically to the Court, recommending potential options for the Court.

(iii) Any decision in this respect shall be taken by the Court.

This amendment may have an impact on the Myanmar military junta's attitude toward compliance with the provisional measures, possibly even inducing its withdrawal from the proceedings, because they would find any such *ad hoc* monitoring committee a troubling prospect.[320]

On the third point, increasing public criticism of the *coup* and the junta's human rights violations may inspire more intervention over and above the previously mentioned existing such participants of Maldives, Canada, and the Netherlands, with the UK being one probable candidate.[321] While there had been no movement in the ICJ for an extended period following the *coup*, the ICJ issued a press release on January 19, 2022 announcing that it would hold oral arguments on the preliminary objections raised by Myanmar on February 21–28, 2022, as mentioned above.[322] On April 6, 2021, the Committee for Representing Pyidaungsu Hluttaw (CRPH), a group of parliamentarians from the National League for the pre-*coup* government, issued a statement that it had received 180,000 items of evidence of post-*coup* human rights violations by the military.[323]

On February 1, 2022, the NUG announced that it "has advised the International Court of Justice (ICJ) that Myanmar accepts the jurisdiction of the Court and withdraws all preliminary objections in the case of *The Gambia v. Myanmar* concerning the military operations against the Rohingya in 2016 and 2017."[324] As of mid-February 2022, there appears to be no response from the ICJ. In light of the fact that the ICJ is the main judicial organ of the United Nations under Article 92 of the UN Charter, it has been pointed out that if the ICJ does not directly address government representation, it might create a discordance of views on this issue among the various organs of the UN,[325] and could also have an impact on the ICC.[326] It is possible, however, that the ICJ may see this as a political issue and thus be awaiting the decision of the credentials committee.

On February 21, 2022, the military junta represented Myanmar at the aforementioned oral arguments. At the start, presiding judge Joan E. Donoghue held that: "the parties to a contentious case before the Court are States, not particular governments. The Court's judgments and its provisional measures orders bind the States that are

---

[320] Pillai (2021).

[321] Ibid.

[322] International Court of Justice Press Release (2022a).

[323] Sebastian (2021).

[324] Republic of the Union of Myanmar National Unity Government (2022).

[325] Weller (2022).

[326] Ibid.

parties to a case."[327] Ko Ko Hlaing, the junta's Minister of International Cooperation, then began arguments, alluding to the change of government by claiming that "[t]here have been some changes in the composition of the Court and representation of the Parties since the last public sitting in this case."[328] He was followed by Dr. Christopher Staker, who continued to represent the Myanmar government after the *coup*, and Professors Stefan Talmon and Robert Kolb also spoke on the government's behalf. Regarding the first preliminary objection, as previously described, Dr. Staker claimed that it cannot be possible for the OIC, an international organization, to bring a case before the ICJ by using a state as an agent.[329] The second preliminary objection, also as previously described, relates to lack of standing on the part of The Gambia.[330] The third preliminary objection, again as previously described, is that Myanmars reservation to Article VIII of the 1948 Genocide Convention precludes the exercise of jurisdiction by the ICJ in this case.[331] The fourth preliminary objection, as previously described, is "that the Court lacks jurisdiction, or that the Application is inadmissible, as there was no dispute between The Gambia and Myanmar when the Application instituting proceedings was submitted."[332]

As anticipated, the ICJ's decision to have the junta represent the Myanmar government in court has been criticized, with Professor Yanghee Lee, former UN Special Rapporteur on the situation of human rights in Myanmar, said of the decision that "[t]hese hearings, with the junta claiming to represent Myanmar, are a disgrace."[333]

On February 23, 2022, The Gambia denied Myanmars first preliminary objection on the grounds that The Gambia was the applicant.[334] According to Professor Pierre d'Argent, one of The Gambia's advocates, Myanmars new government representatives will also contest The Gambia's eligibility to be an applicant in the case, as it has renewed some of its counsels.[335] Next came standing, in which regard The Gambia emphasized the *erga omnes partes* obligations of the Genocide Convention,[336] and further, that there were no indispensable third parties.[337] Tafadzwa Pasipanodya, another advocate for The Gambia, continued that Article VIII of the convention, and Myanmar's reservation thereon, is irrelevant to calling on the Court,[338] arguing that Article VIII governs appeals to United Nations organs at a political level, and thus has no bearing on calling on the Court to resolve legal disputes between States Parties.[339]

---

[327] Verbatim Record (2022a), p. 11.

[328] Ibid., p. 13.

[329] Ibid., p. 26, para. 60.

[330] Ibid., pp. 27–39, paras. 5–61.

[331] Ibid., pp. 40–49, paras. 1–55.

[332] Ibid., pp. 49–60, paras. 1–67.

[333] Special Advisory Council for Myanmar (2022).

[334] Verbatim Record (2022b), pp. 19–28, paras. 1–37.

[335] Ibid., p. 30, para. 6.

[336] Ibid., p. 32, para. 14.

[337] Ibid., p. 27, para. 33.

[338] Ibid., p. 40, para. 3.

[339] Ibid., p. 40, para. 5.

The last advocated for The Gambia, Arsalan Suleman, asserted that the parties' exchanges at the United Nations demonstrate that The Gambia and Myanmar "held clearly opposite views concerning Myanmar's fulfilment of its obligations under the Genocide Convention, and that they disagreed about the facts and legal implications of Myanmar's anti-Rohingya "clearance operations" in Rakhine state."[340] The hearing were adjourned on the afternoon of February 28, 2022.

4.11 Implications of the Application of the Genocide Convention in Ukraine and Russia on the Application of the Genocide Convention in Myanmar

As previously mentioned, the situation in Myanmar is not the only case simultaneously pending at the ICC and the ICJ. The situation in Ukraine is also simultaneously pending before these courts. To date, the Ukrainian case at the ICJ is progressing more rapidly than the Myanmar case, which has been attributed to the COVID-19 pandemic and the 2021 *coup*.[341] In any case, there is no doubt that the inter-state conflict between Ukraine and Russia has commanded the attention of the international community since 2022.

In connection with the Russian Special Military Operation launched against Ukraine on February 24, 2022, Ukraine filed a complaint with the ICJ against Russia as early as February 26, 2022, alleging that Russia is falsely claiming that acts of genocide are occurring in Luhansk and Donetsk and is conducting military actions against Ukraine without legal basis under the Genocide Convention.[342] Since both Russia and Ukraine are parties to the convention, Ukraine has based its claim on the fact that under Article 9 of the convention, both states have agreed to refer disputes concerning the interpretation, application, and implementation of the Genocide Convention to the ICJ. On March 2, the ICC decided to open an official investigation into the situation in Ukraine, meaning that, as previously described, the same dispute would be pending before the ICC and the ICJ, as with the situation in Myanmar, even though the ICC and the ICJ would play different roles, respectively pursuing individual criminal responsibility and state responsibility. In other words, judicial international institutions are being actively used in the form of these simultaneous ICC and ICJ proceedings to stop ongoing gross human rights violations as soon as possible and to pursue criminal responsibility for culpable parties thereto.

As described elsewhere, both ICJ cases were brought using the compromissory clause of Article 9 of the Genocide Convention. Regarding the conflict between Ukraine and Russia, however, it is unlikely that both parties would consent to refer the matter to the ICJ. As for the situation in Myanmar, it is unlikely to be heard by the ICJ, as its jurisdiction extends only to inter-state disputes, and the Rohingya

---

[340] Ibid., p. 52, para. 24.

[341] Pillai (2022).

[342] Government of Ukraine (2022).

104   4 The Relationship Between the Rohingya Case Before the International ...

issue is one of persecution of a domestic minority within a state. It is thus unlikely
as well that both parties to an ongoing armed conflict would agree to make a referral
to the ICJ in order to address gross human rights violations in said conflict. If states
had sufficient communication and compromise among themselves to make such an
agreement, then it would seem possible for them to conclude an armistice or peace
treaty instead.

The most significant difference between the Myanmar and the Ukraine cases
before the ICJ lies in the differences in the subjects of their disputes: the former seeks
to interrogate Myanmar's violations of its obligation under the Genocide Convention
to prevent genocide, while the latter seeks to stop the use of force by Russia on the
basis of Russia having violated its obligation under the Genocide Convention to
prevent genocide and to question the illegality of the use of force, also under the
convention. Thus, the question arises as to the contours of the subject matter of the
dispute; specifically, whether Russia's obligation to suspend its use of force against
Ukraine can be considered a dispute concerning the application and interpretation of
the Genocide Convention.

4.12   Conclusion

The promotion of democratization in the world in the post-Cold War era has accel-
erated the momentum for international cooperation and diversified international and
regional dispute settlement mechanisms. The complementary relationship between
state and individual criminal responsibility for acts that constitute crimes under international law, in particular human rights violations, has long been noted.[343] In many
cases, these responsibilities should be pursued simultaneously. Yet, it appears that
there is currently no unified approach to systemic understanding international law
of dual-track pursuit of state and individual responsibility for serious violations of
international law, such as violations of peremptory norms. However, the spirit of the
eradication of impunity requires that every effort be made to hold both individuals and
states accountable for human rights violations wherever possible. In this context, this
chapter makes clear the necessity to rethink the impact of such dual-track pursuits
of responsibility. Such a renewed understanding will make the international legal
system more effective in preventing and punishing serious crimes within its jurisdiction. In other words, a systematic understanding of international criminal law,
international human rights law, and international humanitarian law will enhance the
effectiveness of the ICC. This view is open to criticism as overly optimistic, and it
is indeed subject to the condition that such investigations and prosecutions follow
international human rights standards, to wit, that domestic criminal investigation and
prosecution mechanisms in developed countries meet these selfsame standards.

Myanmar is a party to the Genocide Convention and the Geneva Conventions, but
not the Additional Protocols to the Geneva Conventions, the Statute of the ICC, or the

---

[343] Trindade (2020), p. 372.

4.12 Conclusion

Convention against Torture. It is therefore premature to expect Myanmar to fulfill its obligations to prevent and punish violations of international law under human rights treaties and humanitarian law. The fulfillment of the state's obligation to investigate and prosecute must itself be a genuine effort in accordance with international human rights standards. Sham trials and scapegoating cannot be considered as fulfilling this obligation.

Following the *coup*, the Rohingya issue is no longer the only issue of gross human rights violations in Myanmar. Calls to hold Myanmars military accountable have shifted to encompass all serious human rights violations by the military, not just those committed against the Rohingya.[344]

Karim A. A. Khan QC was sworn in as Chief Prosecutor for the ICC in June 2021. There is no prospect of the military junta cooperating with the ICC's investigation and prosecution, and Mr. Khan's prosecution strategy is unclear as of this writing. Under these circumstances, it is uncertain to what extent pressure from the international community to hold both individuals and the state accountable will affect the Myanmar junta.

On July 22, 2022, Myanmar were the majority of the ICJ judges rejected Myanmar's preliminary objections, with the junta present for the ruling. If junta officials are present at future ICJ proceedings, the possibility of their arrest in the Netherlands cannot be ruled out, subject to the timing of any ICC warrants.

Sadly, attempts to use the ICC and the ICJ to hold the junta accountable will not be enough to overcome the current situation in Myanmar. The ICC cannot be independent of domestic and international politics, given that like the ICTY, the ICC is nothing more than "a giant without arms and legs[, needing] artificial limbs" to function.[345] States' cooperation with the ICC represents those very limbs. While continuing to pursue responsibility for the Rohingya issue and the other ongoing gross human rights violations in Myanmar, the international community should also consider other means to resolve the situation. Regarding the Ukraine crisis, the Group of Seven (G7) immediately declared that it would preserve evidence in cooperation with the ICC prosecutor.[346] To avoid further Rohingya ethnic cleansing, it will be necessary to improve the human rights situation in Myanmar itself, utopian though it may seem, by ratifying human rights treaties and forming an inclusive society beyond ethnic nationalism, thereby transforming the values of Myanmarese society.[347]

As the *coup* further exacerbates the crisis, keeping the matter pending before the ICJ and the ICC has the added benefit of retaining the attention of the international community.

---

[344] Cheung (2021).

[345] Cassese (1998), p. 13.

[346] European Council (2022), 'G7 Leaders' Statement - Brussels, 24 March 2022', (24 March 2022) available at < https://www.consilium.europa.eu/en/press/press-releases/2022/03/24/g7-leaders-statement-brussels-24-march-2022/ > (last accessed, 28 March 2022) para. 2.

[347] Alam, Khan (2022), pp. 369–371.

References

Alam J (2021) Responsibility to protect in international criminal law: the case of the Genocide against the Rohingya. In: Mulaj K (ed) Postgenocide: interdisciplinary reflections on the effects of Genocide. Oxford University Press, Oxford, pp 112–133

Alam J, Khan BU (2022) Complexities and challenges in reconciling international human rights with international criminal law: an introduction. In: Human rights and international criminal law. Brill, Leiden, pp 351–376

Almuhana SA (2019) The international criminal court (ICC) and the Rohingya crisis - jurisdiction and future perspectives. Kilaw J 7(4):45–87

Baghdassarian A (2022) The legal significance of U.S. recognition of the Armenian Genocide: implications for strategic litigation. Harvard Int Law J Online. https://harvardilj.org/2022/05/the-legal-significance-of-u-s-recognition-of-the-armenian-genocide-implications-for-strategic-litigation/

Berschinski R (2018) Trump administration notches a serious human rights win. No, really. Just security. https://www.justsecurity.org/50846/trump-administration-notches-human-rights-win-no-really/

Bonafè BI (2009) The relationship between state and individual responsibility for international crimes. Martinus Nijhoff, Leiden, Boston

Cassese A (1998) On the current trends towards criminal prosecution and punishment of breaches of international humanitarian law. Euro J Int Law 9:2–17

Cheung C (2021) Beyond the Coup in Myanmar: the need for an inclusive accountability. Just security. https://www.justsecurity.org/76234/beyond-the-coup-in-myanmar-the-need-for-an-inclusive-accountability/

Chinkin CM (1986) Third-party intervention before the international court of justice. Am J Int Law 80(3):495–531

Declaration of Judge *Ad Hoc* Kress (2020) Order. Application of the convention on the prevention and punishment of the crime of Genocide (the Gambia v. Myanmar). International Court of Justice

Declaration of Judge *Ad Hoc* Kress (2022) Application of the Convention on the Prevention and Punishment of the Crime of Genocide (The Gambia v. Myanmar) Preliminary Objections. International Court of Justice.

Delegation of the European Union to the United Nations in New York (2021) Statement on behalf of the European Union and its Member States delivered by Ambassador Silvio Gonzato, Deputy Head of the Delegation of the European Union to the United Nations, at the 75th Session of the United Nations General Assembly. https://www.eeas.europa.eu/delegations/un-new-york/eu-statement---united-nations-general-assembly-meeting-myanmar_en?s=63

Dissenting Opinion of Judge Xue (2022) Application of the Convention on the Prevention and Punishment of the Crime of Genocide (The Gambia v. Myanmar) Preliminary Objections. International Court of Justice.

Dissenting Opinion of Vice-President, Al-Khasawneh (2007) Application of the convention on the prevention and punishment of the crime of Genocide (Bosnia and Herzegovina v. Serbia and Montenegro) merits. International Court of Justice

Domino J (2020) Gambia v. Facebook: what the discovery request reveals about Facebook's content moderation. Just security. https://www.justsecurity.org/71157/gambia-v-facebook-what-the-discovery-request-reveals-about-facebooks-content-moderation/

Duffy H (2018) Strategic human rights litigation: understanding and maximising impact. Hart Publishing, Oxford

Elie Wiesel Genocide and Atrocity Prevention Act (S. 1158) (2018). https://www.congress.gov/bill/115th-congress/senate-bill/1158

Elie Wiesel Genocide and Atrocity Prevention Report (2019). https://trumpwhitehouse.archives.gov/wp-content/uploads/2019/09/ELIE-WIESEL-GENOCIDE-AND-ATROCITIES-PREVENTION-REPORT.pdf

References

European Council (2022) G7 Leaders' statement - Brussels, 24 March 2022. https://www.consilium. europa.eu/en/press/press-releases/2022/03/24/g7-leaders-statement-brussels-24-march-2022/

European Union (2022) Myanmar: joint ministerial statement marking the 5th anniversary of the Myanmar military's attack against Rohingya and ensuing crisis. https://www.eeas.europa.eu/eeas/myanmar-joint-ministerial-statement-marking-5th-anniversary-myanmar-military%E2%80%99s-attack-against

Federal Foreign Office of Germany (2022) Federal foreign office on the fifth anniversary of the attacks against Rohingya communities in Myanmar and the refugee crisis they triggered. https://www.auswaertiges-amt.de/en/newsroom/news/-/2548384

Gepp MGM (2021) The road not taken: failure to protect from atrocity crimes in Myanmar. Groningen J Int Law 9(1):78–100

Glanville L (2021) Sharing responsibility: the history and future of protection from atrocities. Princeton University Press, Princeton

Global Justice Center (2020) Press releases: Myanmar files second report to world court on compliance with order to protect Rohingya. https://www.globaljusticecenter.net/press-center/press-releases/1392-myanmar-files-second-report-to-world-court-on-compliance-with-order-to-protect-rohingya

Global Magnitsky Human Rights Accountability Act (S. 284) (2016). https://www.congress.gov/bill/114th-congress/senate-bill/284/text

Governments of Canada & The Netherlands (2020) Joint statement of Canada and the Kingdom of the Netherlands regarding intention to intervene in The Gambia v. Myanmar case at the International Court of Justice. https://www.government.nl/documents/diplomatic-statements/2020/09/02/joint-statement-of-canada-and-the-kingdom-of-the-netherlands-regarding-intention-to-intervene-in-the-gambia-v.-myanmar-case-at-the-international-court-of-justice

Governments of Canada & Netherlands (2022) Joint statement of Canada and the Kingdom of the Netherlands regarding today's decision of the International Court of Justice in the Rohingya genocide case between The Gambia and Myanmar

Government of the Republic of the Gambia (2019) Application instituting proceedings and request for provisional measures. Application of the convention on the prevention and punishment of the crime of Genocide (the Gambia v. Myanmar)

Government of the United Kingdom (2022) Fifth anniversary of the Rohingya crisis in Myanmar: UK statement. https://www.gov.uk/government/news/uk-statement-on-the-5th-anniversary-of-the-rohingya-crisis

Government of the Maldives (2020) Speech: statement by his excellency Abdulla Shahid Minister of Foreign Affairs of the Republic of Maldives at the high level segment of the 43rd session of the United Nations Human Rights Council. https://www.gov.mv/en/news-and-communications/statement-by-his-excellency-abdulla-shahid-minister-of-foreign-affairs-of-the-republic-of-maldives

Government of Ukraine (2022) Application instituting proceedings. Dispute relating to allegations of Genocide (Ukraine v. Russian Federation), the International Court of Justice

Huneeus A (2013) International criminal law by other means: The Quasi-Criminal Jurisdiction of the Human Rights Courts. Am J Int Law 107(1):1–44

International Court of Justice (1984) Order. Military and paramilitary activities in and against Nicaragua (Nicaragua v. United States of America), declaration of intervention

International Court of Justice (2007) Judgment. Application of the convention on the prevention and punishment of the crime of Genocide (Bosnia and Herzegovina v. Serbia and Montenegro) Merits

International Court of Justice (2011) Judgment. Application of the international convention on the elimination of all forms of racial discrimination (Georgia v. Russian Federation), preliminary objections

International Court of Justice (2015) Judgment. Case concerning application of the convention on the prevention and punishment of the crime of Genocide (Croatia v. Serbia) merits

International Court of Justice (2019) Judgment. Certain Iranian Assets (Islamic Republic of Iran v. United States of America) preliminary objections

International Court of Justice (2021) Order. Application of the convention on the prevention and punishment of the crime of Genocide (the Gambia v. Myanmar)

International Court of Justice (2022) Judgment. Application of the convention on the prevention and punishment of the crime of Genocide, preliminary objections (the Gambia v. Myanmar).

International Court of Justice Press Release (2020) Press Release No. 2020/38

International Court of Justice Press Release (2022a) Press Release No. 2022a/11

International Court of Justice Press Release (2022b) Press Release No. 2022b/28

International Criminal Court Official Journal Publication (2016) Memorandum of understanding between the international criminal court and the Inter-American Court of Human Rights. ICC-PRES/17-01-16. https://www.icc-cpi.int/sites/default/files/iccdocs/oj/MoU_CR_En.pdf

International Criminal Tribunal for the Former Yugoslavia (1998) Prosecutor v. Anto Furundzija, 'Judgment', Trial Chamber, IT-95-17/1-T

International Criminal Tribunal for the Former Yugoslavia (2016) Prosecutor v. Radovan Karadžić, 'Judgment', trial chamber, IT-95-5/18-T

Islam MR (2022) The Gambia v. Myanmar: an analysis of the ICJ's decision on jurisdiction under the Genocide convention. ASIL Insights 26(9):1–7

Islam MR, Muquim N (2020) The Gambia v. Myanmar at the I.C.J.: Good samaritans testing state responsibility for atrocities on the Rohingya. California Western Int J 51(1):77–131

Kapucu VT (2022) The Rohingya of Myanmar: R2P, international justice and accountability. In: Ercan PG (ed) The responsibility to protect twenty years on: rhetoric and implementation. Palgrave Macmillan, Cham, pp 221–243

Karazsia ZA (2018) An unfulfilled promise: the Genocide convention and the obligation of prevention. J Strat Secur 11(4):20–31

Kassim YR (2014) The geopolitics of intervention: Asia and the responsibility to protect. Springer, Singapore

Khan B (2022) Complexities and challenges in reconciling international human rights with international criminal law: an introduction. In: Human rights and international criminal law. Brill, Leiden, pp XXII-XXXIV

Kittichaisaree K (2022) The Rohingya, justice and international law. Abingdon, Routledge

Kreß C (2007) The international court of justice and the elements of the crime of Genocide. Euro J Int Law 18(4):619–629

LaGrand Case (Germany v. United States of America) (2001) Judgment. International Court of Justice

Lee R (2021) Myanmar's Rohingya Genocide: Identity, history and hate speech. I.B. Tauris, London

Lyngdorf S, Van der Wilt H (2009) Procedural obligations under the European convention on human rights: useful guidelines for the assessment of 'unwillingness' and 'inability' in the context of the complementarity principle. Int Crim Law Rev 9(1):39–75

Manti NP, Islam DNC (2022) Genocide, forced migration, and forced labor: a case study on Rohingya people under international law. In: Bülbül K, Islam MN, Khan MS (eds) Rohingya refugee crisis in Myanmar: ethnic conflict and resolution. Palgrave Macmillan, Singapore

Mcintyre J (2022) The new wave of Article 63 interventions at the international court of justice. EJIL:Talk!. https://www.ejiltalk.org/the-new-wave-of-article-63-interventions-at-the-international-court-of-justice/

Mennecke M (2021) The international court of justice and the responsibility to protect: learning from the case of The Gambia v Myanmar. Glob Respons Protect 13:324–348

Messmer A (2021) Rohingya Refugees Sue Meta for $150B, say failure to stop hate speech led to Genocide. Newsweek. https://www.newsweek.com/rohingya-refugees-sue-meta-150b-say-failure-stop-hate-speech-led-genocide-1656988

Mettraux G (2009) The law of command responsibility. Oxford University Press, Oxford; New York

Ministry of Foreign Affairs of the Maldives (2020) News: Maldives welcomes the joint statement by Canada and the Kingdom of the Netherlands announcing their intention to intervene in The

References

Gambia v. Myanmar case at the International Court of Justice. https://www.gov.mv/en/news-and-communications/maldives-welcomes-the-joint-statement-by-canada-and-the-kingdom-of-the-netherlands-announcing-their-intention-to-intervene-in-the-gambia-v-myanmar-case-at-the-international-court-of-justice

Ministry of International Cooperation of the Government of Republic of the Myanmar (2022) "Press Statement" judgement of the international court of justice (ICJ) on the preliminary objections raised by Myanmar. https://myanmar.gov.mm/home

Murad N (2019) Awkward exchanges as trump meets religious persecution survivors – Video. The Guardian. https://www.theguardian.com/global/video/2019/jul/19/where-is-that-exactly-donald-trump-asks-rohingya-refugee-seeking-us-help-video

Nachemson A (2021) Justice in the balance as UN considers recognition question. Frontier Myanmar. https://www.frontiermyanmar.net/en/justice-in-the-balance-as-un-considers-recognition-question/

National Unity Government (2021) Press Statement, 1/2021. https://gov.nugmyanmar.org/2021/05/30/press-statement-1-2021/

Nishikawa Y (2020) The reality of protecting the Rohingya: an inherent limitation of the responsibility to protect. Asian Secur 16(1):90–106

Nollkaemper A (2003) Concurrence between individual responsibility and state responsibility in international law. Int Compar Law Q 52(3):615–640

Pérez-León-Acevedo J, Pinto TA (2021) Disentangling law and religion in the Rohingya case at the international criminal court. Nordic J Human Rights 39(4):458–480

Pillai P (2019) The Gambia v Myanmar at the international court of justice: points of interest in the application. Opinio Juris. http://opiniojuris.org/2019/11/13/the-gambia-v-myanmar-at-the-international-court-of-justice-points-of-interest-in-the-application/

Pillai P (2021) Myanmar Coup d'état – implications for international justice. Opinio Juris. http://opiniojuris.org/2021/02/11/myanmar-coup-detat-implications-for-international-justice/

Pillai P (2022) The Gambia v. Myanmar and Ukraine v. Russian Federation: a tale of two cases at the international court of justice. Opinio Juris. https://opiniojuris.org/2022/07/14/the-gambia-v-myanmar-and-ukraine-v-russian-federation-a-tale-of-two-cases-at-the-international-court-of-justice/

Pre-Trial Chamber III of the International Criminal Court (2019) Decision Pursuant to Article 15 of the Rome Statute on the authorisation of an investigation into the situation in the People's Republic of Bangladesh/Republic of the Union of Myanmar. ICC-01/19-27

Ractcliffe R (2020) Amal Clooney to pursue Rohingya case at The Hague. The Guardian. https://www.theguardian.com/world/2020/feb/27/amal-clooney-to-pursue-rohingya-case-at-the-hague

Ramsden M (2021) Accountability for crimes against the Rohingya: strategic litigation in the international court of justice. Harvard Negot Law Rev 26(2):153–191

Ramsden M, Gledhill K (2019) Defining strategic litigation. Civ Justice Q 38(4):407–426

Reid NL (2005) Bridging the conceptual chasm: superior responsibility as the missing link between state and individual responsibility under international law. Leiden J Int Law 18(4):795–828

Renshaw C (2021) Myanmar on Trial: is the country's military on the run from international law?', Asia and the Pacific Policy Society Policy Forum. https://www.policyforum.net/myanmar-on-trial/

Republic of the Union of Myanmar (2021) Preliminary objections of the Republic of the Union of Myanmar. Application of the convention on the prevention and punishment of the crime of Genocide (the Gambia v. Myanmar). International Court of Justice

Republic of the Union of Myanmar National Unity Government (2022) Announcement (2/2022) – Myanmar withdraws all preliminary objections to the international court of justice hearing on the Genocide Case. https://gov.nugmyanmar.org/2022/02/01/announcement-2-2022-myanmar-withdraws-all-preliminary-objections-to-the-international-court-of-justice-hearing-on-the-genocide-case/

Rodman KA (2011) Duty to prosecute. In: Chatterjee DK (ed) Encyclopedia of global justice. Springer, Berlin

Roht-Arriaza N (1990) State responsibility to investigate and prosecute grave human rights violations in international law. Calif Law Rev 78(2):449–513

Rome Statute of the International Criminal Court (1998) United Nations Treaty Series 2187(38544):3–158.

Schabas WA (2011) Synergy or fragmentation? International criminal law and the European convection on human rights. J Int Crim Justice 9(3):609–632

Schabas WA (2018) Prevention of crimes against humanity. J Int Crim Justice 16(4):705–728

Schabas WA (2022) Preventing Genocide and the Ukraine/Russia Case. EJIL Talk!. https://www.ejiltalk.org/preventing-genocide-and-the-ukraine-russia-case/

Schiffbauer B (2018) The duty to prevent Genocide under international law: naming and shaming as a measure of prevention. Genocide Stud Prevent Int J 12(3):83–94

Sebastian S (2021) The pitfalls of international justice in Myanmar: Will threats of international criminal prosecutions against the junta's leaders make compromise more likely – or less? The Diplomat/ https://thediplomat.com/2021/04/the-pitfalls-of-international-justice-in-myanmar/

Separate Opinion of Judge Cançado Trindade (2020) Order. Application of the convention on the prevention and punishment of the crime of Genocide (the Gambia v. Myanmar). International Court of Justice

Separate Opinion of Vide-President Judge Xue (2020) Order. Application of the convention on the prevention and punishment of the crime of Genocide (the Gambia v. Myanmar). International Court of Justice

Shubin G & Radhakrishnan A (2021) Beyond the coup in Myanmar: a crisis born from impunity. Just Security. https://www.justsecurity.org/76182/beyond-the-coup-in-myanmar-a-crisis-born-from-impunity/

Simpson A (2022) Myanmar's Genocide overshadowed by Ukraine. East Asia Forum. https://www.eastasiaforum.org/2022/10/05/myanmars-genocide-overshadowed-by-ukraine

Spadaro A (2020) The situation in the People's Republic of Bangladesh/Republic of the Union of Myanmar decision to authorize investigation (I.C.C.) and the Gambia V. Myanmar order for provisional measures (I.C.J.). Int Legal Mater 59(4):616–693

Special Advisory Council for Myanmar (2022) Disgraceful ICJ decision irresponsible and unnecessary delay to justice. https://specialadvisorycouncil.org/wp-content/uploads/2022/02/SAC-M-PR-ICJ-Hearings-ENGLISH.pdf

Spokesman for the UN Secretary General (2020) Statement attributable to the spokesman for the secretary-general - on the international court of justice order in the case "The Gambia vs. Myanmar". https://www.un.org/sg/en/content/sg/statement/2020-01-23/statement-attributable-the-spokesman-for-the-secretary-general-the-international-court-of-justice-order-the-case-the-gambia-vs-myanmar

Statute of the International Court of Justice (1945) Treaties and Other International Agreements of the United States of America 3:1179–1195.

Tams CJ (2014) Article I. In: Tams CJ, Berster L, Schiffbauer B (eds) Convention on the prevention and punishment of the crime of Genocide: a commentary. Munich, Oxford, Baden-Baden, C.H. Beck, Hart, Nomos

Towey H (2021) Facebook is fighting to keep records of its own investigation into the genocide of Rohingya Muslims in Myanmar out of court. Business Insider. https://www.businessinsider.com/facebook-mark-zuckerberg-myanmar-rohingya-genocide-case-whistleblower-2021-10

Trindade AAC (2020) Conceptual constructions: responsibility for international crimes and universal jurisdiction. In: International law for humankind. Brill, Leiden, Boston, pp 367–390

UN Doc. A/56/10 (2001)

UN Doc. A/70/621–S/2015/978 (2015)

UN Doc. A/74/10 (2019)

UN Doc. A/75/L.85/Rev.1 (2021)

UN Doc. A/C.3/76/L.30 Rev.1 (2021)

References

UN Doc. A/CN.4/SER.A/2001/Add.1 (2001)

UN Doc. A/HRC/31/13 (2015)

UN Doc. A/HRC/39/CRP.2 (2018)

UN Doc. A/HRC/S-29/L.1 (2021)

UN Doc. A/RES/180(II) (1947)

UN Doc. A/RES/60/1 (2005)

UN Doc. A/RES/75/287 (2021)

UN Doc. S/PRST/2021/5 (2021)

UN Doc. SC/14430 (2021)

U.S. Department of State (2022) Secretary Antony J. Blinken at the United States Holocaust Memorial Museum. https://www.state.gov/secretary-antony-j-blinken-at-the-united-states-holocaust-memorial-museum/

U.S. Department of Treasury (2022) Press release: treasury sanctions military leaders, military-affiliated cronies and businesses, and a military unit prior to armed forces day in Burma. https://home.treasury.gov/news/press-releases/jy0679

U.S. District Court, District of Columbia (2021) Order. In re Application Pursuant to 28 U.S.C. § 1782 of The Republic of the Gambia. Petitioner, v. Facebook, Inc. Respondent, Civil Action No. 20-mc-36-JEB-ZMF

U.S. Embassy and Consulates in China (2021) Secretary Blinken on the The Signing of the Uyghur Forced Labor Prevention Act. https://china.usembassy-china.org.cn/secretary-blinken-on-the-the-signing-of-the-uyghur-forced-labor-prevention-act%E2%80%AF/

U.S. President Donald J. Trump (2017) Executive Order 13818 of December 20, 2017: blocking the property of persons involved in serious human rights abuse or corruption. Federal Register 82(246):60839–60843

U.S. President Joseph R. Biden Jr. (2021) Executive Order 14014 of February 10, 2021: blocking property with respect to the situation in Burma. Federal Register 86(28):9429–9432

Uddin N (2022) Voices of the Rohingya people : a Case of Genocide, Ethnocide and 'Subhuman' Life. Palgrave Macmillan, Cham

United Nations Commission of Experts (1995) The final report on the evidence of grave breaches of the Geneva conventions and other violations of international humanitarian law committed in the territory of the former Yugoslavia. UN Doc. S/1994/674 (1994). https://www.icty.org/x/file/About/OTP/un_commission_of_experts_report1994_en.pdf

United Nations Human Rights Office of the High Commissioner (2017) Zeid Ra'ad Al Hussein: opening statement by Zeid Ra'ad Al Hussein: darker and more dangerous: high commissioner updates the human rights council on human rights issues in 40 countries

Verbatim Record of the International Court of Justice (2019a), CR 2019a/18

Verbatim Record of the International Court of Justice (2019b), CR 2019b/19

Verbatim Record of the International Court of Justice (2022a) CR 2022/1

Verbatim Record of the International Court of Justice (2022b) CR 2022b/2

Verbatim Record of the International Court of Justice (2022c) CR 2022c/5

Weller M (2022) Is the ICJ at risk of providing cover for the alleged Genocide in Myanmar?. EJIL Talk! https://www.ejiltalk.org/is-the-icj-at-risk-of-providing-cover-for-the-alleged-genocide-in-myanmar

White House (2021) Statement by President Joe Biden on Armenian remembrance day. https://www.whitehouse.gov/briefing-room/statements-releases/2021/04/24/statement-by-president-joe-biden-on-armenian-remembrance-day/

Wolf J (2016) Individual responsibility and collective state responsibility for international crimes: separate or complementary concepts under international law?. In: Fitzmaurice M, Okowa P (eds) Prosecuting international crimes: a multidisciplinary approach. Leiden, Brill

Zaman M (2021) After the UN Resolution on Rohingya Crisis, what comes next?'. The Daily Star. https://www.thedailystar.net/views/opinion/news/after-the-un-resolution-rohingya-crisis-what-comes-next-2900446

Chapter 5
The Legitimacy, Effectiveness, and Efficiency of the ICC

Abstract There have long been doubts about the viability and productivity of the International Criminal Court (ICC). At one point, African countries were actively hostile to it, owing to a perceived inequity of the African continent being overly represented in its investigations and prosecutions. Against this backdrop, it is significant that the ICC's Office of the Prosecutor (OTP) launched investigations into the problems of Asian countries such as Bangladesh/Myanmar and Afghanistan. However, both of these have been met with strong opposition from Non-State Oarties, owing to of the potential for criminal charges involving same, raising the question of what impact this may have on the legitimacy of the ICC. This chapter critically examines the Bangladesh/Myanmar situation before the ICC from the perspective of the latter's legitimacy in the course of reviewing that very legitimacy, as well as the ICC's effectiveness and efficiency.

5.1 The Meaning and Indicators of the ICC's Legitimacy

5.1.1 Legitimacy Discourse in International Law

Although traditional international law may occasionally demand legitimacy on the part of governments to access the arenas of global diplomacy in the capacity of sovereign States,[1] the notion of legitimacy itself in contrast to that of legality has only recently begun to receive significant attention in the international community.[2] The long-time indifference to legitimacy in the context of international society and

---

[1] *See* Falk (2012), p. 17.

[2] Taking the last five years as an example, a number of publications dealing with the issue of legitimacy in international law have been published, including: Wolfrum, Röben (2008); Meyer (2009); Murphy (2009), pp. 1147–1156; Brunnée, Toope (eds.), (2010); Falk (2012).

This chapter first appeared as Hitomi Takemura, "An Analysis of Legitimacy Discourses in International Criminal Justice through Comparative Research on the ICC and the ECCC," *the Journal of International Law and Diplomacy*, vol. 112, no. 1 (2013), pp. 56–79.

© The Author(s), under exclusive license to Springer Nature Singapore Pte Ltd. 2023
H. Takemura, *The Rohingya Crisis and the International Criminal Court*,
https://doi.org/10.1007/978-981-99-2734-0_5

international law can be attributed to several factors. First, the structure of international society, as opposed to that of domestic society, may not provide individuals with a sense of relevant authority or legal constraint.[3] Second, traditional international law consists mainly of consensual obligations and bilateral treaties, and such a "consensualist basis of obligation has tended to moot the issue of legitimacy."[4] Third, international institutions are regarded as exercising little authority.[5] The end of the Cold War strengthened the role of the UN; thus, there emerged the need to discuss the legitimacy of the use of force in light of the UN Charter, as well as of the Security Council. Fourth, the interests of international society have been gradually shifting from the protection of State sovereignty to that of individual human rights, and for better or for worse, this shift has been used to attempt to justify some humanitarian interventions, as typified by the North Atlantic Treaty Organization (NATO) intervention in Kosovo.[6] The case has often been made that "legality could be challenged by the ethical, humanitarian or political demands of legitimacy."[7] It is in this atmosphere that the aforementioned discussion regarding the legitimacy of international law and international institutions began.

Such humanitarian demands for legitimacy partly account for the advent of the Nuremberg and Tokyo tribunals, and thus, legitimacy discourse in international law is in some ways related to legitimacy discourse in international criminal justice. One of the features of the latter relates to the trend of international organizations having direct influence on individuals.[8] In other words, as most international criminal tribunals and the ICC are international institutions by definition, awareness of legitimacy in international law can also be shared by the aforementioned legitimacy discourse in international criminal justice. The enabling of the Security Council following the end of the Cold War fostered practices for the establishment of international criminal tribunals by the Council as its subsidiary organs, as well as so-called hybrid tribunals set up by agreement between the UN and the relevant States on the initiative of the Council.[9] The resulting precedents attracted controversy over the legitimacy of the Council and the legality of its actions.

---

[3] Bodansky (1999), p. 597.

[4] Ibid.

[5] Ibid. *See also* Kumm (2004), p. 911; Koskenniemi (2011), p. 103. Koskenniemi wrote: "During the Cold War, issues of legitimacy and justifiability such as those raised in this memorandum could not arise as it was clear that there was no such 'system of general government' to which they could be dealt by reference."

[6] It is also well known that the Independent International Commission on Kosovo "concludes that NATO military intervention was illegal but legitimate." The Independent International Commission on Kosovo (2000), p. 4.

[7] Popovski, Turner (2012), p. 439.

[8] Apart from international criminal institutions, the impact of international organizations on private persons can be seen in the examples of economic sanctions imposed by the United Nations Security Council, large-scale infrastructure projects financed by the World Bank, and decisions made by the Settlement Body of the World Trade Organization. *See* Sato (2009), p. 16.

[9] For the Special Court for Sierra Leone, UN Doc. S/RES/1315 (14 August 2000); for the Special Tribunal for Lebanon, UN Doc. S/RES/1664 (29 March 2006).

5.1.2 Legitimacy Discourse in International Criminal Law

Three significant periods may be identified in the history of legitimacy discourse in international criminal justice: (i) "illegal but legitimate," as seen before Nuremberg and Tokyo; (ii) having equated legitimacy with legality, indifference to distinctions between these; and (iii) the future of international criminal justice, which should involve closing the gaps between legality and legitimacy.

The meanings and indicatives of "legitimacy" and "legitimate" have drawn much attention in connection to international criminal justice. This has been true from the very beginning of the modern history of individual criminal responsibility in international law, namely, the trials before the International Military Tribunal (Nuremberg tribunal) and the International Military Tribunal for the Far East (Tokyo tribunal). There are two features of the early history of legitimacy discourse in international criminal justice. First, the Nuremberg and Tokyo tribunals have long been criticized as "victor's justice," and thereby their legitimacies have been under attack. As applicable to any international criminal institution including the ICC, "the one-sidedness of the prosecution did not contribute to strengthening the legitimacy of the trials."[10] Second, the legality of the tribunals was more severely criticized than their legitimacy. One reason why the Nuremberg tribunal's legitimacy has not been seriously questioned lies in its Charter,[11] specifically Article 3, which provides that "Neither the Tribunal, its members nor their alternates can be challenged by the prosecution, or by the Defendants or their Counsel [...]."[12] Another reason is that bringing the Nazi leaders to trial in the name of the Allies is obviously more legitimate than summary execution.[13] In other words, this is as per the aforementioned case of legitimacy discourse in international law following the end of the Cold War.

Even though international criminal tribunals always uphold their own legitimacy and legality, the issues are raised constantly. Before the Tokyo tribunal, the defense challenged its legality and jurisdiction on the grounds that there was no authority of the Allies acting through the Supreme Commander to include crimes against peace in its Charter and *ex post facto* legislation.[14] In rejecting this contention, the Tokyo tribunal ruled that the law of the Charter was decisive and binding, and also referred to the Nuremberg judgment's reasoning,[15] holding that it "prefers to express its

---

[10] Tomuschat (2006), p. 833.

[11] Schabas (2006), p. 50.

[12] United Nations (1945).

[13] Popovski (2012), p. 395.

[14] Majority Judgment, reprinted in Boister, Cryer (2008), p. 80.

[15] "The Charter is not an arbitrary exercise of power on the part of the victorious nations but is the expression of international law existing at the time of creation [...] The maxim 'nullum crimen sine lege' is not a limitation of sovereignty but is in general a principle of justice. To assert that it is unjust to punish those who in the defence of treaties and assurances have attacked neighboring states without warning is obviously untrue for in such circumstances the attacker must know that he is doing wrong, and so far from it being unjust to punish him, it would be unjust if his wrong were allowed to go unpunished." ibid., pp. 80–81.

116   5 The Legitimacy, Effectiveness, and Efficiency of the ICC

unqualified adherence to the relevant opinions of the Nuremberg Tribunal [...]."[16]
The Tokyo tribunal cited the following passage from Nuremberg Tribunal Judgment
in addressing the question of its own legality: "The Charter is not an arbitrary exercise
of power on the part of the victorious nations but is the expression of international
law existing at the time of its creation. [...] The maxim *nullum crimen sine lege* is
not a limitation of sovereignty but is in general a principle of justice. To assert that
it is unjust to punish those who in defiance of treaties and assurances have attacked
neighboring States without warning is obviously untrue for in such circumstances
the attacker must know that he is doing wrong, and so far from it being unjust to
punish him, it would be unjust if his wrong were allowed to go unpunished."[17]

To be more specific, issues of legitimacy and legality of international criminal
tribunals often appear undifferentiated in legitimacy discourse before international
criminal institutions, as the issue of the legitimacy of the parent organ of an international criminal institution is sometimes seen as identical with the question of
the legality of the international criminal institution itself. Forty-five years after the
Nuremberg and Tokyo tribunals, the end of the Cold War enabled the UN Security
Council to establish tribunals for the genocidal situations in the former Yugoslavia
and Rwanda. It is well known that Duško Tadić, the first defendant to stand trial at the
ICTY, questioned the legality of the Tribunal, to wit, the legitimacy of the act by the
Security Council, as a political organ of the UN, to establish an international criminal
tribunal. The Trial Chamber of the ICTY referred to "legitimacy of creation" when it
discussed "the legality of the creation of the International Tribunal."[18] Subsequently,
the ICTY Appeals Chamber denied Tadić's challenge, ruling "that the International
Tribunal is empowered to pronounce upon the plea challenging the legality of the
establishment of the International Tribunal."[19] The chamber thus chose the term
"legality," rather than "legitimacy," in its interlocutory decision. When faced with a
similar challenge in Kanyabashi, the Trial Chamber II of the ICTR used neither term
when it rejected the argument that it was empowered to review Security Council decisions, ruling that "the Security Council has a wide margin of discretion in deciding
when and where there exists a threat to international peace and security. By their
very nature, however, such discretionary assessments are not justifiable since they
involve the consideration of a number of social, political and circumstantial factors
which cannot be weighed and balanced objectively by this Trial Chamber."[20] No
appeal was filed.

It would appear to be more difficult for any defendant to successfully challenge the
legality of their trials at least in front of the ICTY or ICTR after Tadić and Kanyabashi.
The reason is that the Judges of the ICTY and the ICTR adopted Rules of Procedure
and Evidence (RPE), equivalent to the aforementioned Article 3 of the Nuremberg

---

[16] Ibid., p. 81.

[17] International Military Tribunal (1947), pp. 216–217.

[18] International Criminal Tribunal for the Former Yugoslavia (1995a), para. 40.

[19] International Criminal Tribunal for the Former Yugoslavia (1995b), para. 146.

[20] International Criminal Tribunal for Rwanda (1997), para. 20.

5.1 The Meaning and Indicators of the ICC's Legitimacy

Charter, to prevent the defense from raising such issues.[21] In 2000, Rule 72 (D) was introduced to both the ICTY and the ICTR in order to prevent challenges to what was termed "jurisdiction," but were in fact challenges to legality.[22] Rule 90 (E) of the Special Tribunal for Lebanon (STL) RPE is almost identical to Rule 72 (D),[23] and it too acts to block similar challenges. Motions were raised before the Special Court for Sierra Leone (SCSL), which was established by agreement between Sierra Leone and the UN, which challenged its jurisdiction and legality as well. While this tribunal did not have rules preventing such motions, the Court rebutted such arguments by skillfully describing the Special Court as "a *sui generis* organ."[24] The term also appeared in the Report of the Secretary-General on the Establishment of a Special Court for Sierra Leone.[25]

Theoretically, the ICC is less problematic regarding the victor's justice problem, given that it is a permanent institution. In practice, both geographical imbalances between States Parties and the regional overrepresentation on the part countries which the OTP has targeted for investigation has discontented some. Such dissatisfaction is derived from a sense of selective justice, analogous to the abovementioned victor's justice criticism for the Nuremberg and Tokyo tribunals. There is an insufficient sense of universal criminal justice, giving rise to a feeling of unfairness in its place.[26]

Whereas the Nuremberg and Tokyo tribunals may be regarded as good examples of a disconnection between legitimacy and legality, the creation of the ICC was intended to permanently bridge this gap.[27] In other words, the ICC is expected to take "legitimacy" seriously, while both the ICC's and its States Parties' abidance by stringent legal procedures is required under the Rome Statute, especially the

---

[21] *See* Rule 72 (D) of the International Criminal Tribunal for the Former Yugoslavia Rules of Procedure and Evidence, as amended 28 August 2012, IT/32/Rev.47 and the ICTR Rules of Procedure and Evidence, as amended 13 May 2015, ITR/3/Rev.1, respectively. The Rules are almost identical.

[22] Special Tribunal for Lebanon (2012), para. 31.

[23] Special Tribunal for Lebanon, Rules of Procedure and Evidence, amended on 8 February 2012, STL/BD/2009/01/Rev.4. Rule 90 (E) of the STL RPE stipulates, "For the purpose of paragraphs (A) (i) and (B) (i), a motion challenging jurisdiction refers exclusively to a motion that challenges an indictment on the ground that it does not relate to the subject-matter, temporal or territorial jurisdiction of the Tribunal, including that it does not relate to the Hariri Attack or an attack of a similar nature and gravity that is connected to it in accordance with the principles of criminal justice."

[24] The Appeals Chamber of the SCSL repeatedly argued that "the Security Council had not abandoned its primary responsibility for the maintenance of international peace and security, but rather, had created a *sui generis* organ to exercise judicial functions that the Security Council could not exercise itself." Special Tribunal for Lebanon (2004a), para. 5; Special Tribunal for Sierra Leone (2004b), paras. 21–22.

[25] UN Doc. S/2000/915 (4 October 2000), para. 9.

[26] In a similar vein but more radically, Brown attacks legitimacy of the ICC by casting a doubt as to "whether there exists a sufficient global consensus on basic values to support the extension to the international human rights regime that an ICC would entail." For Brown, only in Europe was there an effective enforcement mechanism for human rights. Brown (2002), p. 222.

[27] Popovski, Turner (2012), pp. 448–449.

complementarity principle.[28] It is only natural to hold international criminal institutions to such high standards, as the freedom of individuals should be restricted only in limited instances, such as by means of a judgment passed in accordance with a lawful process, irrespective of international or domestic spheres.[29]

5.1.3 The Meaning of Legitimacy

The year 2022 marks the ICC's twentieth anniversary. The institution has entered what we might call adolescence, and as such, its effectiveness and legitimacy will be increasingly questioned. However, neither concept has a fixed definition in international law, and different actors have discussed them in various ways thus far. For instance, former ICC Chief Prosecutor Fatou Bensouda described the ICC as having "gained a status and legitimacy as a crucial actor on the international scene regarding peace and justice."[30] At the Eighteenth Session of the Assembly of States Parties to the Rome Statute, the Japanese delegation noted that "[i]n order to strengthen the legitimacy of the ICC, what is important is to increase the number of States Parties, and not to increase the number of cases that attract political attention."[31]

These are just a few of the ways in which legitimacy on the part of international criminal institutions has been and continues to be discussed. Such discussion may be divided into the following categories, for convenience's sake: (i) democratic legitimacy; (ii) formal legitimacy; and (iii) social legitimacy. While the first category might fit into the second, those who argue against the democratic legitimacy of international criminal institutions tend to evaluate it from the perspective of the democratic legitimacy of a national government. The last two categories of the concept of legitimacy appear to introduce inherent aspects of an international legal system to which international criminal law also belongs. Referring back to the first category, if one simply applies the notion of legitimacy of State authority rooted in national domestic governance to international law, without considering the intrinsic difficulties of enhancing said democratic legitimacy of international criminal institutions, then international law consequently lacks legitimacy, with the attendant risk of undermining constitutional lawmaking processes.[32] No one can escape the cliché

---

[28] Article 21(3) of the Rome Statute requires that "The application and interpretation of law pursuant to this article must be consistent with internationally recognized human rights,"while the principle of complementarity is prescribed in article 1 and preambular paragraph 10. Rome Statute of the International Criminal Court (1998) 2187 UNTS 90.

[29] See Article 9(1) of the International Covenant on Civil and Political Rights: "Everyone has the right to liberty and security of person. No one shall be subjected to arbitrary arrest or detention. *No one shall be deprived of his liberty except on such grounds and in accordance with such procedures as are established by law* (emphasis added)." G.A. Res. 2200A (XXI), 21 U.N. GAOR Supp. (No. 16) at 52, UN. Doc. A/6316 (1966), 999 UNTS. 1.

[30] The Office of the Prosecutor of the International Criminal Court (2012).

[31] Japan Statement (2019).

[32] See Young (2003), p. 529.

5.1 The Meaning and Indicators of the ICC's Legitimacy

that there is neither government nor *demos* in international society, that latter being part and parcel of democracy in the domestic arena.[33] Accordingly, this claim may also refute these attacks on democratic legitimacy. Although the domestic analogy of the concept of democracy poses some difficulties, the model is not completely unrelated to the condition that international institutions may enhance their legitimacy by abiding by such procedural criteria common to domestic democratic principles as accountability, consent of participants, and transparency.[34] Consent-based legitimacy is arguably most common in relations between international organizations and their member states because such relations are based not on a mere hypothetical social contract, but on binding treaties.[35] At present, however, the ICC continues to open investigations into situations potentially concerning Non-States Parties, and there is scope to consider whether the consensual justification is valid in that sense as well.

The rest of this chapter considers the aforementioned concepts of democratic, procedural, and social legitimacy, as propounded by scholars and States alike. It is useful and generally accepted to draw distinctions between procedural (otherwise known as legal, formal, input-oriented,[36] or normative) and social (otherwise known as sociological, substantive, empirical, perceptive, output-oriented, or outcome-oriented) aspects of legitimacy.[37] The thrust of procedural legitimacy is that an authority can be considered legitimate because it exercises its powers through procedures that are seen as adequate or fair.[38] This theory of legitimacy appraises authority in terms of general criteria set out by the theory's proponents. When one speaks of the legal or normative legitimacy of an authority, they sometimes deal virtually with legality, and this normative aspect of legality overlaps with the question of legality. Nonetheless, normative legitimacy, as described above, is not identical with legality to the extent that legitimacy discourse is more than the issue of legality, even though they are taken to be cognate.[39] While procedural fairness is undoubtedly a

---

[33] Weiler (2004), p. 560, where he argues that: "The international system form of governance with government and without demos means there is no purchase, no handle whereby we can graft democracy as we understand it from Statal settings on to the international arena."

[34] Buchanan, Keohane (2008), pp. 25–62.

[35] Sato (2009), p. 14.

[36] Scharpf distinguishes between input-oriented and output-oriented legitimizing beliefs: "Input-oriented democratic thought emphasizes 'government by the people.' Political choices are legitimate if and because they reflect the 'will of the people'—that is, if they can be derived from the authentic preferences of the members of the community. By contrast, the output perspective emphasizes 'government for the people.' Here, political choices are legitimate if and because they effectively promote the common welfare of the constituency in question." Scharpt (1999) p. 6.

[37] Weiler (1991), p. 2468; Bodansky (1999), p. 601; Wolfrum (2012), p. 809; Clark (2005), pp. 18–19; Nollkaemper (2001), p. 13.

[38] Wolfrum, *supra* note 15, p. 809.

[39] Müllerson wrote, "Legitimacy is a wider concept than the concept of lawfulness because it includes legality, i.e. lawfulness of norms, institutions, situations (orders) or behavior of various actors. Lawfulness is one, in 'normal' cases the most important, element or aspect, of legitimacy. However, legitimacy is more than simply lawfulness. It includes morality or a sense of fairness or justice. Although ideally these properties have to coincide, if not completely, then at least quite substantially, in practice, they may clash, and in such a case we may indeed be able to say that

120 5 The Legitimacy, Effectiveness, and Efficiency of the ICC

necessary condition for international criminal justice, it is not a sufficient condition and not "convincing enough in itself when the defendant has a strong theory about the illegitimacy of the trial."[40] Therefore, a sociological perspective of legitimacy is also worth consideration. Today, it is even said that the legitimacy of the ICC should be understood in this second sense of the word.[41]

Social legitimacy takes as its focus the belief systems of those subject to that authority.[42] Traced back through the work of Max Weber,[43] such legitimacy is synonymous with perceived legitimacy.[44] As evaluation thereof by its stakeholders tends to be output-oriented, the concept of legitimacy in general, as opposed to legality, is "highly subjective" by nature,[45] with social legitimacy most subjective of all.[46] For those who take legitimacy as "the belief by an actor that a rule or institution ought to be obeyed," social legitimacy has a great deal to do with procedural legitimacy,[47] to the extend that the latter is in fact sublimated into the former, as Popovski shrewdly points out: "Compliance with legal rules helps to confer legitimacy, but the effect is conditioned by the perceived legitimacy of these rules in the circumstances of the time."[48] For the purpose of scrutinizing these factors of legitimacy, however, this book maintains this generally accepted divide between procedural and social legitimacy.

---

something is illegal but legitimate or, vice versa, legal but illegitimate." Müllerson (2008), p. 191. *See also* Clark (2005), p. 210.

[40] Glasius, Meijers (2012), p. 251.

[41] McIntyre (2020), p. 26.

[42] Clark (2005), p. 18.

[43] Weber wrote: "Conduct, especially social conduct, and quite particularly a social relationship, can be oriented on the part of the actors toward their *idea* (*Vorstellung*) of the existence of a *legitimate order*. [...] Today the most common form of legitimacy is the belief in legality, i.e., the acquiescence in enactments which are formally correct and which have been made in the accustomed manner." Weber (1954), pp. 3, 9.

[44] Kotecha (2020), p. 111.

[45] Popovski (2012), p. 389. Hurd also stresses the subjectivity of the concept. Hurd (1999), p. 381.

[46] *See* Ramji-Nogales (2010), p. 12. Koskenniemi notes that "The perspective is control. The normative framework is in place. Action has been decided. The only remaining question is how to reach the target with minimal cost. This is where legitimacy is needed—to ensure a warm feeling in the audience." Koskenniemi (2007), p. 16.

[47] Hurd (2007), p. 30.

[48] Popovski (2012), p. 389. A similar point has been made by Suchman, writing that: "[l]egitimacy is a perception or assumption in that it represents a reaction of observers to the organization as they see it; thus, legitimacy is possessed objectively, yet created subjectively." Suchman (1995), p. 574.

5.1 The Meaning and Indicators of the ICC's Legitimacy

5.1.4 Legitimacy of the ICC

5.1.4.1 Democratic Legitimacy

The issues surrounding the democratic legitimacy of international institutions may be distilled into whether international criminal institutions are established democratically, and whether these institutions function democratically once established, which particularly raises the question of transparency.[49] The first question relates to consent legitimacy, as described above.[50] In answer, it appears that the ICC was founded through democratic procedures,[51] as it was established by treaty, videlicet, the Rome Statute, and because fully 120 States took part in the Rome Conference at which that statute was adopted. As of this writing, 24 years later, there are 123 signatories to the Rome Statute. However, consent legitimacy in this context is derived from the consent of States and not the citizens of those States, as per the general process of making international law.[52] Consent legitimacy in the meaning of domestic democratic legitimacy then depends on the degree of democracy in each domestic society for the internalization of international norms in their respective legal systems.

Regarding the second question, the ICC is criticized as lacking a democratic linkage with those Non-State Party nationals over whom it exercises authority, based on the principle of territoriality under Article 12(2)(a) of the statute,[53] whereas regarding the exercise of the ICC's jurisdiction over Non-States Parties, in the case of Security Council referrals, it is generally accepted that that the consensual legitimacy of member states to the UN Charter is granted under Article 25 thereof.[54] Counter-arguments have been made, however. For instance, even the US, which has spearheaded the criticism of the democratic deficit of the ICC, adheres to various treaties that require States Parties to prosecute or extradite persons in their territory who are alleged to have committed defined offenses, regardless of their nationality.[55] Another counter-argument holds that the right to a fair trial is far more important

---

[49] Glasius (2012), p. 47.

[50] Cassese described "consent legitimacy" as: "body of a politic, or a domestic or international institution is considered legitimate when the majority of the population, or the majority of the institution's constituency, express a high degree of *consent and approval for it* (emphasis original)." Cassese (2012), p. 492.

[51] Glasius (2012), p. 48.

[52] When Hurd studied the legitimacy of the UN Security Council, he confined himself to the perspective of its legitimacy among states, rather among the citizens of those states. *See* Hurd (2007), p. 9.

[53] Morris (2002), pp. 591–6.

[54] Wallerstein (2015), p. 135; McIntyre (2021), p. 514.

[55] Orentlicher (2003), p. 509. The referenced treaties are the Geneva Convention Relative to the Protection of Civilian Persons in Time of War, Aug. 12, 1949, art. 146, 75 UNTS 287, 386; Convention against Torture and Other Cruel, Inhuman or Degrading Treatment or Punishment, Dec. 10, 1984, arts. 5 & 7, 1465 UNTS 85; International Convention Against the Taking of Hostages, G.A. Res. 146, U.N. GAOR, 34th Sess., Supp. No. 46, at 245, U.N. Doc. A/34/36 (1979); Convention on the Prevention and Punishment of Crimes Against Internationally Protected Persons, Including Diplomatic Agents, arts. 3(2) & 7, 28 U.S.T. 1975, 1979–81; Convention on the Suppression of

than the right to democratic governance, and the assurance of a fair trial is essential for a liberal understanding of democratic legitimacy.[56] Ironically, the cynical and hostile attitudes of Non-States Parties to the ICC arguably undermine the democratic legitimacy of the ICC, as the more universal the ICC becomes, the more democratic the ICC may be.

Apart from the legitimacy of the ICC itself, the democratic legitimacy of the ICC vis-à-vis States Parties is strengthened by the complementarity principle.[57] Under this principle, the ICC may investigate and prosecute core international crimes only when national jurisdictions are genuinely unable or unwilling to do so. While we cannot expect robust democracy and respect for human rights in some States Parties whose situations have come to the attention of the ICC due to this selfsame complementarity principle,[58] conversely, the ICC pressures most States Parties, other than those that refer their own situations to the ICC, to adopt higher standards of due process, fair trial, victim protection, and independence from political pressure, again, by way of the complementarity principle.[59] Thus, while the principle may serve to promote democratic principles among States Parties in theory, there is little evidence of this in practice.

The low degree of democratic legitimacy of the ICC's exercise of jurisdiction over Non-States Parties has become a particular problem in recent years, and it is hoped that the ICC will come up with a convincing explanation for its democratic legitimacy,[60] as failure to do so will not only weigh heavily in its judges, but also impair its very sociological legitimacy. It is suggested, albeit in the context of denial of immunity for heads of State of third countries, that "[w]hile poorly reasoned rulings may not in themselves undermine the short-term deterrent effect of the ICC, there is a real risk that the problematic jurisprudence described above may indirectly affect deterrence negatively by undermining the Court's legitimate authority."[61]

5.1.4.2 Procedural Legitimacy

Procedural legitimacy is said to be the most significant focus of scholarly attention of the ICC's legitimacy.[62] This aspect of legitimacy is also known as "legitimacy of

---

Unlawful Seizure of Aircraft, Dec. 16, 1970, arts. IV & VII, 22 U.S.T. 1641, 1645–46, 860 UNTS 105, 108–09; and the Convention for the Suppression of Unlawful Acts Against the Safety of Civil Aviation, Sept. 23, 1971, arts. 5 & 7, 24 U.S.T. 564, 570–71.

[56] Fichtelberg (2006), pp. 765–785.

[57] The ICC's complementarity principle is enshrined in preambular Paragraph 10 and Article 1 of the Rome Statute. Rome Statute of the International Criminal Court (1998).

[58] Glasius (2012), p. 49.

[59] Popovski (2012), p. 405.

[60] McIntyre (2021), p. 541.

[61] Kjeldgaard-Pedersen (2021), p. 956.

[62] DeGuzman (2018), p. 74.

5.1 The Meaning and Indicators of the ICC's Legitimacy

exercise" or "input legitimacy,"[63] and as such, fairness clearly an important factor thereof.[64] Regarding the ICTY, for example, Judge Theodor Meron noted that fairness and due process rights are the basis of the legitimacy and credibility of the tribunal's proceedings.[65] The right to a fair trial is a key element of human rights protection and serves as a procedural means for safeguarding rule of law.[66] This right requires impartiality, independence, public hearings, and expeditiousness.[67,68] The mechanism of controlling prosecutorial discretion is also important for procedural legitimacy, as prosecutors must exercise their discretionary powers in a nondiscriminatory manner.[69] Other factors relevant to both procedural and democratic legitimacy may include an institution's answerability to a founding authority; the transparency of organs of the institution; and its accountability to the institution's constituency.[70,71] Concerning accountability to the institution's constituency, the ICC allows victim participation through representatives of victims, which enhances the procedural legitimacy of these institutions.[72] However, the difference is that the former may award the victim reparations on an individual or collective basis by means of a trust fund established for the benefit of the victims, and the latter may award only collective and moral reparations to civil parties.[73]

The ICC takes pride in its permanence, impartiality, and adherence to international treaty standards governing the rights of defendants and prisoners under the Rome Statute. The ICC has already overcome its first great challenge, that of securing its procedural legitimacy, which it appears to have maintained, at least in its Trial Chambers. The situation was as follows. In the first case tried at the ICC, against Thomas Lubanga Dyilo, the prosecutor refused to disclose potentially exculpatory evidence. The Trial Chamber ordered a stay, ruling that "the trial process [had] been ruptured to such a degree that it [was] now impossible to piece together the

---

[63] Ibid.

[64] Luban (2010), p. 579.

[65] Meron (2021), pp. 92–93, 185.

[66] Human Rights Committee, General Comment No. 32, UN Doc. CCPR/C/GC/32 (23 August 2007), para. 2.

[67] Ibid. paras. 23, 25 and 27.

[68] For the factor of independence, *see e.g.,* Bellingham (2012). "So the International Criminal Court came into being at a time when the importance of international justice was becoming increasingly recognized. At its heart, the Court is an independent judicial body; and it is this judicial independence that is both the source of its legitimacy and the means by which it dispenses with justice."

[69] Danner A M (2003), p. 536. See also Greenawalt (2007), pp. 583–673; Struett (2009) pp. 107–132; Falligant (2010), pp. 727–751; Greenawalt (2009), pp. 107–162.

[70] Cassese named the legitimacy that takes into account these factors "performance legitimacy." Cassese (2012), p. 493.

[71] There is a counterargument that the responsibility to explain itself to affected communities is not necessarily taken for granted in the pursuit of normal domestic criminal justice. Glasius (2012), p. 46.

[72] *See* Article 68(3) of the Rome Statute and Articles 23, 23bis, 23ter, 23quarter, and 23quinquies of the Internal Rules (Rev. 8), rev. August 3, 2011.

[73] *See* Articles 75 and 77 of the Rome Statute and 23quinquies of the Internal Rules (Rev. 8).

constituent elements of a fair trial."[74] The Lubanga trial was thus the ideal test of the ICC's procedural legitimacy, although the mistake was, of course, unwelcome to begin with, and as indicated above, expeditiousness is also part and parcel of the right to a fair trial.[75]

Turning to impartiality, as a permanent institution upholding the legality principle, the ICC is, in theory, free from the victor's justice problem, apart from the aforementioned situation of governments of States Parties referring themselves to the ICC with malicious intent. In this respect, Article 16 of the Rome Statute grants the Security Council a privileged status that could be interpreted as allowing it to defer investigations and prosecutions indefinitely.[76] The ICC resolution on the crime of aggression at the Kampala Review Conference of the Rome Statute is said to be another source of eroding impartiality on the part of the ICC, as Article 15*bis*(5) of the statute generally excludes jurisdiction over the alleged crime of aggression by Non-States Parties and provides for an opt-out declaration for States Parties,[77] and such jurisdictional exceptions constitute significant limitations that may undermine the Court's legitimacy[78] by the selfsame erosion of its impartiality.

5.1.4.3 Social Legitimacy

Social legitimacy as defined above differs significantly from stakeholder to stakeholder. Stakeholders in international criminal institutions might consist of afflicted populations, perpetrators,[79] States, and the UN. The latter is a particularly important stakeholder in the ICC where matters referred to the Court by the Security Council are concerned. Factors of social legitimacy range from outcomes of prosecution cases and situation selection decisions[80] to the sharing of common goals.[81]

It is apparent that the outcomes of the Prosecutor's situation- and case-selection decisions affect the ICC's social legitimacy among States and eventually could have an impact on the Court's aforementioned procedural legitimacy, i.e., its fairness. For example, in its first decade and more, all ICC cases originated from Africa, a fact that damaged the Court's social legitimacy among parts of its constituency. Even today, all ICC conviction to-date are from Africa. It should be noted, however, that some

---

[74] Trial Chamber I of the International Criminal Court (2008).

[75] *See* Anoushirvani (2010), pp. 213–239.

[76] Article 16 provides that "No investigation or prosecution may be commenced or proceeded with under this Statute for a period of 12 months after the Security Council, in a resolution adopted under Chapter VII of the Charter of the United Nations, has requested the Court to that effect; that request may be renewed by the Council under the same conditions." Rome Statute of the International Criminal Court (1998).

[77] The Assembly of States Parties of the International Criminal Court, Resolution RC/Res.6 (2010).

[78] Ambos (2010), p. 508.

[79] Ramji-Nogales enumerates afflicted populations, perpetrators, and political elites. *See* Ramji-Nogales (2010), p. 12.

[80] DeGuzman (2009), p. 1404.

[81] Cassese (2012), p. 492.

5.1 The Meaning and Indicators of the ICC's Legitimacy

of these first cases were filed with the ICC by African States Parties themselves, possibly in the calculated hope of neutralizing rebels in their own borders, in an instance of the aforementioned malicious intent. Such political motives on the part of African States' became blatantly obvious in this regard[82] after 2005, when the OTP targeted governmental figures in Kenya and Darfur, the latter being a Non-State Party to the ICC, only in response to Security Council referral. In response to the latter, the African Union (AU) adopted many resolutions of its own rejecting ICC proceedings against Sudanese President Omar Hassan Al-Bashir, calling on its member states not to cooperate with the ICC pursuant to the head-of-State immunity and privileges provisions of Article 98 of the Rome Statute.[83]

If the ICC's target is uncooperative African States, but ICC African member states are themselves uncooperative, then the ICC's effectiveness, which, as will be discussed hereinafter, is a factor in evaluating its procedural legitimacy, is accordingly impaired.[84] In other words, the failure of African ICC parties to comply with the Court's request that Sudan extradite Bashir, as described elsewhere, was clearly damaging to the legitimacy of the Court's authority.[85] This issue also relates to the aforementioned sense of unfairness among stakeholders towards case selection on the part of the ICC Prosecutor. It is a hard truth that "[t]he actions of the former colonial powers are free of international criminal accountability today as they ever were"[86] and the manner in which the OTP chooses cases attracts criticism that "only non-Western governments can be norm violators; Western governments can only be norm setters and enforcers,"[87] even though such case selection by independent parties is indeed the desired outcome of applying the principle of complementarity. Thus, if the OTP turns its attention to State government without working with State jurisdiction, the state will view the ICC as merely selecting politically expedient targets in line with the perceived Western model of interventionist bullying of the weak.[88] The AU has sought an ICJ advisory opinion on the issue of sovereign immunity, there has been no response as of March 2022.[89] In the meantime, the ICC Appellate Chamber issued a decision denying immunity to Non-State Party heads of State in the context of relations between the ICC and State Party to which the ICC requests

---

[82] *See* Niang (2017), p. 617.

[83] African Union, Assembly (2009), para. 10; African Union, Assembly (2010), paras. 5–6; African Union, Assembly (2011a), para. 5; Assembly of the African Union (2011b); Assembly of the African Union (2012), paras. 3–8; Assembly of the African Union (2013), paras. 3–6; Assembly of the African Union (2016a), paras. 2–4; Assembly of the African Union (2016b), paras. 2–4; Assembly of the African Union (2018), paras. 2–5.

[84] The Republic of Malawi and the Republic of Chad, both African States Parties to the ICC, were accused by the Pre-Trial Chamber of failing to cooperate with the ICC. *See* Pre-Trial Chamber I of the International Criminal Court (2011); la Chambre Préliminaire I (2011).

[85] Makaza (2017), p. 283.

[86] Thakur (2012), p. 56.

[87] Ibid., p. 57.

[88] Stegmiller (2017), p. 269.

[89] Assembly of the African Union (2018), para. 5.

the extradition of Non-State Party heads of State.[90] If the ICJ issues its requested opinion in these circumstances, and it reinforces the aforementioned ICC requests, it would accordingly strengthen ICC social legitimacy. Regardless, AU has become less hostile to the ICC since the April 2019 *coup* in Sudan that ousted Bashir, and there is much less impetus behind the aforementioned advisory opinion request as a result as well. The geographical bias in ICC case selection, particularly vis-à-vis Africa, has also been overcome to some extent since 2016, when the OTP opened its first investigation outside Africa, in Georgia.[91] As of this writing, the OTP has been authorized to conduct 17 investigations, of which Palestine, Bangladesh/Myanmar, Afghanistan, the Philippines, and Ukraine, in addition to Georgia, are outside of Africa.

Inherent bias in domestic and international criminal justice proceedings alike inevitably impairs ICC sociological legitimacy, especially where victims are concerned. It has been pointed out, however, that "[j]urisdiction over some cases is better than jurisdiction over no cases."[92] In this regard, Africa's active involvement in the ICC, including providing the Court's second Chief Prosecutor, as well as judges and defense lawyers, has resulted in the Court's current achievements. This indicates that African grievances should not be ignored by the ICC or its member states, but rather confronted and solutions sought, thereby further strengthening the ICC's legitimacy. Ultimately, the "legitimacy debate ensures that voices that would have otherwise been muted and ignored can be heard and taken seriously."[93]

5.2 ICC Effectiveness and Efficiency

Generallly, effectiveness may be defined as the fact of producing a successful result, and efficiency as the ratio of work to energy inputted. While it is pointed out that "there is a considerable gap in researchers' understanding of the ICC's effectiveness and functioning,"[94] there seems to be rough agreement among these selfsame researchers in that effectiveness and efficiency are related to the goals of the Court and its outcomes.[95] The notion of the effectiveness and efficiency thus relates to, and may be subsumed into, sociological legitimacy.

With this in mind, the Assembly of States Parties of the Rome Statute established the Independent Expert Review (IER),[96] whose members[97] have a mandate to

---

[90] Appeals Chamber of the International Criminal Court (2019).

[91] Pre-Trial Chamber I of the International Criminal Court (2016).

[92] Meron (2021), p. 92.

[93] Vasiliev (2017), p. 91.

[94] Muhammad, Holá, Dirkzwager (2021), p. 128.

[95] Shany (2014), p. 14.

[96] The Assembly of States Parties of the International Criminal Court (2019).

[97] Nicolas Guillou (France), Mónica Pinto (Argentina), Mike Smith (Australia), Anna Bednarek (Poland), Ian Bonomy (U.K.), Mohamed Chande Othman (Tanzania), Hassan Jallow (Gambia), and

5.2 ICC Effectiveness and Efficiency

produce "concrete, achievable and actionable recommendations aimed at enhancing the performance, efficiency and effectiveness of the Court."[98] In September 2020, the IER issued a report on the ICC's procedural effectiveness.[99] This was "the first systematic assessments of the ICC's procedural effectiveness,"[100] and as such, offers 384 recommendations of the aforementioned kind, both short and long-term.[101]

According to the report, efficiency means internal performance, and effectiveness is viewed in terms of impact.[102] Quantitative indicators are needed to measure Court activity if its efficiency is to be assessed. For measuring activities, the data relate to administration of justice, key aspects whereof include number of sitting hours, time taken to issue specific decisions, and accuracy of expected timelines, whereas it is stressed that actual judicial or prosecutorial decisions are not themselves being evaluated.[103] The report clarifies that assessing the Court's effectiveness means evaluating the impact of the ICC on affected local communities and victims, as well as deterrent effects.[104] It further asserts that civil society organizations and academics can play an essential role in such objective assessments of the Court.[105]

If we consider the purpose of international criminal tribunals to be to bring to trial those who have committed serious violations of international law, then the efficiency of these tribunals would be the ratio of public trials to monetary costs, with the complexity of the trials taken into account.[106] In this respect, efficiency may be equated with cost-effectiveness, although, as it is generally agreed among relevant parties that the number of convictions obtained by the ICC is an inappropriate measure of the Court's effectiveness,[107] the prosecution may be at issue in this instance rather than the aforementioned number of convictions obtained. In addition, from the perspective of the principle of complementarity, the efficiency of the ICC is higher when no case is pending before it. In this regard, it is well known that Luis Moreno Ocampo, first Chief Prosecutor of the ICC, made the following statement about effectiveness at his swearing-in ceremony:

Cristina Schwansee Romano (Brazil), with Richard Goldstone (South Africa) Chairman. Independent Expert Review of the International Criminal Court and the Rome Statute System Final Report (2020), p. 7, para. 3.

[98] Ibid., para. 6.

[99] Independent Expert Review of the International Criminal Court and the Rome Statute System Final Report (2020).

[100] Muhammad, Holá, Dirkzwager (2021), p. 128.

[101] Independent Expert Review of the International Criminal Court and the Rome Statute System Final Report (2020), p. 11, para. 23.

[102] Ibid., p. 116, para. 363.

[103] Ibid., p. 117, para. 367.

[104] Ibid., p. 117, para. 368.

[105] Ibid., p. 117, para. 368.

[106] Ford (2014), p. 37.

[107] Muhammad, Holá, Dirkzwager (2021), p. 148.

The effectiveness of the International Criminal Court should not be measured by the number of cases that reach it. On the contrary, complementarity implies that the absence of trials before this Court, as a consequence of the regular functioning of national institutions, would be a major success.[108]

In other words, in theory, as long as the ICC abides by the aforementioned complementarity principle, the Court will function more efficiently by assisting genuine investigations and prosecutions in national courts. In practice, however, one can hardly expect a State to exercise universal jurisdiction or a disputing or post-dispute State to fairly and impartially investigate and prosecute criminal acts occurring during its own disputes. The ICC exists precisely to prepare for the possibility of impunity, i.e., therein lies its raison d'être. This is why some believe that the ratio of expenses to persons indicted before the ICC is an unambiguous metric of efficiency, as indicated above. And between its first indictment, in July 2005, and 2012, 30 people were indicted in all, which means that €27.6 million was appropriated per person on average, exactly €27,589,391, making the ICC less efficient than the ICTY.[109] However, assessment of legitimacy in such a simple manner should not diminish the institution and role of such tribunals. If the convenience and efficiency of national and international criminal trials are considered to all that matters, to the extent that their significance as guardians of law is underestimated, then such proceedings will not be seen as legitimate.

It has also been noted that the ICC's system of judicial appointments, in which one-third of the Court's 18 judges are replaced at a time in three-year cycles, poses a threat to the ICC's efficiency and judicial consistency.[110] Similarly, it has been considered necessary to increase the effectiveness and efficiency of victim participation procedures as well. Victims admitted to participate in proceedings within the meaning of Article 68(3) of the Statute must demonstrate their victimhood through application forms in accordance with Rule 89 of the Rules and Procedure and Evidence of the Court,[111] which has tried to streamline this admissions process, chiefly by the Presidency of the Court approving a revised one-page version of the application form.[112] Other shortcomings in the efficiency of the Rome Statute have also been observed, including the lack of a time limit for preliminary hearings.

In order to ensure consistency of proceedings and enhance efficiency, the Chambers Practice Manual was adopted on September 4, 2015.[113] Although designed to reflect best practices as identified by ICC judges, some of aspects have been criticized as appearing to depart from established practice. For instance, the Manual state

---

[108] Statement of Luis Moreno-Ocampo (2003), p. 3.

[109] Bassiouni, Hansen (2016), p. 313.

[110] Meron (2021), p. 315.

[111] Delagrange (2018), p. 545.

[112] Ibid., p. 547.

[113] The International Criminal Court Pre-Trial Practice Manual (2015), revised February 1, 2016 (the ICC Chambers' Practice Manual (2016)), May 12, 2017 (the ICC Chambers' Practice Manual (2017)), November 29, 2019 (the ICC Chambers' Practice Manual (2019)), and March 25, 2022 (the ICC Chambers' Practice Manual (2022)).

that in-depth analysis charts that had been utilized by the Court are not required.[114] Moreover, while the Manual is intended as a reference for the Chambers, it is in fact taken as an alternative to normative amendments to the Rules and Regulations, as well as the Statute itself.[115] Needless to say, therefore, the ICC should not distort its legal stability or deviate too far from its nature as an institution established by treaty in the pursuit of efficiency, lest it risk States questioning its procedural legitimacy, which might in turn lead to a crisis of legitimacy for the Court overall.

5.3 Evaluating Legitimacy and Effectiveness vis-à-vis Bangladesh/Myanmar

5.3.1 Evaluating Legitimacy

The ICC is presently confronted with doubts about its legitimacy from two directions: the AU and Non-States Parties. First of all, the ICC's legitimacy, in this context arguably its sociological legitimacy, is questioned by the AU, primarily with regard to violations of sovereign immunity, as described previously.[116] Where Non-States Parties are concerned, it is the ICC's democratic and procedural legitimacy that is questioned instead. In the latter regard, it has been pointed out that "[t]here is no democratic linkage between the ICC and those Non-State Party nationals over whom it would exercise authority."[117] However, the ICC's mandate is so important that this lack of democracy has gone unquestioned to-date.[118] At the same time, democratic legitimation in the context of the ICC may be understood as access for the marginalized rather than the consent of the majority, as in domestic society.[119] The ICC's system of victim participation will thus undoubtedly have a positive impact on the ICC's democratic legitimacy. Normally, the exercise of domestic territorial jurisdiction over foreigners is not in question from the viewpoint of democratic legitimacy. In the Bangladesh/Myanmar case, however, the exercise of jurisdiction by the ICC, an international organization established by treaty, is at stake. The Pre-Trial Chamber of the ICC justified the Court's exercise of jurisdiction in this matter by the objective territorial principle and the constitutive element theory,[120] given that at least one constitutive element of the crime occurred on the territory of a State Party, as previously described. It is possible that democratic legitimacy regarding Bangladesh/Myanmar with respect to the alleged crime of deportation of the Rohingyas may be

---

[114] McDermott (2017), pp. 888–889.

[115] Ibid., p. 891.

[116] Kerr (2020), pp. 211–212.

[117] Morris (2002), p. 596.

[118] Ibid.

[119] Glasius (2012), p. 62.

[120] Pre-Trial Chamber III of the International Criminal Court (2019), p. 28, para. 62.

supported by the fact that said crime, being enumerated in Nuremberg Principle IV(b), has long been considered part of customary international law,[121] if the democratic legitimacy of customary international law itself is supported.[122] This also argues *nullum crimen sine lege* for ICC procedural legitimacy with respect thereto.

That said, such procedural legitimacy, to wit, the exercise of ICC jurisdiction over nationals of Non-States Parties raises the following additional question: may the ICC legitimately subject to its jurisdiction such Non-State Party nationals for crimes committed on the territory of a Non-State Party, where the customary status of the crimes charged may be in doubt?[123] The ICC is accordingly well advised ensure said customary status in attempting such exercise of jurisdiction, whether retroactively or when prosecuting alleged crimes occurring on the territory of Non-States Parties that have not ratified treaties prohibiting the alleged conduct or method of warfare and committed by nationals of same.[124]

Regarding social legitimacy, as previously described, both the NUG and the Bangladeshi authorities seem to be cooperating with the ICC since the February 2021 *coup*. On February 27, 2022, the Chief Prosecutor of the ICC made a five-day trip to Bangladesh, visiting Dhaka and Cox's Bazar.[125] Such a trip would not have been possible without the cooperation of the Bangladeshi authorities. The ICC's taking on situations in Asia will enhance its social legitimacy in terms of claims of bias on the Court's part. Ensuring universality and the universal application of law is key to the ICC burnishing its credentials among stakeholders, especially States. Like Africa, Asia is not monolithic; some countries are relatively active in the ICC, while others are reluctant or, like the Philippines, have withdrawn. On the one hand, the Bangladesh/ Myanmar situation could definitely be a touchstone for the ICC to address ongoing issues, including the concerns about its evenhandedness. On the other hand, if the ICC were to involve itself in situations concerning Non-States Parties, it would not be able to obtain the cooperation of the countries concerned, which would hinder its investigations and prosecutions, which in turn would again impair its effectiveness and efficiency, and ultimately its legitimacy. Therefore, barring regime change, it is highly unlikely that the ICC will effectively deal with crimes in which Non-States Parties to the Rome Statute are suspects. It thus remains to be seen how the ICC's relationship with Myanmar will evolve; i.e., whether the ICC will engage with the ruling junta or the NUG.

---

[121] *See* Principles of International Law Recognized in the Charter of the Nürnberg Tribunal and in the Judgment of the Tribunal (1950), pp. 181–195.

[122] For the democratic legitimacy of customary international law, *see* Lepard (2010), p. 256.

[123] Hayashi, Bailliet, Nicholson (2017), p. 8.

[124] Bartels (2017), pp. 160, 166.

[125] Press Release of the International Criminal Court (2022).

5.3.2 Effectiveness: Likelihood of Trials in Domestic Courts

5.3.2.1 Argentina

If the ICC's efficiency and effectiveness are enhanced by the burden sharing between it and domestic jurisdictions, it is important to consider the possibility of the allegations of serious violation of human rights against Rohingya in such domestic fora, as described previously. Currently, Argentina has the most potential to play a role in respect of the Bangladesh/Myanmar situation before the ICC, in terms of the aforementioned principle of complementarity. To recap, the criminal lawsuit to hold Myanmars political and military leaders accountable for the plight of the Rohingya was filed in an Argentine court on November 13, 2019 by a Latin-American NGO and Rohingya activist Maung Tun Khin.[126] However, on July 12, 2021, the court decided not to open an investigation because the ICC's OTP had launched its investigation.[127] Khin appealed and the a hearing was held on August 17, 2021.[128] On November 26, 2021, the Federal Criminal Court of Argentina overturned the lower court decision that had denied plaintiffs' request to investigate the alleged genocide and crimes against humanity committed against the Rohingya.[129] Based as it is on an assertion of universal jurisdiction, this case is considered one of the most important attempts to promote the common interest of the international community in ensuring that grave human rights violations do not go unpunished. While it is impossible to predict at this point whether this case will continue, it deserves attention in terms of the role of States in complementing the ICC, especially in light of the latter's limited resources and the number of alleged perpetrators.

5.3.2.2 Bangladesh

As of this writing, it is claimed that the International Crimes Tribunal, Bangladesh (ICT-BD) arguably has jurisdiction to investigate and prosecute the crime against humanity of deportation of Rohingya from Myanmar to Bangladesh.[130] Bangladesh government passed the International Crimes (Tribunals) Act in 1973 to address crimes under international law that occurred during the Bangladesh Liberation War,[131] which Bangladesh secured independence from Pakistan. Article 3(1) of the Act states, "Tribunal shall have the power to try and punish any individual or group of individuals, or organisation, or any member of any armed, defence or auxiliary forces, irrespective of his nationality, who commits or has committed, in the territory of Bangladesh, whether before or after the commencement of this Act, any of the crimes mentioned in

---

[126] Fortify Rights Press Release (2021) Argentina: Prosecute Crimes against Rohingya in Myanmar.

[127] ibid.

[128] ibid.

[129] Independent Investigative Mechanism for Myanmar (2022), p. 4.

[130] Foysal (2021).

[131] The International Crimes (Tribunals) Act, 1973 (1973) (Amendment, 2013).

sub-section (2)." Article 3(2) provides that crimes against humanity, crimes against peace, and genocide are crimes within the jurisdiction of a Tribunal for which there shall be individual responsibility. Although this subject matter jurisdiction gives the impression that the ICT-BD is international, it is deemed domestic in nature,[132] because no non-Bangladeshi judges are seated on the panel. The Act was invoked following amendment in 2009, as part of a movement in the country to punish war crimes.

If the ICT-BD genuinely exercises territorial jurisdiction over crimes of deportation into territory of Bangladesh, such exercise might enhance the ICC's complementarity scheme and eventually make the ICC more efficient. It has also been pointed out, however, that Bangladesh, including the ICT-BD, is not the appropriate forum for complementary investigation and prosecution of crimes within the ICC's jurisdiction.[133] It may therefore not be realistic to investigate and prosecute crimes against the Rohingya in Bangladesh. The exercise of universal jurisdiction in a third country, where fairness and impartiality can be assured, would instead be more suitable to the aforementioned objective of making the ICC more efficient.

5.3.2.3 Turkey

On March 29, 2022, the London-based Myanmar Accountability Project filed a criminal case with the Public Prosecutor's Office in Istanbul, Turkey. The group's allegations do not directly relate to the alleged crimes against Rohingya by the Myanmar military, but instead cover allegations of widespread torture since the 2021 *coup*, in the hope that the Turkish court will exercises universal jurisdiction on that basis,[134] given that Turkey ratified the Torture Convention in 1988, whereas Myanmar has neither signed nor ratified it. The motivation for filing this lawsuit was thus to prevent ongoing human rights violations by the Myanmar junta, rather than to prevent impunity on the part of those responsible for the persecution of the Rohingya.

In June 2022, it was reported that the Turkish authorities had initiated a preliminary investigation into members of the Myanmar junta.[135] There was a similar call in Indonesia.[136]

---

[132] Menon (2016), para. 7.

[133] Guerica 37 International Justice Chambers (2018). "It cannot be argued that the ICT is either fair, or competent, and thus it cannot it all conscience, be considered an appropriate route to accountability to the hundreds of thousands of Rohingya victims." ibid., p. 54.

[134] Myanmar Accountability Project Press Release (2022).

[135] Ibid.

[136] Baboolal (2022).

5.3 Evaluating Legitimacy and Effectiveness vis-à-vis Bangladesh/Myanmar

5.3.2.4 Indonesia

In September 2022, Indonesian activists Marzuki Darusman and Busyro Muqoddas, along with Aliansi Jurnalis Independen/Alliance of Independent Journalists (AJI) in Jakarta, formally submitted a petition to the Constitutional Court, requesting review of the Law on the Court of Human Rights so as to enable Indonesia to try non-Indonesian citizens for human rights abuses.[137] Particularly, the petition was filed in order to permit a case before Indonesian courts against the Myanmar junta, accused of crimes against humanity, war crimes, and genocide against the Muslim population of the country. Currently, Article 5 of the Law on the Court of Human Rights stipulates that a trial of perpetrators of human rights violations can only be carried out if the crimes are committed "by Indonesian citizens".[138] That condition limits the case of the Rohingya atrocities handled by the Indonesian authorities at present.

5.3.2.5 Germany

On January 20, 2023, Fortify Rights, a human rights group for Myanmarese people, and sixteen individual complainants from Myanmar filed under universal jurisdiction a criminal complaint in Germany against Myanmar military officials and others for genocide, war crimes, and crimes against humanity.[139] In international law, increased domestic prosecution is highly valued from the complementarity principle, whereby the ICC complements domestic criminal jurisdiction, and from the perspective that domestic courts can prosecute a wider range of crimes than the ICC in terms of the scope of subject-matter jurisdiction (*ratione materiae*) against Myanmar, a Non-State Party.[140] Moreover, the case filed in Germany requests the German Federal Prosecutor to investigate crimes committed against Rohingya people between 2016 and 2017 and against other civilians since the Myanmar *coup* of February 2021. The case is a comprehensive one tackling human rights violations in Myanmar, and Germany has been active in the exercise of universal jurisdiction, willing to end impunity for crimes under international law. There are currently more than one-hundred investigations by German prosecutors in Germany into cases of crimes under international law.[141] Given the legal workload, there is no doubt the German Federal Prosecutor's Office will need time to investigate and build a case against the Rohingya atrocities.

---

[137] Ariyanti (2022).

[138] Tirtasari (2022).

[139] Strangio (2023).

[140] Pelliconi and De Gregorio (2023).

[141] Permanent Mission of the Federal Republic of Germany in New York (2022).

5.4 Conclusion

One *raison d'être* of legitimacy discourse is legitimatization of authority. That is to say, legitimacy discourse is meant to contribute to the power to promote commitment to and compliance with authority. It is hoped that enhancing authority's prestige will lead to its effective operation. It is preferable to utilize legitimacy evaluations to that end, although well-intentioned critical analyses of such evaluations are surely important to improving international criminal institutions. On the one hand, the Bangladesh/Myanmar situation could be an opportunity to restore the ICC's reputation for legitimacy regarding accusations of bias toward Africa in its investigations and prosecutions. On the other hand, the case will have an impact on the social legitimacy of the ICC, given the lack of progress in ICC proceedings in the matter and the ongoing suggestion of bias on the part of the OTP, the latter whereof contributing to the low legitimacy ratings that the ICC receives from African and developing countries.[142] To resolve this situation, the OTP itself must proactively publish its criteria for selecting cases for investigation and prosecution and its prosecution strategies, as well as clarify the universal values of investigation and prosecution in specific situations. Moreover, the ICC's procedural legitimacy ultimately hinges on "the quality of its procedure and decisions," and its democratic legitimacy on consent of States, which is described as the Court's "lifeblood."[143]

The ICC is underpinned by the principle of complementarity, which states that the ICC cannot deal with serious crimes around the world on its own. Its effectiveness and efficiency depend not only on its strong reputation for legitimacy, but also on this very principle functioning adequately. That is to say, its success hinges not on how many cases it handles, but on its ability to use both domestic and international criminal jurisdiction to reduce the gap between impunity and punishment.[144] Perhaps its effectiveness and efficiency should also be considered in terms of collaboration between the ICC and domestic criminal jurisdictions. Looking at the Myanmar/Bangladesh situation, it is clear that the willingness of a few States, especially those that are States Parties to the ICC, to exercise universal jurisdiction over the Rohingya crisis will lend credence to ICC complementarity, even actual prosecution does not result.

As of 2022, it is said that the support of States for the ICC regarding the situation in Ukraine has enhanced the Court's legitimacy.[145] The OTP decision to open an investigation into the situation in Ukraine was marked by the referral of more than 40 States Parties and the active cooperation of the United States with the ICC. It is hoped that this greater interest on the part of countries in the ICC will bring about a virtuous circle in the progress of the ICC's investigation and prosecution of the Rohingya issue.

---

[142] Santurio, Rosa (2022), p. 30.

[143] Lanza (2022), p. 61.

[144] Stegmiller (2017), p. 271.

[145] Dutton, Sterio (2023), p. 31.

References

African Union, Assembly (2009) Decision on the Meeting of African States Parties to the Rome Statute of the International Criminal Tribunal (ICC) Doc. Assembly/AU/13(XIII). Assembly/AU/Dec.245(XIII) Rev.1

African Union, Assembly (2010) Decision on the Progress Report of the Commission on the Implementation of Decision Assembly/AU/Dec.270(XIV) on the Second Ministerial Meeting on the Rome Statute of the International Criminal Court (ICC) Doc. Assembly/AU/10(XV). Assembly/AU/Dec.296(XV)

African Union, Assembly (2011a) Decision on the Implementation of the Decisions on the International Criminal Court (ICC) Doc. EX.CL/639(XVIII)', 30–31 January 2011, Assembly/AU/Dec.334(XVI)

African Union, Assembly (2011b) Decision on the Implementation of the Assembly Decisions on the International Criminal Court—Doc. EX.CL/670(XIX),' 30 June–1 July 2011, Assembly/AU/Dec.366(XVII)

Ambos K (2010) The crime of aggression after Kampala. German Yearbook Int Law 53:463–509

Anoushirvani S (2010) The future of the international criminal court: the long road to legitimacy begins with the trial of Thomas Lubanga Dyilo. Pace Int Law Rev 22(1):213–239

Appeals Chamber of the International Criminal Court (2019) Judgment in the Jordan Referral re Al-Bashir Appeal. ICC-02/05-01/09-397-Corr

Ariyanti R (2022) AJI files to prosecute Myanmar human rights violations in Indonesia. International Federation of Journalists. https://www.ifj.org/media-centre/news/detail/category/press-freedom/article/aji-files-to-prosecute-myanmar-human-rights-violations-in-indonesia.html

Assembly of the African Union (2012) 18th Ordinary Session, 29–30 January 2012, Assembly/AU/Dec.397(XVIII)

Assembly of the African Union (2013) 21st Ordinary Session, 26–27 May 2013, Assembly/AU/Dec.482(XXI)

Assembly of the African Union (2016a) 26th Ordinary Session, 30–31 January 2016. Assembly/AU/Dec.590(XXVI)

Assembly of the African Union (2016b) 27th Ordinary Session, 17–18 July 2016, Assembly/AU/Dec.616 (XXVII)

Assembly of the African Union (2018) 30th Ordinary Session, 28–29 January 2018, Assembly/AU/Dec.672(XXX)

Baboolal S (2022) Indonesia activists ask court to allow human rights case against Myanmar Junta. Jurist. https://www.jurist.org/news/2022/09/indonesia-activists-ask-court-to-allow-human-rights-case-against-myanmar-junta/

Bartels R (2017) Legitimacy and ICC jurisdiction following security council referrals: conduct on the territory of non-party states and the legality principle. In: Hayashi N, Bailliet CM (eds) Legitimacy of international criminal tribunals. Cambridge University Press, Cambridge, pp 141–178

Bassiouni MC, Hansen A (2016) The inevitable practice of the office of the prosecutor. In Steinberg RH (ed) Contemporary issues facing the international criminal court. Brill Nijhoff, Leiden, pp 309–236

Bellingham H (2012) The international criminal court, ten years on: foreign office minister Henry Bellingham spoke about the achievements of and prospects for the international criminal court at a conference marking its tenth anniversary. http://www.fco.gov.uk/en/news/latest-news/?view=Speech&id=778932082

Bodansky D (1999) The legitimacy of international governance: a coming challenge for international environmental law? Am J Int Law 93(3):596–624

Boister N, Cryer R (eds) (2008) Documents on the Tokyo international military tribunal. Oxford University Press, Oxford

Brown C (2002) Sovereignty, rights and justice: international political theory today. Polity Press, New York

Brunnée, Toope (eds) (2010) Legitimacy and legality in international law: an interactional account. Cambridge University Press, Cambridge

Buchanan A, Keohane RO (2008) The legitimacy of global governance institutions. In: Wolfrum R, Röben V (eds) Legitimacy in international law. Springer, Berlin, pp 25–62

Cassese A (2012) The legitimacy of international criminal tribunals and the current prospects of international criminal justice. Leiden J Int Law 25(2):491–501

Clark I (2005) Legitimacy in international society. Oxford University Press, New York

Danner AM (2003) Enhancing the legitimacy and accountability of prosecutorial discretion at the international criminal court. Am J Int Law 97(3):510–552

DeGuzman MM (2009) Gravity and the legitimacy of the international criminal court. Fordham Int Law J 32(5):1400–1465

DeGuzman MM (2018) The global-local Dilemma and the ICC's legitimacy. In: Grossman N, Cohen HG, Follesdal A, Ulfstein G (eds) Legitimacy and international courts. Cambridge University Press, Cambridge, pp 62–82

Delagrange M (2018) The path towards greater efficiency and effectiveness in the victim application processes of the international criminal court. Int Crim Law Rev 18(3):540–562

Dutton Y, Sterio M (2023) The war in Ukraine and the legitimacy of the international criminal court. Am Univ Law Rev, Forthcoming. https://ssrn.com/abstract=4235675

Falk R (2012) Introduction: legality and legitimacy: necessities and problematics of exceptionalism. In: Falk R, Juergensmeyer M, Popovski V (eds) Legality and legitimacy in global affairs. Oxford University Press, New York, pp 3–42

Falligant J (2010) The prosecution of Sudanese president Al Bashir: why a security council deferral would harm the legitimacy of the international criminal court. Wisconsin Int Law J 27(4):727–751

Fichtelberg A (2006) Democratic legitimacy and the international criminal court: a liberal defence. J Int Crim Justice 4(4):765–785

Ford S (2014) Complexity and efficiency at international criminal courts. Emory Int Law Rev 29(1):1–69

Fortify Rights Press Release (2021) Argentina: Prosecute crimes against Rohingya in Myanmar. https://www.fortifyrights.org/mya-inv-2021-09-30/

Foysal QO (2016) The prospects of prosecuting Rohingya deportation before the international crimes Tribunal, Bangladesh (ICT-BD). Opinio Juris. http://opiniojuris.org/2021/02/11/the-prospects-of-prosecuting-rohingya-deportation-before-the-international-crimes-tribunal-bangladesh-ict-bd/

Glasius M (2012) Do international criminal courts require democratic legitimacy? Eur J Int Law 23(1):43–66

Glasius M, Meijers T (2012) Constructions of legitimacy: the Charles Taylor trial. Int J Transitional Justice 6:229–252

Greenawalt AKA (2007) Justice without politics? Prosecutorial discretion and the, international criminal court. New York Univ J Int Law Politics 39(3):583–673

Greenawalt AKA (2009) Complementarity in crisis: Uganda, alternative justice, and the international criminal court. Virginia J Int Law 50(1):107–162

Guerica 37 International Justice Chambers (2018) Amicus curiae observations by Guernica 37 International Justice Chambers pursuant to Rule 103 of the Rules. ICC-RoC46(3)-01/18-24. https://www.icc-cpi.int/sites/default/files/CourtRecords/CR2018_03129.PDF

Hayashi N, Bailliet CM, Nicholson J (2017) Introduction. In: Hayashi N, Bailliet CM (eds) Legitimacy of international criminal tribunals. Cambridge University Press, Cambridge, pp 1–22

Hurd I (1999) Legitimacy and authority in international politics. Int Organ 53(2):379–408

Hurd I (2007) After anarchy: legitimacy and power in the united nations security council. Princeton University Press, Princeton

ICC Chambers Practice Manual (2016). https://www.icc-cpi.int/iccdocs/other/Chambers_practice_manual--FEBRUARY_2016.pdf

References

ICC Chambers Practice Manual (2017). https://www.icc-cpi.int/iccdocs/other/170512-icc-chambers-practice-manual_May_2017_ENG.pdf

ICC Chambers Practice Manual (2019). https://www.icc-cpi.int/sites/default/files/191129-chamber-manual-eng.pdf

ICC Chambers Practice Manual (2022). https://www.icc-cpi.int/sites/default/files/2022-06/20220323-chambers-practice-manual-fifth-edition-eng_2.pdf

Independent Expert Review of the International Criminal Court and the Rome Statute System Final Report (2020). https://asp.icc-cpi.int/iccdocs/asp_docs/ASP19/IER-Final-Report-ENG.pdf

Independent Investigative Mechanism for Myanmar (2022) Bulletin 6

International Criminal Tribunal for Rwanda (1997) Prosecutor v. Joseph Kanyabashi. Decision on the Defence Motion on Jurisdiction. Trial Chamber II. ICTR-96-15-T

International Criminal Tribunal for Rwanda Rules of Procedure and Evidence (2015) ITR/3/Rev.1

International Criminal Tribunal for the Former Yugoslavia (1995a) Prosecutor v. Duško Tadić. Decision on the Defence Motion on Jurisdiction. Trial Chamber II. IT-94-1-T

International Criminal Tribunal for the Former Yugoslavia (1995b) Prosecutor v. Duško Tadić. Decision on the Defence Motion of Interlocutory Appeal on Jurisdiction. Appeals Chamber. IT-94-I-T

International Criminal Tribunal for the Former Yugoslavia Rules of Procedure and Evidence (2012) IT/32/Rev.47

International Military Tribunal (1947) Judicial decisions: international military tribunal (Nuremberg) judgment and sentence (1 October 1946). Am J Int Law 41(1):172–333

Japan Statement by H. E. Mr. Horinouchi Hidehisa: Ambassador of Japan to the Netherlands at the Eighteenth Session of the Assembly of States Parties to the Rome Statute of the International Criminal Court (2019)

Kerr C (2020) Sovereign immunity, the AU, and the ICC: legitimacy undermined. Michigan J Int Law 41(1):195–225

Kjeldgaard-Pedersen A (2021) Is the quality of the ICC's legal reasoning an obstacle to its ability to deter international crimes? J Int Crim Justice 19(4):939–957

Koskenniemi M (2007) Formalism, fragmentation, freedom: Kantian themes in today's international law. No Found J Extreme Legal Positivism 2007(4):7–28

Koskenniemi M (2011) The politics of international law. Hart Publishing, Oxford

Kotecha B (2020) The international criminal court's selectivity and procedural justice. J Int Crim Justice 18(1):107–139

Kumm M (2004) The legitimacy of international law: a constitutionalist framework of analysis. Eur J Int Law 15(5):907–931

Lanza G (2022) Indirect perpetration in the Rome statute: the search for independence from domestic law and doctrines. Revue Int De Droit Pénal 93(1):59–84

La Chambre préliminaire I de la Cour pénale internationale (2011) Décision rendue en application de l'article 87-7 du Statut de Rome concernant le refus de la République du Tchad d'accéder aux demandes de coopération délivrées par la Cour concernant l'arrestation et la remise d'Omar Hassan Ahmad Al Bashir. ICC-02/05-01/09-140

Lepard BD (2010) Customary international law: a new theory with practical applications. Cambridge University Press, Cambridge

Luban D (2010) Fairness to rightness: jurisdiction, legality, and the legitimacy of the international criminal law. In: Besson S, Tasioulas J (eds) The philosophy of international law. Oxford University Press, Oxford, pp 569–588

Makaza D (2017) African supranational criminal jurisdiction: one step towards ending impunity or two steps backwards for international criminal justice? In: Hayashi N, Bailliet CM (eds) The legitimacy of international criminal tribunals. Cambridge University Press, Cambridge, pp 272–296

McDermott Y (2017) The international criminal court's chambers practice manual: towards a return to judicial law making in international criminal procedure? J Int Crim Justice 15(5):873–904

McIntyre G (2020) The impact of a lack of consistency and coherence: how key decisions of the international criminal court have undermined the court's legitimacy. Questions Int Law Zoom In 67:25–57

McIntyre G (2021) The ICC, self-created challenges and missed opportunities to legitimize authority over non-states parties. J Int Crim Justice 19(3):511–542

Menon P (2016) International crimes tribunal in Bangladesh. Max Planck Encyclopedia of International Law, Oxford University Press. https://www.mpi.lu/fileadmin/mpi/medien/research/MPEiPro/IC_Tribunal_in_Bangladesh_law-mpeipro-e3092.pdf

Meron T (2021) Standing up for justice: the challenges of trying atrocity crimes. Oxford University Press, Oxford

Meyer L (2009) Legitimacy, justice and public international law. Cambridge University Press, Cambridge

Morris M (2002) The democratic Dilemma of the international criminal court. Buffalo Crim Law Rev 5(2):591–600

Muhammad S, Holá B, Dirkzwager A (2021) Reimagining the ICC: exploring practitioner's perspectives on the effectiveness of the international criminal court. Int Crim Law Rev 21(1):126–153

Müllerson R (2008) Aspects of legitimacy of decisions of international courts and tribunals: comments. In: Wolfrum R, Röben V (eds) Legitimacy in international law. Springer, Berlin, pp 189–201

Murphy SD (2009) Aggression, legitimacy and the international criminal court. Eur J Int Law 20(4):1147–1156

Myanmar Accountability Project Press Release (2022) Unprecedented criminal procedure against Myanmar Junta launched in Turkey criminal complaint for torture and crimes against humanity filed in Istanbul. https://the-world-is-watching.org/2022/03/29/unprecedented-criminal-proced ure-against-myanmar-junta-launched-in-turkey/

Myanmar Accountability Project Press Release (2022) Turkish authorities open unprecedented investigation into Myanmar Junta. https://the-world-is-watching.org/2022/06/02/turkish-author ities-open-unprecedented-investigation-into-myanmar-junta/

Niang M (2017) Africa and the legitimacy of the ICC in question international. Crim Law Rev 17(4):615–624

Nollkaemper A (2001) The legitimacy of international law in the case law of the international criminal tribunal for the former Yugoslavia. In: Vandamme TAJA, Reestman JH (eds) Ambiguity in the rule of law: the interface between national and international legal systems. Europa Law Publishing, Groningen, pp 13–23

Orentlicher DF (2003) Judging global justice assessing the international criminal court. Wisconsin Int Law J 21:495–512

Pelliconi AM, De Gregorio FS (2023) New universal jurisdiction case filed in Germany for crimes committed in Myanmar before and after the coup: on complementarity, effectiveness, and new hopes for old crimes. EJIL: Talk! https://www.ejiltalk.org/new-universal-jurisdiction-case-filed-in-germany-for-crimes-committed-in-myanmar-before-and-after-the-coup-on-com plementarity-effectiveness-and-new-hopes-for-old-crimes/

Permanent Mission of the Federal Republic of Germany in New York (2022) Statement of Germany in the UNGA Sixth Committee, "The Scope and Application of the Principle of Universal Jurisdiction", October 12th, 2022. https://new-york-un.diplo.de/un-en/news-corner/-/2558190

Popovski V (2012) Legality and legitimacy of international criminal tribunals. In: Falk R, Juergensmeyer M, Popovski V (eds) Legality and legitimacy in global affairs. Oxford University Press, New York, pp 388–413

Popovski V, Turner N (2012) Conclusion: legitimacy as complement and corrective to legality. In: Falk R, Juergensmeyer M, Popovski V (eds) Legality and legitimacy in global affairs. Oxford University Press, New York, pp 439–450

Press Release of the International Criminal Court (2022) ICC Prosecutor, Karim A. A. Khan QC, Concludes First Visit to Bangladesh, Underlines Commitment to Advance Investigations into

References

Alleged Atrocity Crimes against the Rohingya. https://www.icc-cpi.int/news/icc-prosecutor-karim-khan-qc-concludes-first-visit-bangladesh-underlines-commitment-advance

Pre-Trial Chamber I of the International Criminal Court (2011) Decision Pursuant to Article 87(7) of the Rome Statute on the Failure by the Republic of Malawi to Comply with the Cooperation Requests Issued by the Court with Respect to the Arrest and Surrender of Omar Hassan Ahmad Al Bashir. ICC-02/05-01/09-139

Pre-Trial Chamber I of the International Criminal Court (2016) Decision on the Prosecutor's Request for Authorization of an Investigation. ICC-01/15-12

Pre-Trial Chamber III of the International Criminal Court (2019) Decision Pursuant to Article 15 of the Rome Statute on the Authorisation of an Investigation into the Situation in the People's Republic of Bangladesh/Republic of the Union of Myanmar. ICC-01/19-27

Principles of International Law Recognized in the Charter of the Nürnberg Tribunal and in the Judgment of the Tribunal (1950) Yearbook of the International Law Commission, vol 2, pp 181–195

Ramji-Nogales J (2010) Designing bespoke transitional justice: a pluralist process approach. Michigan J Int Law 32(1):1–72

Rome Statute of the International Criminal Court (1998) 2187 UNTS 90

Santurio SL, Rosa PNM (2022) The international criminal court and the symbolic purpose of trials: rescuing the court's legitimacy in developing and least developed countries. RIDP 93(1):17–34

Sato T (2009) Legitimacy of international organizations and their decisions: challenges that international organizations face in the 21st century. Hitotsubashi J Law Politics 37:11–30

Schabas WA (2006) The UN international criminal tribunals: the former Yugoslavia, Rwanda and Sierra Leone. Cambridge University Press, Cambridge

Scharpf FW (1999) Governing in Europe: effective and democratic? Oxford University Press, Oxford

Shany Y (2014) Assessing the effectiveness of international courts. Oxford University Press, Oxford

Special Tribunal for Lebanon (2004a) Prosecutor v. Augustine Gbao. Decision on Preliminary Motion on the Invalidity of the Agreement Between the United Nations and the Government of Sierra Leone on the Establishment of the Special Court. Appeals Chamber. SCSL-04-15-AR72(E)

Special Tribunal for Lebanon (2004b) Prosecutor v. Moinina Fofana Decision on Preliminary Motion on Lack of Jurisdiction Materiae: Illegal Delegation of Power by the United Nations. Appeals Chamber. SCSL-2004b-14-AR72(E)

Special Tribunal for Lebanon (2012) Prosecutor v. Salim Jamil Ayyash, Mustafa Amine Badreddine, Hussein Hassan Oneissi and Assad Hassan Sabra Decision on the Defence Challenges to the Jurisdiction and Legality of the Tribunal. Trial Chamber. STL-11-01/PT/TC

Statement made by Mr. Luis Moreno-Ocampo (2003) Ceremony for the Solemn Undertaking of the Chief Prosecutor of the International Criminal Court. https://www.icc-cpi.int/news/statement-made-mr-luis-moreno-ocampo-ceremony-solemn-undertaking-chief-prosecutor-icc

Stegmiller I (2017) Positive complementarity and legitimacy—is the international criminal court shifting from judicial restraint towards interventionism? In: Hayashi N, Bailliet CM (eds) The legitimacy of international criminal tribunals. Cambridge University Press, Cambridge, pp 247–271

Strangio S (2023) Rights group files complaint in Germany against Myanmar's generals. The Diplomat. https://thediplomat.com/2023/01/rights-group-files-complaint-in-germany-against-myanmars-generals/

Struett MJ (2009) The politics of discursive legitimacy: understanding the dynamics and implications of prosecutorial discretion at the international criminal court. In: Roach SC (ed) Governance, order, and the international criminal court: between realpolitik and a cosmopolitan court. Oxford University Press, Oxford, pp 107–132

Suchman MC (1995) Managing legitimacy: strategic and institutional approaches. Acad Manag Rev 20(3):571–610

Thakur R (2012) Law, legitimacy and the united nations. In: Falk R, Juergensmeyer M, Popovski V (eds) Legality and legitimacy in global affairs. Oxford University Press, New York, pp 45–71

The Assembly of States Parties of the International Criminal Court (2010) Resolution RC/Res.6

The Assembly of States Parties of the International Criminal Court, Review of the ICC and the Rome Statute System, ICC-ASP/18/Res.7 (2019)

The Independent International Commission on Kosovo (2000) The Kosovo Report. Oxford University Press, New York

The International Crimes (Tribunals) Act, 1973 (1973) (Amendment, 2013). http://bdlaws.minlaw. gov.bd/act-435.html; https://ihl-databases.icrc.org/en/national-practice/international-crimes-tri bunals-act-1973-amendment-2013

The International Criminal Court Pre-Trial Practice Manual (2015). https://www.icc-cpi.int/sites/ default/files/iccdocs/other/Pre-Trial_practice_manual_(September_2015).pdf

The Office of the Prosecutor of the International Criminal Court (2012) OTP Briefing 127

Tomuschat C (2006) The legacy of Nuremberg. J Int Crim Justice 4(4):830–844

Tirtasari P (2022) Unprecedented case brought against Myanmar Junta in Indonesia. Aliansi Jurnails Independen. https://aji.or.id/read/press-release/1441/festivalmedia.html

Trial Chamber I of the International Criminal Court (2008) Decision on the Consequences of Non-Disclosure of Exculpatory Materials Covered by Article 54(3)(e) Agreements and the Application to Stay the Prosecution of the Accused, Together with Certain other Issues Raised at the Status Conference on 10 June 2008. ICC-01/04-01/06

UN. Doc. A/6316 (1966)

UN Doc. CCPR/C/GC/32 (2007)

UN Doc. S/2000/915 (2000)

UN Doc. S/RES/1315 (2000)

UN Doc. S/RES/1664 (2006)

United Nations (1945) Charter of the international military tribunal, annex to the agreement for the prosecution and punishment of the major war criminals of the European Axis ("London Agreement"), 8 August 1945

Vasiliev S (2017) Between international criminal justice and injustice: theorising legitimacy. In: Hayashi N, Bailliet CM (eds) The legitimacy of international criminal tribunals. Cambridge University Press, Cambridge, pp 66–91

Wallerstein S (2015) Delegation of powers and authority in international criminal law. Crim Law Philos 9:123–140

Weber M (1954) Economy and society, 2nd ed. (trans. Shils E, Rheinstein M). Cambridge Harvard University Press

Weiler JHH (1991) The transformation of Europe. Yale Law J 100(8):2403–2483

Weiler JHH (2004) The geology of international law—governance, democracy and legitimacy. Die Zeitschrift für ausländisches öffentliches Recht und Völkerrecht (ZaöRV) 64:547–562

Wolfrum R (2012) Legitimacy in international law. In: Wolfrum R (ed) The Max Planck encyclopedia of public international law 6. Oxford University Press, Oxford, pp 808–813

Wolfrum R, Röben V (eds) (2018) Legitimacy in international law. Springer, Berlin

Young EA (2003) The trouble with global constitution. Texas Int Law J 38(3):527–545

Chapter 6
Conclusion

Abstract The International Criminal Court (ICC) would resolve the issue of geographic equity by dealing with the Rohingya crisis. On the other hand, Myanmar, where evidence on the human rights situation of the Rohingya would be found, is a Non-State Party to the ICC, and the prospects of a successful investigation and prosecution by the ICC's Office of the Prosecutor (OTP) are currently low. However, the persecuted Rohingya are within the territory of Bangladesh, a State Party to the ICC, and there is a good chance that they will be able to testify. Given that the ICC advocates the principle of complementarity, in which the ICC complements a state's jurisdiction, there is also an expectation that Myanmar itself will seriously address the issue of human rights violations related to the Rohingya crisis.

6.1 Rule of Law in a World in Chaos

In the early twenty-first century, we are witnessing textbook examples of ethnic cleansing[1] and aggression[2] that mankind had banned in the previous century through treaty and customary international law. The international community must deal with such scourges rationally, in accordance with that selfsame international law. The international community is learning the importance of expressing concern about violations of international law and of human rights, regardless of considerations of non-interference in domestic affairs. With Ukraine filing suit with the ICJ[3] and States Parties referring the matter to the ICC,[4] the Ukraine case follows that of Myanmar in being simultaneously referred to both courts. In both instances, the Security Council

---

[1] Office of the United Nations High Commissioner for Human Rights (2017).

[2] The wording used by Professor Ryan Goodman, *see* Wolf (2022).

[3] International Court of Justice (2022).

[4] Although Lithuania submitted a communication under Article 15(2) of the Rome Statute on February 28, 2022, it made a referral under Article 14 of the Statute to speed up the investigative procedure. Minister of Justice of the Republic of Lithuania (2022). The other 38 States jointly submitted a referral under Article 14(1). Government of the United Kingdom of Great Britain and Northern Ireland (2022).

© The Author(s), under exclusive license to Springer Nature Singapore Pte Ltd. 2023   141
H. Takemura, *The Rohingya Crisis and the International Criminal Court*,
https://doi.org/10.1007/978-981-99-2734-0_6

was not expected to intervene due to the threat of Russian or Chinese vetoes. Given that the ICJ lacks enforcement powers, there would likely no alternative but to turn to judicial solutions when the Security Council is paralyzed. Even if provisional measures in *ex parte* cases based on Article IX of the Genocide Convention are ineffective, they may constitute a powerful message to the international community and to the persecuted.

The COVID-19 crisis that began in 2020 and the 2021 *coup* in Myanmar are not improving the Rohingya crisis. Further human rights violations have in fact resulted in their wake. Amid the pandemic, the Rohingya refugee camps in Bangladesh are said to be in even more dire sanitary conditions, with people who are particularly vulnerable to the disease mingled inseparably with other refugees.[5] As for the foregoing, the Office of the United Nations High Commissioner for Human Rights (OHCHR) estimates that crimes against humanity have likely been committed since, including murder, persecution, imprisonment, sexual violence, enforced disappearance, and torture. Even if these acts constitute war crimes or crimes against humanity, however, they are taking place within Myanmar, complicating efforts to treat them as having been committed within the territory of an ICC State Party, thus forestalling ICC initiatives to assert jurisdiction to investigate and prosecute same.

Notwithstanding, the international community continues to maintain a focus on the Rohingya plight.[6] Once the international community recognizes the existence of state-sponsored genocide, the responsible state comes in for severe criticism. It will be hard for such a state to rehabilitate itself. Judge Kriangsak Kittichaisaree concluded his book on the Rohingya by stating that "a delayed justice is still better than no justice at all."[7] The multifaceted pursuit of responsibility for crimes under the international law before the ICJ and the ICC also further strengthens the movement of the fight against impunity.

In the face of the Security Council's inability to take concerted action on the plight of the Rohingya, individual states have begun to recognize the persecution of the Rohingya as genocide. On March 21, 2022, US Secretary of State Antony J. Blinken formally recognized that members of the Burmese military committed genocide and crimes against humanity against the Rohingya,[8] which was welcomed by the NUG.[9] While such a finding of genocide on the part of an individual state may not have a significant direct impact on the ICJ and ICC, it would certainly set a precedent in terms of state practices. It is thus important that the various actors on the international stage not demonstrate indifference to the Rohingya issue.

Several countries have sanctioned individuals responsible for Myanmar's human rights violations against the Rohingya, beginning with the US, which issued Executive Order 14,014, "Blocking Property with Respect to the Situation in Burma,"[10]

---

[5] Bülbül et al. (2022), p. 391.

[6] Human Rights Council (2022), p. 13, para. 67.

[7] Kittichaisaree (2021), p. 291.

[8] U.S. Department of State (2022)

[9] Republic of Myanmar, National Unity Government (2022).

[10] U.S. President Joseph R. Biden Jr. (2021), pp. 9429–9432.

6.2 Proposed Solutions

a declaration of a national emergency to deal with an unusual and extraordinary threat to the national security and foreign policy of the US following the February 2021 *coup*. Pursuant to this Executive Order, in light of the US government's conclusion that the Burmese military committed genocide, crimes against humanity, and ethnic cleansing against Rohingya, on March 25, 2022, the US government designated five individuals and five entities connected to Burma's military regime,[11] with Canada and the UK following suit.[12] By way of these sanctions, listed persons in these countries and nationals outside these countries are prohibited from engaging in any activity related to any property of these persons or providing financial or related services to them. Known as "smart" or "targeted" sanctions, these are considered lawful countermeasures.[13]

6.2 Proposed Solutions

As described herein, short- and long-term solutions alike have been proposed to the Rohingya plight. The reason is that international criminal justice rulings alone will not solve the problem; all avenues to aiding the Rohingya must be pursued.

The long-term solution is to improve refugee policy. This means that the international community, including Japan, must find consensus concerning Rohingya human rights violations, using mechanisms such as third-country relocation and resettlement, so that the burden does not fall solely on neighboring countries such as Bangladesh. Rohingya growing up in Bangladesh are particularly interested in settling in a third country.[14] At the same time, however, the indifference of the international community has complicated such third-country resettlement, and some have pointed out that the only possible option is voluntary repatriation.[15] In order to facilitate same, measures are needed that include the creation of Rohingya safe zones in Rakhine State and education to reduce Myanmarese hatred of Rohingya.[16]

To this end, on June 6, 2018, the OHCHR and the United Nations Development Programme (UNDP) signed a tripartite Memorandum of Understanding (MoU) with the Government of Myanmar,[17] which was aimed at creating conducive conditions for the voluntary, safe, dignified and sustainable repatriation of refugees from Bangladesh.[18] However, the Myanmar government has been assessed as having not taken the necessary steps to put conditions for the return of the refugees in place.[19]

---

[11] U.S. Department of the Treasury (2022).

[12] Government of Canada (2022); Government of the UK (2022), *see* Government of the UK (2021).

[13] Tzanakopoulos (2019), p. 136; Baran (2022).

[14] Siddiqi (2022), p. 355.

[15] Islam et al. (2022), p. 330.

[16] Ibid., p. 331.

[17] United Nations Human Rights Council (2019), p. 14, para. 85.

[18] Ibid.

[19] Ibid.

Although the MoU was renewed in May 2020,[20] the Myanmar government still has yet to provide a concrete roadmap for the return of the Rohingya and the granting of citizenship. Given that the freedoms of Rohingya and Myanmarese citizens alike are being restricted under the junta, the Myanmar government must work with the UN and other organizations in a sincere effort to improve the human rights situation there. In revising the MoU, it was suggested that Rohingya themselves, especially female Rohingya, need to be involved in refugee policy.[21]

Agreements had been signed between the Myanmar and Bangladesh governments for the return of refugees prior to the *coup*. The Arrangement on Return of Displaced Persons from Rakhine State Between the Government of the People's Republic of Bangladesh and the Government of the Republic of the Union of Myanmar was signed on July 23, 2017,[22] followed by the Physical Arrangement for Repatriation of Displaced Myanmar Residents from Bangladesh under the Arrangement on Return of the Displaced Persons from Rakhine State, on January 16, 2018.[23] It is expected that the Myanmar government will take action to ensure that the Rohingya are granted citizenship when they are repatriated.

ASEAN is also expected to play a role with regard to the return of refugees. Although in 2019, the ASEAN Coordinating Centre for Humanitarian Assistance on Disaster Management (AHA Centre) was given a mandate to identify areas of cooperation in which ASEAN and Myanmar would work toward the repatriation and resettlement of the Rohingya. While the AHA Centre has produced a Preliminary Needs Assessment Report,[24] ASEAN has still not shown much enthusiasm about encouraging member states to help the Rohingya.[25] Under these circumstances, it is suggested that the international community exert additional pressure on ASEAN members, especially Indonesia and Malaysia, to encourage the group to take steps to resolve the situation.[26]

There are no courts of human rights in Asia. Nor does Myanmar participate in the International Covenant on Civil and Political Rights (ICCPR), and although Myanmar has ratified several human rights treaties, it does not accept individual communication procedures to ensure compliance. In the long run, it goes without saying that it would be desirable for Myanmar to voluntarily participate in human rights treaties and to act in a manner consistent with international human rights standards.

---

[20] United Nations High Commissioner for Refugees (2020).

[21] Parveen and Sahana (2022), p. 371.

[22] Arrangement on Return of Displaced Persons from Rakhine State Between the Government of the People's Republic of Bangladesh and the Government of the Republic of the Union of Myanmar (2017).

[23] Physical Arrangement for Repatriation of Displaced Myanmar Residents from Bangladesh under the Arrangement on Return of Displaced Persons from Rakhine State (2018).

[24] Gonsalves and Pathak (2022), p. 83.

[25] Ibid.

[26] Ibid., p. 84.

6.2 Proposed Solutions

In the short term, Myanmar must comply with the ICJ's provisional measures order, as the order is binding, and actively cooperate with the ICC investigation. To say the least, however, the junta is unlikely to accede. It would be also unacceptable for the Myanmar authorities to conduct compromised and otherwise unfair domestic investigations and prosecutions in an attempt to evade ICC investigations and prosecutions, if any. Although the NUG is now cooperating with the UN, the ICJ, and the ICC, the ICJ appears to instead recognize the military regime's standing as defendant, and in light of the ICC's silence on the NUG's declaration of acceptance of the ICC's jurisdiction, there is no guarantee that the ICC will recognize the NUG as the legitimate government either. Even if the NUG does not receive such endorsement, however, its efforts to collect evidence and otherwise participate in the IIMM could prompt the ICJ and ICC to act. Aside from attempts by the ICJ and ICC to hold the Rohingya accountable for their plight, there is also hope for the exercise of universal jurisdiction, as seen in the pursuit of responsibility in Argentina for violations of Rohingya rights.

Other short-term actions would include supplying food and medicine to the Rohingya, guaranteeing educational opportunities for Rohingya refugees, and providing means for communication online.[27] At a minimum, the right to life of the Rohingya would need to be secured through a stable food supply. The human rights situation in Myanmar has created a humanitarian crisis for the general population as well as the Rohingya. The World Health Organization (WHO) estimates that unless the situation is improved, health service disruptions will result in an additional 47,156 avoidable deaths in 2022.[28] As March 2022, the junta has killed at least 1600 civilians and displaced over 500,000.[29] In comparison with the international community's swift reaction to the situation in Ukraine, the Special Rapporteur on the Situation of Human Rights in Myanmar "notes the strong and swift action taken by member states on behalf of the people of Ukraine and implores the international community to act similarly to protect the people of Myanmar."[30]

For short-term measures such as the foregoing to improve the Rohingya's situation, it will be crucial that not only the state but also various international actors, including companies, take an interest in the human rights situation in Myanmar. Multinational companies and investors are also expected to ensure that their actions are consistent with international human rights standards, especially in light of the Guiding Principles on Business and Human Rights[31] and the Organisation for Economic Cooperation and Development (OECD) Due Diligence Guidance for Responsible Business Conduct,[32] even though neither is enforceable.[33] For instance, Japanese beverage company Kirin Holdings Company has decided to withdraw from

---

[27] Ibid., pp. 372–373.

[28] Office of the United Nations High Commissioner for Human Rights (2022), p. 9, para. 37.

[29] Ibid., p. 3, para. 2.

[30] Ibid., p. 3, para. 7.

[31] Office of the United Nations High Commissioner for Human Rights (2011).

[32] Organisation for Economic Cooperation and Development (2018).

[33] Kittichaisaree (2021), pp. 273.

146 6 Conclusion

doing business in Myanmar in order to terminate its joint venture partnership with Myanmar Economic Holdings Public Company Limited (MEHPCL), which provides welfare fund services to Tatmadaw.[34]

6.3 Dual-Track Pursuit of State and Individual Responsibility in the International Legal System

Simultaneous pursuit of responsibility against states and individuals at the ICJ and the ICC, respectively, may help establish synergies in the pursuit of responsibility for crimes under international law in terms of evidence collection, fact-finding, and the like. On the other hand, the standard of proof for the pursuit of individual criminal responsibility is different from that for the pursuit of state responsibility, which makes sense, given the respective penalties. However, those who bear the greatest responsibility for the most serious crimes under international law are often key figures in the running of states, and the ICC's *raison d'être* should accordingly be to hold such persons, shrouded in the veil of sovereignty though they may be, accountable without reserve. Thus, there could very well be an overlap between the assumed facts of state and individual criminal responsibility for crimes under international law committed by such persons.

The simultaneous pursuit of state and individual responsibility for crimes under international law, which, as described herein, are pending simultaneously at the ICJ and ICC in the Bangladesh/Myanmar and Ukraine situations, would not necessarily require the pursuit of individual criminal responsibility at the international level. In contrast, the judicial pursuit of state responsibility, where sovereign immunity is concerned, leaves only the option of pursuing it at that level rather than in the domestic arena. In fact, the number of unilateral suits by states pursuing treaty violations based on compatibility clauses is on the rise, and it is even reported that parties negotiating new treaties are refraining from inserting such clauses to avoid such situations.[35] The creative use of the ICJ to stop ongoing conflicts based on the compromissory clause would produce just such side effects.

It is important to stop criminal acts under international law by simultaneously pursuing state and individual responsibility in various forms, while not providing escape routes for criminals in the process. Such efforts would help with the perception of bias in international criminal justice. At a time of rising interest in the ICC in the wake of the armed conflict between Ukraine and Russia that began in 2022, the international community must increase its support for the ICC in order that those responsible for such crimes are brought to justice. The problem is that, as those responsible for gross human rights violations are often key government and military officials, arresting them is often politically difficult domestically until they leave their positions, all of which necessitates internal societal transformations. Moreover, legal

---

[34] Kirin Holdings Company Limited (2022).

[35] Fontanelli (2021).

proceedings are usually time-consuming and have at best indirect effects on ongoing conflicts and human rights violations. In other words, international law, in the form of the ICJ and the ICC, are not quick fixes to deal with human rights violations in times of trouble. How they are used does matter, however, as pursuing legal accountability in such venues is not the only solution. Rather, it will take awareness on the part of each and every one of us as individuals to resolve such appalling situations as the Rohingya crisis. The international community, and each of us who are part of it, must not let our resolve flag continue our political efforts in support of the internal transformation, in this case, of Myanmar society.

References

Arrangement on Return of Displaced Persons from Rakhine State Between the Government of the People's Republic of Bangladesh and the Government of the Republic of the Union of Myanmar (2017). https://www.theindependentbd.com/assets/images/banner/linked_file/201 71125094240.pdf

Baran D (2022) What is the international law on unilateral sanctions? Examining the Case of unilateral sanctions imposed on Russia. Al Shaq Strategic Research. https://research.sharqf orum.org/2022/04/22/unilateral-sanctions/

Bülbül K, Islam MN, Khan MS (2022) Looking at the past, moving to the future: stories from the spectacle of Rohingyas. In: Bülbül K, Islam MN, Khan MS (eds) Rohingya Refugee Crisis in Myanmar: ethnic conflict and resolution. Palgrave Macmillan, Singapore, pp 379–412

Fontanelli F (2021) The disputes between Armenia and Azerbaijan: the CERD compromissory clause as a one-way ticket to Hague. EJIL: Talk! https://www.ejiltalk.org/the-disputes-between-armenia-and-azerbaijan-the-cerd-compromissory-clause-as-a-one-way-ticket-to-hague/

Gonsalves T, Pathak A (2022) The Rohingya crisis: a long road ahead. In: Mukhopadhyay U (ed) Internal migration within South Asia: contemporary issues and challenges. Springer, Singapore, pp 71–89

Government of Canada (2022) Special economic measures (Burma) regulations (SOR/2007-285), amended by SOR/2022-65

Government of the UK (2021) The Myanmar (Sanctions) regulations 2021 (S.I. 2021, No, 496)

Government of the UK (2022) Press Release: UK announces new sanctions against Myanmar military ahead of Myanmar Armed Forces Day: UK sanctions announced ahead of Myanmar Armed Forces Day in coordination with allies

Government of the United Kingdom of Great Britain and Northern Ireland (2022) Referral letter submitted in coordination with 38 states parties. https://www.icc-cpi.int/itemsDocuments/ukr aine/Article-14-letter.pdf

Human Rights Council (2022) Situation of human rights in Myanmar since 1 February 2021: report of the United Nations High commissioner for human rights. UN Doc. A/HRC/49/72, advance edited version

International Court of Justice (2022) Application instituting proceedings and request for provisional measures, dispute relating to Allegations of Genocide (Ukraine v. Russian Federation)

Islam BAMT, Sammonds P, Alam SMRA, Alam MS, Chakma A, Durrat F, Patwary OH (2022) Sustainable Rohingya repatriation in Myanmar: some criteria to follow. In: Uddin N (ed) The Rohingya Crisis: human rights issues, policy concerns and burden sharing. Sage, Los Angeles, pp 305–337

Kirin Holdings Company Limited (2022) Withdrawal from the Myanmar business. https://pdf.irp ocket.com/C2503/OMfg/VvCP/LpVE.pdf

Kittichaisaree K (2021) The Rohingya, Justice and international law. Abingdon, Routledge

Minister of Justice of the Republic of Lithuania (2022) Lithuania refers to article 14 of the Rome Statute for an investigation into the situation in Ukraine. https://www.icc-cpi.int/itemsDocuments/ukraine/1041.pdf

Office of the United Nations High Commissioner for Human Rights (2011) Guiding principles on business and human rights, HR/PUB/11/04

Office of the United Nations High Commissioner for Human Rights (2017) Zeid Ra'ad Al Hussein: opening statement by Zeid Ra'ad Al Hussein: darker and more dangerous: high commissioner updates the human rights council on human rights issues in 40 countries

Office of the United Nations High Commissioner for Human Rights (2022) Report of the special rapporteur on the situation of human rights in Myanmar, Thomas H. Andrews, advance unedited version. UN Doc. A/HRC/49/76

Organisation for Economic Cooperation and Development (2018) The OECD due diligence guidance for responsible business conduct

Parveen S, Sahana M (2022) Identity and Humanitarian-based approach: resolution and resolving the Rohingya refugee crisis. In: Bülbül K, Islam MN, Khan MS (eds) Rohingya Refugee Crisis in Myanmar: ethnic conflict and resolution. Palgrave Macmillan, Singapore, pp 357–378

Physical Arrangement for Repatriation of Displaced Myanmar Residents from Bangladesh under the Arrangement on Return of Displaced Persons from Rakhine State (2018). https://www.icc-cpi.int/sites/default/files/RelatedRecords/CR2019_06133.PDF

Republic of Myanmar, National Unity Government (2022) Announcement No. (5/2022)—statement on the determination by the United States Government of Genocide and crimes against humanity against the Rohingya

Siddiqi B (2022) The "Myth" of repatriation: the prolonged sufferings of the Rohingya. In: Uddin N (ed) The Rohingya Crisis: human rights issues, policy concerns and burden sharing. Sage, Los Angeles, pp 334–357

Tzanakopoulos A (2019) State responsibility for "targeted sanctions." AJIL Unbound 113:135–139. https://doi.org/10.1017/aju.2019.22

U.S. Department of State (2022) Secretary Antony J. Blinken at the United States Holocaust Memorial Museum. https://www.state.gov/secretary-antony-j-blinken-at-the-united-states-holocaust-memorial-museum/

U.S. Department of the Treasury (2022) Press Release: Treasury Sanctions Military Leaders, Military-Affiliated Cronies and Businesses, and a Military Unit Prior to Armed Forces Day in Burma

U.S. President Joseph R. Biden Jr. (2021) Executive Order 14014 of February 10, 2021: blocking property with respect to the situation in Burma. Federal Reg 86(28):9429–9432

United Nations High Commissioner for Refugees (2020) UNHCR Press Release: UNDP, UNHCR and the Government of the Union of Myanmar extend memorandum of understanding. https://www.unhcr.org/asia/news/press/2020/5/5eb8fe484/undp-unhcr-and-the-government-of-the-union-of-myanmar-extend-memorandum.html

United Nations Human Rights Council (2019) Report of the independent international fact-finding mission on Myanmar. UN Doc. A/HRC/42/50

Wolf ZB (2022) Putin vs. the entire concept of international law. CNN. https://www.egyptindependent.com/putin-vs-the-entire-concept-of-international-law/

Index

A
African Union (AU), 125, 126, 129
Arakan Rohingya Salvation Army (ARSA), 3, 23, 31, 44, 50, 98
Argentina, 3, 28, 38, 82, 126, 131, 145
Assembly of States Parties, 118
Association of Southeast Asian Nations (ASEAN), 47–49, 81, 96, 144
Aung San Suu Kii, 5, 100

B
Bangladesh, 2–4, 6, 11, 12, 20, 21, 23, 27, 28, 34, 37–40, 42–46, 48–50, 52–55, 63, 66, 70, 73, 77, 79, 81, 82, 85, 99, 113, 126, 129–132, 134, 141–144, 146
Biological Weapons Convention, 37

C
Canada, 38, 63, 67, 68, 71, 77, 80, 82, 101, 143
China, 3, 30, 31, 34, 49, 94, 99
Convention on the Elimination of All Forms of Discrimination Against Women, 36
Convention on the Rights of the Child, 36
Coup, 4–6, 8, 19, 21, 24, 27, 34, 35, 47–50, 55, 69, 72, 78–82, 96, 100–103, 105, 126, 130, 132, 133, 142–144
COVID-19, 4–6, 23, 103, 142
Crimes against humanity, 4, 6, 43, 44, 46, 85, 89–92, 94, 95, 99, 131–133, 142, 143

E
Enforced Disappearance Convention, 93
Erga omnes, 38, 63, 64, 66, 69, 70, 76–79, 102
European Union (EU), 6, 30, 46, 47, 71, 72, 81, 82, 105

G
Gambia, 3, 4, 7, 35, 37, 38, 63–66, 68–71, 73–83, 86, 94, 96, 97, 99, 101–103, 126
General Assembly, 3, 12, 34, 42, 52, 53, 75, 81, 82, 85, 87, 88, 94–96, 100
Geneva Conventions, 34, 36, 37, 92, 104, 121
Genocide, 3, 4, 7, 28, 30, 35, 38, 43, 63–66, 69–71, 73, 76, 80, 83, 85–91, 94, 95, 97–99, 103, 104, 131–133, 142, 143
Genocide Convention, 3, 4, 7, 11, 27, 28, 33, 35–38, 47, 63–66, 69–71, 73–79, 82–84, 86–91, 94, 96–98, 102–104, 142
Germany, 67, 68, 133

H
Human Rights Council (UNHRC), 3, 8, 28–30, 32, 33, 35, 67, 81, 142, 143

I
ICC Statute (Rome Statute), 3, 4, 7, 27, 28, 35, 39, 40, 44–47, 55, 82, 85, 89, 91, 92, 117, 118, 121–128, 130, 141
Independent Commission of Inquiry (ICOE), 31, 33

© The Editor(s) (if applicable) and The Author(s), under exclusive license to Springer Nature Singapore Pte Ltd. 2023
H. Takemura, *The Rohingya Crisis and the International Criminal Court*, https://doi.org/10.1007/978-981-99-2734-0

149

Index

Independent Investigative Mechanism for
Myanmar (IIMM), 6, 32, 38, 82,
131, 145
Indonesia, 2, 132, 133, 144
International Court of Justice (ICJ), 1, 3, 4,
7, 11, 12, 28, 31, 35–38, 41, 51–53,
63–90, 96–105, 125, 126, 141, 142,
145–147
International Criminal Court (ICC)
Appeals Chamber [of the ICC], 40, 51,
126
Office of the Prosecutor (OTP) [of the
ICC], 4, 7, 27, 28, 32, 39, 43, 44, 51,
113, 118, 141
Pre-Trial Chamber [of the ICC], 129
Trial Chamber [of the ICC], 45
International Criminal Tribunal for Rwanda
(ICTR), 92, 116, 117
International Criminal Tribunal for the
Former Yugoslavia (ICTY), 84, 85,
87, 90, 92, 105, 116, 117, 123, 128
International Law Commission (ILC), 79,
89, 91
International Military Tribunal for the Far
East (Tokyo tribunal), 115
International Military Tribunal (Nuremberg
tribunal), 115
International Residual Mechanism for
Criminal Tribunals (MICT), 37

J
Japan/Japanese, 2, 11, 17–19, 24, 28, 31,
34, 53, 67, 82, 118, 143, 145
Jus cogens, 38, 64, 89

K
Kachin, 8, 18, 24, 30, 33

L
Legitimacy, 4, 6, 7, 27, 45, 50, 113–126,
128–130, 134

M
Maldives, 67, 101
Muslim, 1, 11–17, 20, 24, 29–31, 35, 38,
65, 81, 82, 133
Myanmar, 1–8, 11, 12, 15, 19–24, 27–40,
42–55, 63–66, 68–86, 89, 90, 94,
96–105, 113, 126, 129–134,
141–147

N
National League for Democracy (NLD), 4,
5, 21, 23, 24
Netherlands, 3, 29, 36, 38, 63, 67, 68, 77,
80, 101, 105

O
Organization of Islamic Cooperation (OIC),
3, 37, 38, 65, 66, 72–74, 82, 86, 102

P
Peremptory norm, 89, 98

R
Rakhine, 3, 4, 11, 12, 15, 17, 19, 23, 24,
28–34, 42, 48, 69, 83–85, 98, 103,
143, 144
Refugee, 1, 2, 6, 20, 21, 23, 24, 37, 38,
46–49, 53, 77, 86, 99, 142–145
Responsibility to Protect (R2P), 94–98
Rohingya, 1–4, 6–8, 11–15, 17–24, 27–31,
33–35, 37–40, 43, 44, 46–50, 52, 54,
63–65, 69–72, 77, 78, 80–86, 94–99,
101, 103, 105, 129, 131–134,
141–145, 147
Russia, 3, 7, 30, 31, 68, 80, 94, 97, 98, 103,
104, 146

S
Security Council, 3, 4, 11, 19, 30–32, 34,
41, 43, 47, 49, 53–55, 72, 81, 82, 87,
94, 95, 97, 99, 114, 116, 117, 121,
124, 125, 141, 142
Superior responsibility, 92, 93
Syria, 94

T
Tatmadaw, 4, 5, 8, 21, 27, 32, 43, 47, 49,
50, 64, 78, 81, 85, 96, 146
Treaty on the Non-Proliferation of Nuclear
Weapons (NPT), 37
Turkey, 132

U
Ukraine, 7, 8, 50, 53, 55, 68, 80, 97, 98,
103–105, 126, 134, 141, 145, 146
United Kingdom (UK), 3, 29, 31, 38, 53,
55, 67, 68, 72, 80, 94, 101, 141, 143

Index

United Nations Commission on Human Rights (UNHCR), 2, 28

United States (US), 2, 28, 31, 37, 40, 41, 68, 72, 80, 82, 98, 99, 121, 134, 142, 143, 147

Universal jurisdiction, 3, 38, 128, 131–134, 145

UN Secretary-General, 28, 34, 35, 40, 51, 71

V

Vienna Convention on the Law of Treaties, 40, 41

W

War crime, 4, 6, 36, 40, 89, 92, 94, 95, 132, 133, 142

Printed in the United States
by Baker & Taylor Publisher Services